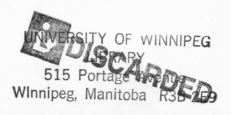

The Yale Ben Jonson

GENERAL EDITORS: ALVIN B. KERNAN AND RICHARD B. YOUNG

Ben Jonson: The Alchemist

EDITED BY ALVIN B. KERNAN

NEW HAVEN AND LONDON:

YALE UNIVERSITY PRESS, 1974

Set in Aldine Bembo type by Wm. Clowes & Sons, Ltd.,
and printed in the United States of America by
The Murray Printing Co., Forge Village, Mass.

Published in Great Britain, Europe, and Africa by
Yale University Press, Ltd., London.
Distributed in Latin America by Kaiman & Polon,
Inc., New York City; in Australasia and Southeast
Asia by John Wiley & Sons Australasia Pty. Ltd.,
Sydney; in India by UBS Publishers' Distributors Pvt.,
Ltd., Delhi; in Japan by John Weatherhill, Inc., Tokyo.

Contents

Preface of the General Editors

The Yale edition of the plays of Ben Jonson is intended to meet two fundamental requirements: first, the need of the modern reader for a readily intelligible text which will convey, as nearly as an edition can, the life and movement which invests the plays on the stage; second, the need of the critic and scholar for a readily available text which represents as accurately as possible, though it does not reproduce, the plays as Jonson printed them. These two requirements are not, we believe, incompatible, but the actual adjustment of one to the other has been determined by the judgment of the individual editors. In details of editorial practice, therefore, the individual volumes of the edition may vary, but in basic editorial principle they are consistent.

The texts are based primarily on the two folio volumes of Jonson's *Works*, the first published in 1616, the second in 1640. The 1616 volume was seen through the press by Jonson himself, and therefore represents to a degree unusual for dramatic texts of the period what the dramatist intended us to have. The 1640 volume presents more difficult textual problems; though Jonson himself began preparing individual plays for it as early as 1631, these were carelessly printed—a fact of which he was painfully aware—and the folio, under the editorship of the eccentric Sir Kenelm Digby, was not completed until after Jonson's death. The quarto editions have also been consulted, and where a quarto reading has been preferred by an editor the necessary information appears in the notes.

In editing Jonson for the modern reader, one of the central problems is that of annotation, a problem that is complicated rather than solved by providing a catalogue of Jonson's immense classical learning or of his contemporary lore. We have believed that annotation is most helpful not when it identifies or defines details but when it clarifies the context of the detail. Consequently, citation of sources, allusions, and analogues, whether classical or colloquial, has been controlled by and restricted to what is relevant in the judgment of the editors to a meaningful understanding of the dramatic and poetic values of the passage in question and of the play as a whole. For the same reason, all editorial apparatus—introductions, notes, and glosses—frequently and deliberately deal with critical and interpretative matters in order to reanimate the topical details and give substance to the imaginative world each play creates.

To provide a readable text it has been necessary to revise some of the printing conventions of the seventeenth-century editions. In order to identify himself with the classical tradition of comedy, Jonson used as a model for his *Works* the first printed editions of Plautus, Terence, and Aristophanes, heading each scene with a list of all characters appearing in it, without marking individual entrances and exits. The present edition follows the more familiar practice of listing only those characters on stage at the beginning of a scene and indicates all entrances and exits. Stage directions, kept to an absolute minimum, have also been added where understanding of the dialogue depends on an implied but not explicit action, or on an unspecified location. With the exception of the first speech ascription in each scene, which is usually omitted by Jonson, all such additions and all other material not in the original text have been enclosed in square brackets.

Where Jonson printed all verse in the metrical unit of the line, whether or not it represents the speech of one or more than one character, this edition divides the parts of such lines according to the speaker, and indicates the metrical unit by echeloning the parts of the line.

The original punctuation has been followed where its rhetorical effect has a dramatic value, but modern pointing has been used wherever necessary to clarify syntactical obscurities and to eliminate obvious errors or mere eccentricity. Spelling has been modernized except where orthographical change affects either meaning or meter. For example, where Jonson prints '*d* to indicate an unstressed ending of a past participle, this edition prints *-ed*, and where Jonson printed *-ed* to indicate stress this edition prints *-èd*. Jonson's frequent elisions, e.g. *th*' or *i*', are retained, and all unusual accents are marked.

In the original text the entrance of a new character usually, though not invariably, initiates a new scene, so that there are many more scenes than a fully modernized text would allow. This edition retains Jonson's act and scene divisions in the belief that in most cases they represent the linking effect, the *liaison des scènes*, characteristic of the developing neoclassic drama; in all cases they represent Jonson's own conception of dramatic form; and the fact of form is part of the meaning of his plays.

Introduction

On those rare occasions in the West when great tragedy has appeared, great comedy, usually the work of a single distinguished comic playwright, has always followed. In fifth-century Athens the tragedies of Aeschylus, Sophocles, and Euripides found their comic counterbalance in Aristophanes; the neo-classical French tragic theater of Corneille and Racine was paralleled by the comic theater of Molière; while the international theater of late nineteenth- and early twentieth-century Europe, which grew up around the realistic tragedy of Ibsen, Strindberg, and Chekhov, found its inevitable nimble comedian in George Bernard Shaw. Comedy and tragedy were more closely linked, less distinct, in the theater of Renaissance London, where king and clown met and talked on the same stage, and the greatest of the tragic writers, William Shakespeare, was also the greatest of the comic writers. But the dramatist who stands out as the professional mocker of the theater of Renaissance London was the author of *The Alchemist*, Benjamin Jonson.

Tragedy and comedy share not only an age but a central idea of man as well, which they treat, however, in different ways. The great comic dramatist always deals with the same ideas, themes, and sense of life which are the subject of tragic drama, but in the wry perspective glass of comedy the heroic subjects of tragedy become strangely transformed. The "swift mind of man," that human wisdom and superb self-confidence which allow Oedipus to solve the riddle of the Sphinx and get the throne of Thebes—and the bed of Jocasta—becomes in *The Clouds* of Aristophanes the sophism of Socrates and his schemes for teaching pupils how to make the worse cause appear the better. The elegant morality and the tortured self-awareness of Racine's Jansenist heroes need only be exposed to the mirror of comedy to become the hilarious hypocritical piety of Molière's Tartuffe. Ibsen's great rebels against the falsehood and stifling convention of nineteenth-century European society—Hedda Gabler or Master Builder Solness—become in comedy such breezy, talkative, commonsensical Shavian heroes as Bluntschli, Caesar, and Joan of Arc.

Similarly, the comedies of Ben Jonson reduce Renaissance tragedy's heroic conception of man and his powers to, as Jonson put it, "deeds and language such as men do use." The most obvious fact about the Renaissance is the appearance, during the fifteenth century in Italy and the sixteenth century in Northern Europe, of a great surge of optimism about the ability of man through the power of his mind, as manifested in his arts and science, to penetrate the mysteries of the world and to remake things to conform to his own desire. This new humanism, which believed everything open to its inquiry and responsive to its shaping hand, found its most dramatic expression in the arts of the time—the paintings of Leonardo, the sculptures of Michelangelo, the buildings of Brunelleschi, the poetry of Petrarch, the learning of Erasmus, the plays of Shakespeare—but it was also the motivating power which drove the new science of Copernicus, Galileo, and Francis Bacon to substitute mind-made mathematical constructs and philosophical theories for the direct appearances of nature. The same energies which gave man the power to reorder the heavens sent him across vast oceans into strange lands to "discover"—as if a land did not exist until seen by European man—and claim for himself the totality of the globe. But perhaps nowhere did man assert his claim to be the central fact in the universe more emphatically than in matters of religion, where theologians like Luther and Calvin discarded the traditional authority of the Catholic church to confront God directly in the words of the Bible and in the depths of their own souls. True, they found in those depths not goodness and beauty but a depravity and ugliness so boundless that salvation could only come, not from human works, but from divine grace. But this is not retreat, it is a form of heroic pride, like that of Marlowe's Doctor Faustus or Satan in *Paradise Lost*, which believes that man's sins are of such cosmic importance that even a God of infinite compassion finds it difficult, if not impossible, to pardon them. Diabolism is not humility but a claim of evil greatness in which Man the sinner is greater in his fall than God the forgiver.

Heroic humanism received perhaps its most extravagant and complex definition in the great tragic heroes created for the Elizabethan stage by such playwrights as William Shakespeare, George Chapman, and John Webster. But the *personnage régnant*[1] who dominated the tragic stage was in the first instance the creation of Christopher Marlowe (1558–93), in whose plays man seeks absolute glory and power in all the ways in which the men of the Renaissance sought fully to realize their humanity. Tamburlaine conquers the world and dies planning to storm the battlements of heaven itself and set his black battle flags in the firmament; Doctor Faustus, the scientist-scholar-magician, sells his soul to the Devil in return for complete knowledge and a "dominion that stretcheth as far as doth the mind of man"; Barabas, the Jew of Malta, the merchant prince and political schemer, channels the treasures of the world into his counting house. In Marlowe's dramatic world, man's greatness realizes itself in many places, on the battlefield, at the council table,

---

1. Walter Kaiser, *Praisers of Folly* (London, 1964), p. 3, calls attention to this most useful concept coined by Hippolyte Taine, *De l'idéal dans l'art* (1867), and defined as the characteristic figure or type of character whose "sentiments and . . . ideas are those of an entire generation." Kaiser argues that the Fool was the *personnage régnant* of the Renaissance, but in the English drama the clown struggled with the king for the crown and the stage.

in the bedroom, in the study and laboratory, and in the great centers of commerce; but though the places may differ, the aim is always the same: the achievement of power, dominance, fullness of being, or, as the conqueror Tamburlaine puts it, "the sweet fruition of an earthly crown."

The great tragic heroes of the post-Marlovian drama—lovers like Romeo and Juliet or Antony and Cleopatra, statesmen like Richard III and Claudius, great captains like Hotspur and Coriolanus, subtle philosophers like Hamlet, and magician-artificers like Prospero— are all more subtle, complex, and psychologically intricate than the oversize Marlovian titans from whom they derive. But all share in claiming that the world declares the glory of man and the heavens showeth his handiwork, the praise which Psalm 19 gives to God the Creator alone. It is true, of course, that a shadow lurks always behind these great images of Renaissance daring and power, a tragic shadow which lingers on to remind the new heroes of what the Middle Ages knew about the weakness of man, the swiftness with which life flashes by, and the inevitable smell of the charnel house. But even when the heroes of humanism are shown, as they regularly are in the tragedy of the age, as baffled, entangled in their own strength, or trapped within the tragic mysteries of a world finally larger than themselves, the emphasis still falls upon the blazing greatness of man, even in the midst of defeat.

The real antagonist of Renaissance optimism about the power of mind and heroic effort was not the bare skull and skeleton left over from some medieval Dance of Death, but a new and sprightly character who insisted from the beginning on sharing the stage with the hero, the Fool.[2] It is remarkable how inseparable hero and fool are in the Renaissance: if Rosinante gallops by with Don Quixote

---

2. The tradition of folly in literature has been well treated in Kaiser, *Praisers of Folly*, and, from a more historical perspective, by Enid Welsford, *The Fool, His Social and Literary History* (London, 1935). Jacob Burckhardt's chapter "Ridicule and Wit" in Part II, "The Development of the Individual," in

in his armor, an ass will surely amble by in a moment carrying Sancho Panza; when the "mirror of all Christian kings," Prince Hal, later to be King Henry V, leads his great army against the noble knight Harry Percy, the rear is inevitably brought up by a tattered regiment commanded by Sir John Falstaff. Even in the scene which stands in all ways at the very center of Renaissance English drama, which is its most solemn moment, the storm scene on the heath in *King Lear*, where the Renaissance encounters the modern world which it is in the process of creating, the great King determined to face directly an indifferent nature and strip man down to his essential nakedness, or nothingness, is followed by a loyal fool who knows only that man must somehow find shelter from a pitiless storm that cares nothing for any living thing.

With his wooden dagger, his jig, his parti-colored suit, and his hood covered with jangling bells, the Fool is everywhere in Renaissance literature: in Sebastian Brandt's *Ship of Fools*, Erasmus' *Praise of Folly*, Rabelais' *Gargantua and Pantagruel*, as well as being omnipresent in the English drama. Sometimes the Fool is "not altogether Fool" and seems wiser than the hero whom he follows, but his presence on the stage at the time, whether he be wise or foolish, is enough to call into question any pretensions to heroism or knowledge. The Fool serves, as it were, as a constant counterbalance to Renaissance man's excessive claims for the power of his mind and hand.

Ben Jonson seems to have been born to create the mirror opposite of Marlowe's heroic world,[3] the comic world of folly, and in none

---

The Civilization of the Renaissance in Italy (1860) remains in many ways the most interesting explanation of the necessary interaction of folly and greatness in the period.

3. The close relationship of "Marlowe's mighty line" (a description created by Jonson in his prefatory verses to the 1623 first folio of Shakespeare's works) to the comically heroic speeches of Jonson was first noted and developed by T. S. Eliot, "Ben Jonson," in *Selected Essays, 1917–1932* (New York, 1932).

of his plays is the heroic subject matter converted to comic reality more obviously and successfully than in *The Alchemist*. Here the aspiration of the Renaissance as a whole to control and remake the world is imaged as a great swindle, alchemy, managed by an impudent servant and a cunning spiel-man, Face and Subtle, who are parodies of those Renaissance philosophers and scientists, such as Bruno and Kepler, to whom Marlowe had given tragic form as the great magician Doctor Faustus. The new Protestantism and the theology of Luther and Calvin become here the Brethren of Amsterdam, the Elder, Zeal-of-the-Land Busy, and his Deacon, Ananias, a pair of greasy, hypocritical knaves spouting biblical phrases while seeking only their own profit. The great Renaissance merchant adventurers who sent their galleons over vast oceans to reap the treasures of new continents—men like Marlowe's Barabas or Shakespeare's Antonio in *The Merchant of Venice*—are reduced by Jonson's comic mirror to the miserable tobacconist, Abel Drugger, stingy, gullible, ingratiating, bowing and scraping to the gentry, and looking for a rich heiress to marry. Military valor no longer takes the form of a Tamburlaine or a Hotspur, but declines to become either the lying Captain Face or the rustic bully Kastril, who has come up to London to learn how to quarrel in the latest Italian fashion so that he can go back down to the country and cut a grand figure while breaking heads in tavern brawls, in one of which he will eventually be killed.[4] Heroic love of the kind in which Romeo and Juliet and Antony and Cleopatra seek perfection of beauty and fulfillment of soul, takes in the house of the alchemists the shape of Mammon's lip-smacking lust and the bedroom skills of a whore, Dol Common, who can "Firk like a flounder, kiss like a scallop, close."

The essence of the Renaissance spirit in England was fully expressed in such historical figures as Sir Philip Sidney and Sir Walter

---

4. "And will go down again and die i' the country" (II.6.62).

Raleigh, and in its comic or perverse form, the Renaissance found its spokesman here in *The Alchemist* in a Fool of heroic proportions, Sir Epicure Mammon. His dream of getting the Philosophers' Stone and using it to transform everything base in the world into something golden, his visions of man triumphant, possessing infinite knowledge, infinite pleasure, and immortal life, voice themselves in a language as marvellous as the world it seeks to create:

> I will have all my beds blown up, not stuffed:
> Down is too hard. And then mine oval room
> Filled with such pictures as Tiberius took
> From Elephantis, and dull Aretine
> But coldly imitated. Then, my glasses
> Cut in more subtle angles, to disperse
> And multiply the figures as I walk
> Naked between my succubae. My mists
> I'll have of perfume, vapored 'bout the room,
> To loose our selves in; and my baths like pits
> To fall into; from whence we will come forth
> And roll us dry in gossamer and roses.
>
> II.2.41–52

The poetry contains perfectly the impulses behind it: as the appetite calls out continually for novel satisfactions, the imagination obliges with rapidly intensifying images of power and pleasure, and the rhetoric soars upward to create, in words at least, the joys which appetite has desired and imagination has envisioned. Enough is never sufficient for the comic overreachers in this play, who seem always out to exhaust nature, to suck things dry, to "milk ... [the] epididimis" of the world. This overgoing or excessiveness seems to be the basic rhythm of the play: Dapper wants more and still more potent charms for gambling; Face and Subtle work Mammon and other victims for more and more money; the alchemist refines his materials over and over again in an attempt to speed nature's processes up and achieve absolute and totally pure gold. The

Jonsonian rhetoric enacts the attempt to achieve "a perpetuity Of life and lust," reaching out to seize on some new object, climb toward some new pleasure, outgo the dizzy heights it has already reached. Even Jonson's heavy punctuation furthers this effect by making each phrase seem like an afterthought, the new but inevitable next reach upwards into the empyrean.

As in the Renaissance, so at the center of the vision in Sir Epicure's lines above stands man, his naked image multiplied to infinity by a series of dazzling mirrors until he fills the world. All things yield to him and take his shape as surely as does the air mattress, the "blown-up" bed on which Sir Epicure will enjoy his pleasures. Desire and language always go too far, of course, and tumble over into such ridiculous excess as rolling dry on rose petals and gossamer; but for all its comic exaggeration, there is in such language a great deal of the real energy and the appetite for transcendence that animated the Renaissance. However inflated the words may be, when Sir Epicure speaks of "the rich Peru" and "the golden mines," he conveys some of the wild excitement that drove the conquistadors across uncharted oceans to the rape of new continents. And when he speaks of discovering the secrets of nature and banishing old age and sickness from the world, we glimpse, even as we laugh, something of the Renaissance's sudden perception that the human mind through art and science could really change the world, that suffering and death need not forever be the lot of man, that things need not always be the way they are. Even when Sir Epicure is at his most idiotic, imagining bedding fifty women a night and eating the rarest foods in all the world, we still can feel something of what the Renaissance must have felt in breaking free from a heavy medieval sense of the pain and sinfulness of flesh to move out into an exquisite realm of feeling, tasting, hearing, and seeing the wonderful sights and things of a wide and joyous world.

But if Jonson's characters are universals, comic versions of the ways in which the Renaissance sought power, knowledge and pleasure, they form at the same time a remarkable cross section, ranging from servant through knight, of London life in the early seventeenth century. Ben Jonson was a London poet, one of that small group of English writers including Swift, Gay, Blake, and Dickens which stands out so prominently in a literary tradition which has most often set its scenes in court and country, and emphasized nature rather than the town. A good deal of the pleasure of *The Alchemist* comes from the extraordinarily skillful way in which Jonson conveys the actual life of the town and of its people by means of a host of small details. All the hopes and aspirations, for example, of the rising new professional men of London are contained in the seeming odds and ends which make up the biography of the lawyer's clerk, Dapper: the small inheritance, the modest education which taught him "small Latin and less Greek," an interest in poetry and the tavern acquaintance of a few minor poets, the practical skills of bookkeeping and the ability to write several hands clearly, the proud possession of a watch, and some fashionable interest in romantic love (disappointed, we later learn). The few details are so specific and so carefully chosen that we seem to know everything about the man. His past and his future are completely determined by his social class and his character type; and if we know nothing of what goes on inside his head, that is because there is nothing to know. In Jonson, unlike Shakespeare, a character is only rarely anything more than the sum of his social attributes.

London itself comes to life before our eyes through Jonson's words. We seem to smell the cooking from the stalls with Subtle as he walks hungry on a cold morning, peer into the dense darkness of Deaf John's Ale House, see the gallant "sons of sword and hazard" on their knees in their velvet cloaks with red linings gambling at Madame Augusta's, hear the Puritan preacher in the meeting house thundering against vanities of dress and such "abominations" as starch, feel the misery of the small shopkeeper when he is taxed eighteen pence to help pay for the new machine which pumps water from under London bridge to some of the nearby houses. Much of Jonson's ironic, mock-epic effect is achieved by this condensation within the same figures of the heroic dreams of the Renaissance and a very solid and lumpy reality. If these men be such things as dreams are made on, then a certain amount of disappointment is inevitable.

But if the characters and the town seem very solid and fixed for Jonson and for us, they are anything but so for the characters themselves. They seek transformation and see themselves as inevitably marked for great things, for mystery, wonder, and magic. It does not surprise the clerk Dapper very much to learn that he was chosen at birth by the supernatural, and that the Queen of Faery is his aunt. This is no more than he had really always thought anyway. The hypocritical Puritans, about as ordinary a pair of rogues as could be found anywhere, assume without question that they commune directly with God and that He speaks through them to the rest of wicked mankind. So blessed, why should they obey any magistrate? acknowledge any law above their own wills? hesitate to counterfeit money? If so poor a thing as Drugger can confidently count on becoming a king of merchants, if a rude booby like Kastril can be made into a "Prince of Cats" and a smooth master of the duello, why should not a rich knight like Sir Epicure Mammon turn all the world to gold and eliminate all sickness and poverty?

In terms of the plot of the play it is to the alchemists and their science, or "art" as it is regularly called in the play, that all of the other characters come in order to have their dreams made real. And just as alchemy is the center of the plot, so is it the central symbol of the play which organizes its diverse parts and irradiates them with meaning.[5] But while Face and Subtle and their confederate Dol use

---

5. As Ray L. Heffner, Jr. ("Unifying Symbols in the Comedy of Ben Jonson," in *English Stage Comedy, English Institute Essays 1954*, ed. W. K. Wimsatt, pp. 74–97 [New York, 1955]) has argued, Jonson always had a great deal of difficulty giving his plays a logical, smoothly developing plot. In consequence, Heffner points out, he tends to rely on central symbols such as

alchemy as their central swindle, they are at the same time the masters of a vast number of other "arts." They cast horoscopes, read palms, are excellent phrenologists, deal with spirits, look into crystal balls to tell the future, make magical charms, arrange marriages, concoct love potions, design store layouts to focus the powers of the universe, instruct in the latest fashions of dress and insult, and all of this by the best scientific principles. The number of arts practiced by these rogues suggests that in them Jonson is caricaturing not just some perversion of alchemy or the beginnings of modern science but the tradition of the "magus," a type of philosopher-scientist-magician to be found only in the Renaissance.[6] In order to understand the magus it is necessary to realize that at the time of the Renaissance a number of men of learning began to believe that the powers of the universe could be found and controlled by bringing together all knowledge from ancient books and manuscripts, which were now being rediscovered and read. Though science may have started in the Renaissance in the work of men like Copernicus, Galileo, and Bacon, the attempt to control nature and understand the cosmic order began with philosophers who were more magicians than scientists—men like Pico della Mirandola, Paracelsus, Bruno, Ficino, Cornelius Agrippa, and the Englishman Dr. John Dee—who dealt with mystic signs, numerology, pneumatology (the science of angels), ancient languages and hieroglyphs, and with alchemy. The Orphic Hymns, the supposed antique books of Hermes Trismegistus,

---

"noise" in *Epicoene* and the question of "warrants" in *Bartholomew Fair* to unify his diverse comic materials. Alchemy is, of course, the comparable unifying symbol of this play.

6. We are only beginning to understand this strange tradition of magic and pseudo-science which was so central to the Renaissance but was ultimately obliterated by the new rational philosophy and science of the modern period. The best book available on the magus is an extraordinarily dense and curious work by Frances Yates, *Giordano Bruno and the Hermetic Tradition* (London, 1964).

the Kabala, books of symbols and mystic signs, as well as more conventional philosophers like Plato, all became treasure houses of knowledge to be searched by the magus for the keys which would reveal to him the harmony of the spheres and the order of the cosmos, which would put into his hands the power of God Himself. All was known and written down, it was thought, by the ancients who had lived in the beginning of time, close to the origin of things. And all could be understood and used if the mind could only study deeply enough and organize the diverse lore that lay spread out before it. In the drama, the magus was represented by figures like Marlowe's Doctor Faustus and Shakespeare's Prospero, but Jonson transforms such heroic knowledge-seekers into comic swindlers, the impudent servant pretending to be Captain Face, the ragged con man pretending to be Doctor Subtle, and the whore Dol Common pretending to be a great and learned lady.

Despite the variety of abstruse arts practiced by Face and Subtle, alchemy is their defining activity, and from its central position in the play this art of arts interprets all other parts. To begin with the most obvious instance of its interpretive function, the constant presence of the concept of alchemy tells us that what the chemist tries to do with base metal like lead is exactly what each of the characters is trying to do with himself. All of the characters are very ordinary clay, about as low on the scale of humanity as lead is on the scale of metals; but all desire to be transformed into something as rich and rare as gold; Dapper into a great gambler, Kastril into a duelist, Sir Epicure into the Emperor of the world. Jonson was thoroughly aware that alchemy serves as a metaphor for character transformation, and in a number of scenes it is impossible to tell whether the raw materials and processes being discussed refer to people or metals. In the opening scene, for example, where Face and Subtle quarrel, each uses alchemical language to describe the way in which he has raised and "sublimed" the other from dung and poverty to fame and riches. The same sort of thing happens again in II.3.95 ff. where it is not at all clear whether Face and Subtle are discussing the stages by which the chemicals are refined and made to yield gold, or whether they are talking about the methods by which the con man in all ages whets his victim's greed in order to take him for the largest possible amount.[7]

In a curious way, what the fools of the play fail to do, the rogues almost achieve. That is, Face and Subtle and Dol do manage to convert the crudest raw materials imaginable, human greed, lust, vanity, and stupidity, into gold by working the fools for all they are worth. If alchemy is ever possible, the play seems to be saying, then its true powers are the wit and the quickness of such clever characters as Face and Subtle, who always manage to turn a dollar somehow. In the end, of course, even these rogues manage to overreach themselves and to lose all the gold and treasure they have stored in the cellar to the master of the house, Lovewit, who returns to town suddenly. But when Lovewit materializes at the beginning of Act V, far from being a *deus ex machina* he is simply the embodiment, in a more respectable form, of that mental agility and histrionic skill, that wit, which we have been watching throughout the play with such fascination as it appears in Face and Subtle, turning the rough opportunities of life into pure gold. Lovewit's marriage with the rich widow and his seizure of all the loot stored in his cellar is the perfect ending of the play, the triumph of true alchemy, the wit which achieves riches and happiness by making the most of such chances as the world throws its way.

---

7. The ability of man to change or to remake himself—man as actor playing many parts—is central to Jonsonian comedy and to the Renaissance conception of man's new possibilities. For excellent discussions of this tradition and the problem it raised see Thomas Greene, "The Flexibility of the Self in Renaissance Literature," and A. Bartlett Giamatti, "Proteus Unbound: Some Versions of the Sea God in the Renaissance." Both articles appear in *The Disciplines of Criticism, Essays in Literary Theory, Interpretation, and History*, ed. Demetz, Greene, and Nelson (New Haven, 1968).

Each of the events and thematic patterns in the play can be usefully looked at and understood as a special instance of alchemy, for Jonson is here showing the world as an endless series of attempts at alchemical transformation. Two more illustrations of the way in which alchemy illuminates the parts of the play will perhaps suggest at least the full range of possibilities for interpretation through the symbol.

It is almost impossible not to notice that the characters of this play are blessed with the "gift of tongues," using language, in most cases, with great facility, if not great precision. Furthermore, the characters are very curious and self-conscious about linguistic questions, speculating, for example, about whether the primitive language spoken by Adam, from which all other languages originated, was Dutch, Hebrew, or some other language. The play even seems, in a curious way, almost to anticipate the theories of modern linguistics about a generative and transformational grammar, a conception or idea of grammar existing in the mind prior to its manifestation in any particular language:

> Where, then, a learned linguist
> Shall see the ancient used communion
> Of vowels and consonants— ...
>   To comprise
> All sounds of voices, in few marks of letters—
>   IV.5.18–23

The characters of the play do indeed seem to possess some key to language, some *langue* which can generate numberless *paroles*, and the play is filled with a variety of special languages created by the characters out of a few words or ideas. There is that special cant language made out of biblical terms and sacred rhetoric which the Puritans create in order to change their mean selves into persecuted saints and the prophets of the Lord. There is the "angry tongue," the special language used for quarrelling, which Face and Lovewit, drawing on Elizabethan books dealing with the management of affairs of honor, teach Kastril in an attempt to change ill-natured quarreling to an elegant skill. There is the mad "tongue of Eber and Javan," that learned philosophical mixture of history and apocalyptic prophecy derived from the writings of Broughton, which Dol spouts in inspired frenzy to drive Mammon out of the house. And soaring above all other voices there are the epic accents and the drumlike thunderous rhetoric of Sir Epicure Mammon transforming greed and lust into a heroic search for eternal love, perfect beauty, endless pleasure and power. But the most remarkably elaborated language is, of course, the incessant jargon of alchemy which fills the play with learned scientific terms and the endless sound of impressive words like "chrysopoeia," "bolt's head," "projection," "the great work," all of which seem to make the achievement of gold so certain and sure. In the light cast by the central alchemical symbol, it is possible to see that in Jonson's view language has become a branch of alchemy, an attempt by means of words to transform a base reality into a golden dream. Neither language nor alchemy need necessarily be a fraud in Jonson's view, but as the characters of this play misuse the great powers given by nature, science, and language, they become mere swindles, perverse distortions of forces innately good.

Ultimately, alchemy contains the play's only judgment on the meaning and the practicality of the Renaissance desire to break at once the shackles of things as they are and to make the world over into gold. Along with the alchemists, the characters of the play seem to believe that nature—the world, that is, as created and given to man, not made by him—is infinitely plastic and will accept any shape that man desires. But by means of the great discussions on alchemy which occupy most of Act II, Jonson manages to insert into the play a conservative conception of the inescapable slowness and limits on the possibility of change and the dependence of any change in man on improvement of his moral nature. Details of the alchemical tradition Jonson uses and the way in which he uses it appear in Appendix I at the end of the text, and here it will be enough to remark that while alchemy in practice is treated in the play as a complete swindle, the *theory* of alchemy as Jonson understood it, and as Subtle spouts it without fully understanding what he is saying, offers a profound criticism of the optimistic dreams of the Renaissance about the speed with and extent to which the world can be changed and improved. Nature, the theory says, moves only very slowly toward making gold out of lead, and any change that occurs will require that man perfect his own moral nature first. By way of example of how the theory of alchemy comments on the action, we can take the scene in Act IV where the alchemical experiment is blown up because, it is said, Sir Epicure has had lustful thoughts about Dol, and this lust has "corrupted" the experiment and exploded it. Face and Subtle are here using good alchemical theory only to delay the time that they will have to show Sir Epicure some real gold; but at the same time the event reminds us that any changes from lead to gold that take place in this imperfect world are going to take place very slowly, at nature's speed, not at man's, and that, to put it in modern terms, our morality has to be as advanced as our science or our science will do us no good, it will only "blow us up."

Speaking of the successful alchemist, Surly remarks,

> Why, I have heard he must be *homo frugi*,
> A pious, holy, and religious man,
> One free from mortal sin, a very virgin.
>
> II.2.97–99

Since no man in Jonson's comic world even approaches the conditions tradition required of the alchemist who would find the stone and make gold, it follows that the best that can be achieved is to accept such good chances as the world offers, as Lovewit does in this play. And such a view also bears on the writing of comedies, for the art of the comic playwright is indeed much like the art of the alchemist: both take base things, refine them by art and try to make gold of what was originally lead. The analogy of comic playwright and alchemist is supported by the fact that the alchemists within the play, Face and Subtle, are at the same time consumate playwrights and actors, changing roles in a flash, playing whatever part the situation requires, setting the stage and improvising the plot in a truly brilliant fashion. But their dramatic skills, like their alchemy, are ultimately swindles, deceptions; not the revelations of great art. Jonson, however, like the true alchemist working in the tradition of honest alchemy around which he builds his play, wished us to think of him as a comic dramatist who worked with nature, not against it; who understood that art could not cheat nature and that the craftsman, "Who casts to write a living line, must sweat";[8] and who asked of his art no more than his play achieves: the revelation of folly and the defeat of villainy by the love of wit.

---

8. Ben Jonson, "To the Memory of My Beloved, the Author Mr. William Shakespeare: And What He Hath Left Us," line 59—the prefatory poem to the 1623 folio edition of Shakespeare's works.

To the Lady, Most
Deserving Her Name,
and Blood:
Mary,
Lady Wroth.

Madam,

In the age of sacrifices the truth of religion was not in the greatness
and fat of the off'rings, but in the devotion and zeal of the sacrificers:
else, what could a handful of gums have done in the sight of a hecatomb? Or, how might I appear at this altar, except with those
affections that no less love the light and witness than they have the   5
conscience of your virtue? If what I offer bear an acceptable odor and
hold the first strength, it is your value of it which remembers where,
when, and to whom it was kindled. Otherwise, as the times are,
there comes rarely forth that thing so full of authority or example,
but by assiduity and custom grows less and loses. This, yet safe in   10
your judgment (which is a Sidney's), is forbidden to speak more,
lest it talk or look like one of the ambitious faces of the time: who,
the more they paint are the less themselves.

Your La[dyship's] true honorer,
Ben. Jonson

WROTH *also spelled and pronounced "worth," therefore "deserving."*
  3 GUMS *incense.*
  3–4 HECATOMB *sacrifice.*
  5 WITNESS *evidence, acts bearing witness to virtue.*
  6 CONSCIENCE *knowledge.*
  10 ASSIDUITY AND CUSTOM *use and familiarity.* THIS *i.e. the dedicatory letter and the
    praise of Lady Mary.*
  11 SIDNEY'S *N. (N. refers throughout to a corresponding note to be found at the end of
    the text.)*
  13 PAINT *make up, use cosmetics.*

To the Reader

If thou beest more, thou art an understander, and then I trust thee.
If thou art one that tak'st up, and but a pretender, beware at what
hands thou receiv'st thy commodity; for thou wert never more fair
in the way to be cozened than in this age in poetry, especially in
5 plays: wherein now the concupiscence of dances and antics so
reigneth as to run away from Nature and be afraid of her is the only
point of art that tickles the spectators. But how out of purpose and
place do I name art, when the professors are grown so obstinate
contemners of it, and presumers on their own naturals, as they are
10 deriders of all diligence that way, and, by simple mocking at the
terms, when they understand not the things, think to get off wittily
with their ignorance? Nay, they are esteemed the more learned
and sufficient for this by the many, through their excellent vice
of judgment. For they commend writers as they do fencers or
15 wrestlers, who, if they come in robustuously and put for it with a

TO THE READER *this critical preface appears in the quarto edition* (Q) *but not in the folio* (F).

2-3 TAK'ST UP . . . COMMODITY N. (N. *refers throughout to a corresponding note at end of text.*)

5 CONCUPISCENCE OF . . . ANTICS *appetite for stage spectacles, wild dances, and grotesque* (antic, antique) *fools.*

6 RUN AWAY FROM NATURE N.

8 PROFESSORS *playwrights, who profess art.*

9 NATURALS *natural, untrained, uninstructed gifts—" a natural" was also a fool.*

11 TERMS *the terminology of neo-classical criticism, e.g. the unities of place, time, action.*

13 MANY Q, *multitude.*

14-15 FENCERS OR WRESTLERS *Fencing and wrestling matches were among the many other kinds of spectacle which, along with plays, were staged in the public theaters.*

great deal of violence, are received for the braver fellows; when many times their own rudeness is the cause of their disgrace, and a little touch of their adversary gives all that boisterous force the foil. I deny not but that these men, who always seek to do more than enough, may some time happen on some thing that is good and 20 great, but very seldom. And when it comes, it doth not recompense the rest of their ill. It sticks out perhaps and is more eminent because all is sordid and vile about it, as lights are more discerned in a thick darkness than a faint shadow. I speak not this out of a hope to do good on any man against his will; for I know, if it were put to the 25 question of theirs and mine, the worse would find more suffrages, because the most favor common errors. But I give thee this warning, that there is a great difference between those that (to gain the opinion of copy) utter all they can, however unfitly, and those that use election and a mean. For it is only the disease of the unskillful to think 30 rude things greater than polished, or scattered more numerous than composed.

17 RUDENESS *lack of skill or art.*
18 FOIL *defeat.*
22 ILL *ill-doing.*
25–26 PUT . . . MINE *"if the popularity of their plays and mine were voted on."*
26 SUFFRAGES *acceptances.*
27 MOST *most people.*
28–29 OPINION OF COPY *reputation for copiousness, easy flow of words and imagination.*
30 ELECTION AND A MEAN *careful selection of materials and moderation in use and placement.*
31–32 SCATTERED . . . COMPOSED *N.*

The Persons of the Play

Subtle, the Alchemist
Face, the Housekeeper
Dol Common, their Colleague
Dapper, a Clerk
Drugger, a Tobaccoman
Lovewit, Master of the House
Epicure Mammon, a Knight
Surly, a Gamester
Tribulation, a Pastor of Amsterdam
Ananias, a Deacon there
Kastril, the Angry Boy
Dame Pliant, his Sister: a Widow

Neighbours
Officers
Mutes

The Scene
LONDON

HOUSEKEEPER *caretaker.* (*Also owner of the playhouse?*)
GAMESTER *gambler, man who lives by his wits.*
AMSTERDAM *various groups of Puritans fled from England to Holland for religious freedom.*
KASTRIL *a small hawk.*
ANGRY BOY *bully, quarreler.*
MUTES *characters who appear but do not speak, such as the Parson in V.5.*

THE ARGUMENT

T he sickness hot, a master quit, for fear,
H is house in town, and left one servant there.
E ase him corrupted, and gave means to know

A cheater and his punk who, now brought low,
5   L eaving their narrow practice, were become
C oz'ners at large; and only wanting some
H ouse to set up, with him they here contract
E ach for a share, and all begin to act.
M uch company they draw, and much abuse,
10   I n casting figures, telling fortunes, news,
S elling of flies, flat bawdry, with the stone;
T ill it, and they, and all in fume are gone.

1 SICKNESS *plague; endemic in London, severe in 1609–10, the year the play was performed.*

4 PUNK *whore.*

5 NARROW PRACTICE *i.e. simple swindling and prostitution.*

10 CASTING FIGURES *drawing up horoscopes.* NEWS *N.*

11 FLIES *gambling charms, familiar spirits.* FLAT *downright.* STONE *the philosopher's stone, which turned base metal into silver and gold.*

12 IN FUME *volatilized.*

PROLOGUE

Fortune, that favors fools, these two short hours
    We wish away, both for your sakes and ours,

1 TWO SHORT HOURS *N.*

Judging spectators, and desire in place,
　To th' author justice, to ourselves but grace.
Our scene is London, 'cause we would make known,　　　　5
　No country's mirth is better than our own.
No clime breeds better matter for your whore,
　Bawd, squire, impostor, many persons more,
Whose manners, now called humors, feed the stage,
　And which have still been subject for the rage　　　　10
Or spleen of comic writers. Though this pen
　Did never aim to grieve, but better men,
Howe'er the age he lives in doth endure
　The vices that she breeds, above their cure.
But, when the wholesome remedies are sweet,　　　　15
　And in their working gain and profit meet,
He hopes to find no spirit so much diseased,
　But will with such fair correctives be pleased.
For here he doth not fear who can apply.
　If there be any that will sit so nigh　　　　20
Unto the stream to look what it doth run,
　They shall find things they'd think, or wish, were done;
They are so natural follies, but so shown
　As even the doers may see, and yet not own.

4 OURSELVES *i.e. the actors of the King's Men, Shakespeare's playing company, who first performed* The Alchemist.
7 MATTER *material, models.*
9 HUMORS *character traits. N.*
10 STILL *always.*
11 SPLEEN *anger.*
19 APPLY *identify the characters as parodies of specific people. N.*
20–21 "*Peer so closely into the play and analyze it.*"
24 OWN *acknowledge as their own (follies). See N. to l. 19 above.*

Act I Scene 1

[*The Scene, London. A Private House.*]

[*Face.*] Believe 't, I will.

Subtle.   Thy worst. I fart at thee.

Dol Common. Ha' you your wits? Why, gentlemen! for love—

Face. Sirrah, I'll strip you—

Subtle.   What to do? Lick figs

Out at my—

Face.   Rogue, rogue, out of all your sleights.

Dol Common. Nay, look ye, Sovereign, General, are you madmen?

Subtle. O, let the wild sheep loose. I'll gum your silks

With good strong water, an' you come.

                [*He threatens to throw a vial at him.*]

Dol Common.   Will you have

The neighbors hear you? Will you betray all?

Hark, I hear somebody.

Face.   Sirrah—

---

1 [*Face.*] N. (*N. refers throughout to a corresponding note at end of text.*)

3 FIGS *piles, or stools.*

5 SOVEREIGN, GENERAL *N.*

6 GUM *ruin.*

7 STRONG WATER *acid.*

Subtle.   I shall mar
All that the tailor has made, if you approach.   10
    Face. You most notorious whelp, you insolent slave,
Dare you do this?
    Subtle.   Yes, faith, yes, faith.
    Face.   Why, who
Am I, my mongrel? Who am I?
    Subtle.   I'll tell you,
Since you know not yourself—
    Face.   Speak lower, rogue.
    Subtle. Yes. You were once (time's not long past) the good,   15
Honest, plain, livery-three-pound-thrum, that kept
Your master's worship's house, here, in the Friars,
For the vacations—
    Face.   Will you be so loud?
    Subtle. Since, by my means, translated suburb-Captain.
    Face. By your means, Doctor Dog?
    Subtle.   Within man's memory,   20
All this I speak of.
    Face.   Why, I pray you, have I
Been countenanced by you, or you by me?
Do but collect, sir, where I met you first.

---

10 ALL . . . MADE *i.e. Face's captain's costume, beneath which he is only the servant Jeremy.*

16 LIVERY . . . THRUM *cheaply dressed, poorly paid (three pounds a year), servant (wearing livery).* THRUM *ends of yarn; also slang for sex, "thrum a wench."*

17 FRIARS *Blackfriars. N.*

18 VACATIONS *periods between terms of court.*

19 SUBURB-CAPTAIN *braggart, mere pretender to rank. Suburbs were the slummy edges of the city.*

22 COUNTENANCED *supported, but with a pun on "given a countenance" or face. Subtle has been changed from a poor thief to a Doctor.*

23 COLLECT *recollect.*

    Subtle. I do not hear well. [*Cupping his ear.*]
    Face.   Not of this, I think it.

25 But I shall put you in mind, sir: at Pie-corner,
    Taking your meal of steam in from cooks' stalls,
    Where, like the father of hunger, you did walk
    Piteously costive, with your pinched-horn nose,
    And your complexion of the Roman wash,
30 Stuck full of black and melancholic worms,
    Like powder-corns shot at th'artillery-yard.
    Subtle. I wish you could advance your voice, a little.
    Face. When you went pinned up in the several rags
    Y'had raked and picked from dunghills before day,
35 Your feet in mouldy slippers, for your kibes,
    A felt of rug, and a thin threaden cloak,
    That scarce would cover your no-buttocks—
    Subtle.   So, sir!
    Face. When all your alchemy, and your algebra,
    Your minerals, vegetals, and animals,
40 Your conjuring, coz'ning, and your dozen of trades,
    Could not relieve your corpse with so much linen
    Would make you tinder but to see a fire;

---

25 PIE-CORNER *area of small eating places near Smithfield, just outside northern city walls.*
28 COSTIVE *constipated (from hunger).* PINCHED-HORN *resembling a shoehorn.*
29 ROMAN WASH *sallow (?).*
30 BLACK . . . WORMS *blackheads.*
31 POWDER . . . YARD *unburnt grains of black powder lying about the firing range.*
32 ADVANCE *raise.*
35 KIBES *sore feet.*
36 FELT OF RUG *hat of rough cloth.*
38 ALGEBRA *associated with alchemy. Mathematics in general was still popularly thought a form of magic.*
39 VEGETALS *plants.*
41 LINEN *underclothing.*
42 TINDER *shreds of linen were used to start fires.*

I ga' you count'nance, credit for your coals,
Your stills, your glasses, your materials,
Built you a furnace, drew you customers,   45
Advanced all your black arts; lent you, beside,
A house to practise in—
    Subtle.   Your master's house!
    Face. Where you have studied the more thriving skill
Of bawdry since.
    Subtle.   Yes, in your master's house.
You and the rats here kept possession.   50
Make it not strange. I know y'were one could keep
The buttery-hatch still locked, and save the chippings,
Sell the dole beer to aqua-vitae men,
The which, together with your Christmas vails
At post-and-pair, your letting out of counters,   55
Made you a pretty stock, some twenty marks,
And gave you credit to converse with cobwebs
Here, since your mistress' death hath broke up house.
           [His voice rises through the speech.]
    Face. You might talk softlier, rascal.
    Subtle.   No, you scarab,

---

43 COALS *special fuels were used in alchemical furnaces.*
44 MATERIALS *the metals used in alchemy.*
46 BLACK ARTS *black magic, as distinguished from white or natural legitimate magic.*
49 BAWDRY *both pimping and prostitution.*
51 MAKE . . . STRANGE "*don't pretend innocence.*"
52–53 N.
54 VAILS *gratuities.*
55 POST-AND-PAIR *a card game.* COUNTERS *chips for gambling. (Is the suggestion that Face ran a game of some kind in the house?)*
56 STOCK *capital.* TWENTY MARKS *about fourteen pounds sterling. Worth much more than today, but a trivial amount compared to the treasure these rogues collect by the end of the play.*
57 GAVE YOU CREDIT *i.e.* "*this is how far it got you.*"
59 SCARAB *dung beetle.*

60 I'll thunder you in pieces. I will teach you
    How to beware to tempt a Fury again
    That carries tempest in his hand and voice.
        Face. The place has made you valiant.
        Subtle.   No, your clothes!
    Thou vermin, have I ta'en thee out of dung,
65 So poor, so wretched, when no living thing
    Would keep thee company, but a spider, or worse?
    Raised thee from brooms, and dust, and wat'ring-pots?
    Sublimed thee, and exalted thee, and fixed thee
    I' the third region, called our state of grace?
70 Wrought thee to spirit, to quintessence, with pains
    Would twice have won me the philosopher's work?
    Put thee in words and fashion? made thee fit
    For more than ordinary fellowships?
    Giv'n thee thy oaths, thy quarreling dimensions?
75 Thy rules to cheat at horse-race, cock-pit, cards,
    Dice, or whatever gallant tincture else?
    Made thee a second in mine own great art?
    And have I this for thank! Do you rebel?

63 NO, YOUR CLOTHES *a sneer at Face's pretense of being a brave captain, i.e.* "*as if valor came from them!*"

64–79 *in these and the following lines Subtle uses alchemy as a metaphor for the transformation of Face. As base metal is changed into gold, so the butler has been made into a captain. For the specific meaning of the alchemical terms in the play see Appendix I, where the alchemical terms used are listed alphabetically and defined, along with a general discussion of alchemical theory.*

71 PHILOSOPHER'S WORK *the end product of alchemical experiment, the* "*stone*" *which turned all metals to gold.*

72 PUT . . . FASHION *taught you to speak and dress in the latest mode.*

74 OATHS *the latest fashions in swearing.* QUARRELING DIMENSIONS *N.*

75 COCK-PIT *cock-fighting.*

76 GALLANT TINCTURE *touch or color (attribute) of gallantry. Tincture is an al-chemical term meaning* "*color.*"

77 ART *i.e. alchemy.*

Do you fly out i' the projection?
Would you be gone now?

    Dol Common.   Gentlemen, what mean you?   80
Will you mar all?

    Subtle.   Slave, thou hadst had no name—

    Dol Common. Will you undo yourselves with civil war?

    Subtle. Never been known past *equi clibanum*,
The heat of horse-dung, underground in cellars,
Or an ale-house darker than Deaf John's; been lost   85
To all mankind but laundresses and tapsters,
Had not I been. [*Shouting.*]

    Dol Common. D'you know who hears you, Sovereign?

    Face. Sirrah—

    Dol Common. Nay, General, I thought you were civil—

    Face. I shall turn desperate if you grow thus loud.

    Subtle. And hang thyself, I care not.

    Face.   Hang thee, collier,   90
And all thy pots and pans, in picture, I will,
Since thou hast moved me—

    Dol Common.   O, this'll o'erthrow all.

    Face. Write thee up bawd in Paul's; have all thy tricks
Of coz'ning with a hollow coal, dust, scrapings,

---

79 FLY OUT *escape, evaporate.* PROJECTION *climax of alchemy, the operation by which base metal is turned to gold.*

83 KNOWN *famed.* PAST EQUI CLIBANUM *"more than the stage of heating with horse manure," i.e. not very advanced (alchemically) or very famous. See Appendix I.*

85 DEAF JOHN'S *a tavern, unknown, but obviously a low dive.*

90 COLLIER *coal carrier; the alchemist works with coals, but there is also a pun on "collar," hangman's noose.*

91 IN PICTURE *drawing. Face is threatening to expose Subtle publicly as alchemist and magician.*

92 MOVED *angered.*

93 WRITE . . . PAUL'S *"publicly advertise you as a procurer" by putting up posters in the aisles of St. Paul's Cathedral, where notices were usually posted.*

95 Searching for things lost with a sieve and shears,
Erecting figures in your rows of houses,
And taking in of shadows with a glass,
Told in red letters; and a face cut for thee,
Worse than Gamaliel Ratsey's.

    Dol Common.   Are you sound?
Ha'you your senses, masters?

100   *Face.*   I will have
A book, but barely reckoning thy impostures,
Shall prove a true philosopher's stone to printers.

    Subtle. Away, you trencher-rascal!

    Face.   Out, you dog-leech!
The vomit of all prisons—

    Dol Common.   Will you be
Your own destructions, gentlemen?

105   *Face.*   Still spewed out
For lying too heavy o' the basket.

    Subtle.   Cheater!

    Face. Bawd!

    Subtle.   Cowherd!

    Face.   Conjurer!

    Subtle.   Cutpurse!

    Face.   Witch!

    Dol Common.   O me!
We are ruined! lost! Ha'you no more regard

94–99 *a catalogue of some of Subtle's swindles.* N.

99 SOUND *sane.*

101 BARELY RECKONING *summing up only a minimal number.*

102 PRINTERS *i.e. the publishers will make a fortune selling such a sensational exposé.*

103 TRENCHER-RASCAL *glutton.* DOG-LEECH *veterinarian (?) or some vermin on dogs (?).*

106 BASKET *stomach, bread-basket.*

To your reputations? Where's your judgment? 'Slight,
Have yet some care of me, o' your republic—   110
   Face. Away this brach! I'll bring thee, rogue, within
The statute of sorcerie, *tricesimo tertio*
Of Harry the Eight; ay, and perhaps thy neck
Within a noose, for laund'ring gold and barbing it.
       She catcheth out Face his sword. Breaks Subtle's glass.
   Dol Common. You'll bring your head within a coxcomb, will you?   115
And you, sir, with your menstrue! Gather it up.
'Sdeath, you abominable pair of stinkards,
Leave off your barking and grow one again,
Or, by the light that shines, I'll cut your throats.
I'll not be made a prey unto the marshal   120
for ne'er a snarling dog-bolt o' you both.
Ha' you together cozened all this while,
And all the world, and shall it now be said
You've made most courteous shift to cozen yourselves?
[*To Face.*] You will accuse him! You will bring him in   125
Within the statute! Who shall take your word?
A whoreson, upstart, apocryphal captain,

---

109 'SLIGHT *"By God's light," a familiar oath.*
110 REPUBLIC *Dol is continuing her political metaphor, but* respublica *means literally, " a public or common thing."*
111 BRACH *bitch.*
112 STATUTE *N.*
114 LAUND'RING . . . BARBING *washing coins in acid and clipping their edges to obtain gold. Defacing coinage was strictly prohibited.*
SD FACE HIS *Face's, the old grammatical form of the possessive.*
116 MENSTRUE *solvent.*
117 'SDEATH *by God's death.*
121 DOG-BOLT *blunt-headed arrow, i.e. noisy but not dangerous.*
124 SHIFT *stratagem.*
127 APOCRYPHAL *phony—from "the Apocrypha," the unauthentic books of the Bible.*

Act I Scene 1

Whom not a Puritan in Blackfriars will trust
So much as for a feather! [*To Subtle.*] And you, too,
130　Will give the cause, forsooth? You will insult,
And claim a primacy in the divisions?
You must be chief? As if you only had
The powder to project with, and the work
Were not begun out of equality?
135　The venter tripartite? All things in common?
Without priority? 'Sdeath, you perpetual curs,
Fall to your couples again, and cozen kindly,
And heartily, and lovingly, as you should,
And lose not the beginning of a term,
140　Or, by this hand, I shall grow factious too,
And take my part and quit you.
　　　Face.　　　　　　　　　'Tis his fault;
He ever murmurs, and objects his pains,
And says the weight of all lies upon him.
　　　Subtle. Why, so it does.
　　　Dol Common.　　　　　How does it? Do not we
Sustain our parts?
145　　*Subtle.*　　　　Yes, but they are not equal.
　　　Dol Common. Why, if your part exceed today, I hope
Ours may tomorrow match it.

128–29 PURITAN . . . FEATHER *Puritan merchants in the Blackfriars area sold feathers and other fashionable items of dress.*
130 CAUSE *i.e. for a quarrel. See* IV.2.22.
131 PRIMACY . . . DIVISIONS *first share in the spoils when they are divided.*
133 POWDER . . . PROJECT *the stone, in powdered form, to change lead to gold.* WORK *alchemy.*
135 VENTER *venture.*
137 FALL . . . COUPLES *joint together.*
139 TERM *period when courts were sitting and there was most activity in London.*
142 OBJECTS HIS PAINS *emphasizes his work.*

Subtle.   Ay, they may.

Dol Common. "May," murmuring mastiff? Ay, and do. Death on
me!

[*To Face.*] Help me to throttle him. [*Chokes Subtle.*]

Subtle.   Dorothy! Mistress Dorothy!
'Ods precious, I'll do anything. What do you mean?   150

Dol Common. Because o' your fermentation and cibation?

Subtle. Not I, by heaven—

Dol Common. Your Sol and Luna—[*To Face.*] Help me.

Subtle. Would I were hanged then! I'll conform myself.

Dol Common. Will you, sir, do so then, and quickly: swear!

Subtle. What should I swear?

Dol Common.   To leave your faction, sir,   155
And labor kindly in the commune work.

Subtle. Let me not breathe if I meant aught beside.
I only used those speeches as a spur
To him.

Dol Common. I hope we need no spurs, sir. Do we?

Face. 'Slid, prove today who shall shark best.

Subtle.   Agreed.   160

Dol Common. Yes, and work close and friendly.

Subtle.   'Slight, the knot
Shall grow the stronger for this breach, with me.

Dol Common. Why so, my good baboons! Shall we go make
A sort of sober, scurvy, precise neighbors,
That scarce have smiled twice sin' the king came in,   165

150 'ODS PRECIOUS *"by God's precious" (body or blood).*
151 FERMENTATION AND CIBATION *alchemical processes, see Appendix I.*
152 SOL AND LUNA *sun and moon; in alchemy gold and silver.*
155 FACTION *divisiveness.*
156 COMMUNE *shared, community.*
160 'SLID *God's eyelid.*
164 PRECISE *puritanical—precise in matters of conscience and biblical interpretation.*
165 KING *James I, king since 1603, seven years before the play.*

A feast of laughter at our follies? Rascals
Would run themselves from breath to see me ride,
Or you t'have but a hole to thrust your heads in,
For which you should pay ear-rent. No, agree.

170 And may Don Provost ride a-feasting long
In his old velvet jerkin and stained scarves,
My noble Sovereign, and worthy General,
Ere we contribute a new crewel garter
To his most worsted worship.

  Subtle.   Royal Dol!

175 Spoken like Claridiana, and thyself!

  Face. For which at supper thou shalt sit in triumph,
And not be styled Dol Common but Dol Proper,
Dol Singular; the longest cut at night
Shall draw thee for his Dol Particular.

           [*Bell rings.*]

180 *Subtle.* Who's that? One rings. To the window, Dol. Pray heav'n
The master do not trouble us this quarter.

  Face. O, fear not him. While there dies one a week
O' the plague, he's safe from thinking toward London.

---

167 RIDE *i.e. in a cart. Whores were stripped and driven through the streets, and
  sometimes whipped.*

168 HOLE *i.e. in the stocks.*

169 EAR-RENT *prisoners in the stocks sometimes had their ears clipped or cut off as
  further punishment.*

170–74 DON PROVOST . . . WORSHIP *N.*

175 CLARIDIANA *heroine of a Spanish romance,* The Mirror of Knighthood.

177–78 COMMON . . . PROPER . . . SINGULAR *ordinary . . . special . . . particular.
  "Not everybody's Dol, but a very special one."*

178 CUT *straw. They will draw to see who gets her all to himself, "particular," this
  night. On less special occasions she was presumably shared.*

181 QUARTER *term of the year.*

Beside, he's busy at his hop-yards now;
I had a letter from him. If he do,   185
He'll send such word for airing o' the house
As you shall have sufficient time to quit it.
Though we break up a fortnight, 'tis no matter.
   Subtle. Who is it, Dol?
   Dol Common.   A fine young quodling.
   Face.   O,
My lawyer's clerk, I lighted on last night   190
In Holborn, at the Dagger. He would have
(I told you of him) a familiar,
To rifle with at horses, and win cups.
   Dol Common. O, let him in.
   Subtle.   Stay. Who shall do't?
   Face.   Get you
Your robes on. I will meet him, as going out.   195
   Dol Common. And what shall I do?
   Face.   Not be seen; away!
                        [Exit Dol.]
Seem you very reserved.
   Subtle.   Enough.
   Face. [Calling out loudly.]
               God b' wi' you, sir.
I pray you, let him know that I was here.
His name is Dapper. I would gladly have stayed, but—

---

184 HOP-YARDS *hops are still grown in Kent, where they ripen in late summer.*
189 QUODLING *green apple; a young lawyer (?).*
191 DAGGER *inn on High Holborn.*
192 FAMILIAR *i.e. a witch's familiar, a spirit, usually in animal form, which does the bidding of its master. Dapper's familiar takes the form of a fly.*
193 RIFLE *gamble.* CUPS *drinks (?) valuable tankards (?).*
199 STAYED *waited.*

Act I Scene 2

[*Dapper calls from without.*]

Dapper. Captain, I am here.

Face.   Who's that? He's come, I think,
Doctor.

[*Enter Dapper.*]

Good faith, sir, I was going away.

Dapper.   In truth,
I'm very sorry, Captain.

Face.   But I thought
Sure I should meet you.

Dapper.   Ay, I'm very glad.
5   I had a scurvy writ or two to make,
And I had lent my watch last night to one
That dines today at the sheriff's, and so was robbed
Of my pass-time. Is this the cunning man?

Face. This is his worship.

Dapper.   Is he a doctor?

Face.   Yes.

Dapper. And ha' you broke with him, Captain?

Face.   Ay.
10   *Dapper.*   And how?

Face. Faith, he does make the matter, sir, so dainty,
I know not what to say—

Dapper.   Not so, good Captain.

Face. Would I were fairly rid on 't, believe me.

Dapper. Nay, now you grieve me, sir. Why should you wish so?

---

6 WATCH *still a rarity and mark of wealth.*

9 DOCTOR *not medical, but in the more original sense of "learned."*

11 MAKE . . . DAINTY *"considers the affair (of the charm) to be of great delicacy."*

I dare assure you I'll not be ungrateful.   15
   Face. I cannot think you will, sir. But the law
Is such a thing—and then, he says, Read's matter
Falling so lately—
   Dapper.   Read! He was an ass,
And dealt, sir, with a fool.
   Face.   It was a clerk, sir.
   Dapper. A clerk?
   Face.   Nay, hear me, sir. You know the law   20
Better, I think—
   Dapper.   I should, sir, and the danger.
You know I showed the statute to you.
   Face.   You did so.
   Dapper. And will I tell then? By this hand of flesh,
Would it might never write good courthand more
If I discover. What do you think of me,   25
That I am a chiaus?
   Face.   What's that?
   Dapper.   The Turk was here.
As one would say, do you think I am a Turk?
   Face. I'll tell the Doctor so.
   Dapper.   Do, good sweet Captain.
   Face. Come, noble Doctor, 'pray thee, let's prevail;
This is the gentleman, and he is no chiaus.   30
   Subtle. Captain, I have returned you all my answer.
I would do much, sir, for your love—But this
I neither may, nor can.
   Face.   Tut, do not say so.

16 LAW *against sorcery.*
17 READ'S MATTER *N.*
24 COURTHAND *the type of script used in legal documents.*
25 DISCOVER *disclose.*
26 CHIAUS *cheat, derived from Turkish word for messenger.* TURK WAS HERE (*who*)
   was here. N.

You deal now with a noble fellow, Doctor,

35   One that will thank you richly; and he's no chiaus.

Let that, sir, move you.

    Subtle.   Pray you, forbear—

    Face.   He has

Four angels here.

    Subtle.   You do me wrong, good sir.

    Face. Doctor, wherein? To tempt you with these spirits?

                     [*Holding up the coins.*]

    Subtle. To tempt my art and love, sir, to my peril.

40   'Fore heav'n, I scarce can think you are my friend,

That so would draw me to apparent danger.

    Face. I draw you? A horse draw you, and a halter,

You, and your flies together—

    Dapper.   Nay, good Captain.

    Face. That know no difference of men.

    Subtle.   Good words, sir.

45   *Face.* Good deeds, sir, Doctor Dogs'-meat. 'Slight, I bring you

No cheating Clim-o'-the-Cloughs or Claribels,

That look as big as five-and-fifty and flush

And spit out secrets like hot custard—

    Dapper.   Captain.

    Face. Nor any melancholic underscribe,

50   Shall tell the vicar; but a special gentle,

That is the heir to forty marks a year,

---

37 ANGELS *coins worth about ten shillings, so called because they bore a figure of the archangel Michael.*

43 FLIES *familiar spirits, for gambling here.*

46 CLIM *legendary outlaw.* CLARIBEL *a lewd knight in Spenser's* Faerie Queene *(4.9.20), but the true reference here is probably lost.*

47–48 N.

50 VICAR *vicar-general, officer of the ecclesiastical court, which would have jurisdiction in sorcery cases.*

51 HEIR TO *has an income of.* MARKS *a mark was worth about fifteen shillings.*

Consorts with the small poets of the time,
Is the sole hope of his old grandmother,
That knows the law, and writes you six fair hands,
Is a fine clerk, and has his ciph'ring perfect,   55
Will take his oath o' the Greek Xenophon,
If need be, in his pocket, and can court
His mistress out of Ovid.

   Dapper.   Nay, dear Captain.

   Face. Did you not tell me so?

   Dapper.   Yes; but I'd ha' you
Use Master Doctor with some more respect.   60

   Face. Hang him, proud stag, with his broad velvet head.
But for your sake I'd choke ere I would change
An article of breath with such a puck-fist!
Come, let's be gone.

   Subtle.   Pray you, le' me speak with you.

   Dapper. His worship calls you, Captain.

   Face.   I am sorry   65
I e'er embarked myself in such a business. [*Going.*]

   Dapper. Nay, good sir; he did call you.

   Face.   Will he take, then?

   Subtle. First, hear me—

   Face.   Not a syllable, 'less you take.

---

54 SIX FAIR HANDS *i.e. a good penman who wrote several of the different styles of writing in use at the time for various purposes.*

55 CIPH'RING *arithmetic; more specifically, bookkeeping.*

56–57 XENOPHON . . . POCKET *N.*

58 OVID *N.*

61 VELVET HEAD *the "velvet" on the growing horns of a stag, and the velvet cap worn by the doctor.*

62 CHANGE *exchange.*

63 PUCK-FIST *puff-ball fungus: airy nothing.*

    Subtle. Pray ye, sir—

    Face.   Upon no terms but an *assumpsit.*

    Subtle. Your humor must be law.

                 He takes the money.

70   *Face.*   Why now, sir, talk.
Now I dare hear you with mine honor. Speak.
So may this gentleman too.

    Subtle.   Why, sir— [*Tries to whisper to Dapper.*]

    Face.   No whisp'ring.

    Subtle. 'Fore heav'n, you do not apprehend the loss
You do yourself in this.

    Face.   Wherein? For what?

75   *Subtle.* Marry, to be so importunate for one,
That, when he has it, will undo you all:
He'll win up all the money i' the town.

    Face. How!

    Subtle.   Yes, and blow up gamester after gamester,
As they do crackers in a puppet-play.

80 If I do give him a familiar,
Give you him all you play for; never set him,
For he will have it.

    Face.   You're mistaken, Doctor.
Why, he does ask one but for cups and horses,
A rifling fly; none o' your great familiars.

85   *Dapper.* Yes, Captain, I would have it, for all games.

---

69 ASSUMPSIT *legal term, verbal promise to perform some act.*
79 CRACKERS *firecrackers, used for sound effects in puppet-plays and other crude drama.*
80 FAMILIAR *familiar spirit, a demon in animal form (such as a fly) controlled by owner.*
81 SET *bet against.*
84 GREAT FAMILIAR *a major demon, such as Mephistopholes, to whom Marlowe's Dr. Faustus sells his soul in order to gain him as a familiar.*

Subtle. I told you so.

Face.   'Slight, that's a new business.
I understood you, a tame bird, to fly
Twice in a term, or so, on Friday nights,
When you had left the office, for a nag
Of forty or fifty shillings.

Dapper.   Ay, 'tis true, sir;   90
But I do think, now, I shall leave the law,
And therefore—

Face.   Why, this changes quite the case!
D' you think that I dare move him?

Dapper.   If you please, sir;
All's one to him, I see.

Face.   What! for that money?
I cannot with my conscience. Nor should you   95
Make the request, methinks.

Dapper.   No, sir, I mean
To add consideration.

Face.   Why, then, sir,
I'll try. [*Turns to Subtle.*] Say that it were for all games, Doctor?

Subtle. [*Speaking sotto voce.*] I say, then, not a mouth shall eat for
    him
At any ordinary, but o' the score,   100
That is a gaming mouth, conceive me.

Face.   Indeed!

Subtle. He'll draw you all the treasure of the realm,

---

93 MOVE *urge.*
94 ALL'S ONE *"it's all the same." Subtle's magic can call either great or small demons.*
99–101 *"No gambler will any longer have enough cash to pay for a meal, but will
    have to charge it."*
99 FOR *because of.*
100 ORDINARY *inn.* O' THE SCORE *"on the cuff," charged or scored up on the books.*
101 CONCEIVE *understand.*

If it be set him.

    Face.   Speak you this from art?

    Subtle. Ay, sir, and reason too, the ground of art.

105 He's o' the only best complexion

The Queen of Faery loves.

    Face.   What! Is he?

    Subtle.   Peace.

He'll overhear you. Sir, should she but see him—

    Face. What!

    Subtle.   Do not you tell him.

    Face.   Will he win at cards too?

    Subtle. The spirits of dead Holland, living Isaac,

110 You'd swear, were in him; such a vigorous luck

As cannot be resisted. 'Slight, he'll put

Six o' your gallants to a cloak, indeed.

    Face. A strange success that some man shall be born to!

    Subtle. He hears you, man—

    Dapper.   Sir, I'll not be ingrateful.

115   *Face.* Faith, I have a confidence in his good nature.

You hear, he says he will not be ingrateful.

    Subtle. Why, as you please; my venture follows yours.

    Face. Troth, do it, Doctor. Think him trusty, and make him.

He may make us both happy in an hour;

120 Win some five thousand pound, and send us two on't.

    Dapper. Believe it, and I will, sir.

    Face.   And you shall, sir.

104 GROUND *basis.*

105 COMPLEXION *temperament, mixture of humors.*

109 DEAD HOLLAND, LIVING ISAAC *N.*

112 TO A CLOAK *i.e. by winning all their other clothing.*

117 MY . . . YOURS *"I'll go along with you."*

118 MAKE *enrich; but also in this play of transformations the word carries its literal sense of "creating" a new Dapper.*

119 HAPPY *fortunate, rich—Latin* beatus.

You have heard all? *Face takes him aside.*
  Dapper.   No, what was't? Nothing, I, sir.
  Face. Nothing?
  Dapper.   A little, sir.
  Face.   Well, a rare star
Reigned at your birth.
  Dapper.   At mine, sir? No.
  Face.   The Doctor
Swears that you are—
  Subtle.   Nay, Captain, you'll tell all now.   125
  Face. Allied to the Queen of Faery.
  Dapper.   Who? That I am?
Believe it, no such matter—
  Face.   Yes, and that
You were born with a caul o' your head.
  Dapper.   Who says so?
  Face.   Come,
You know it well enough, though you dissemble it.
  Dapper. I' fac, I do not. You are mistaken.
  Face.   How!   130

Swear by your fac, and in a thing so known
Unto the Doctor? How shall we, sir, trust you
I' the other matter? Can we ever think,
When you have won five or six thousand pound,
You'll send us shares in 't, by this rate?
  Dapper.   By Jove, sir,   135

---

126 ALLIED *related.*
128 CAUL *cap; a portion of the "inner membrane inclosing the foetus before birth . . .
    sometimes enveloping the head of the child at birth, superstitiously regarded as of
    good omen . . ." (OED).*
130 I'FAC *in faith, a very mild oath, which Face pretends to take very seriously.*
135 BY THIS RATE *"acting in this way."*

I'll win ten thousand pound, and send you half.
I' fac's no oath.

    Subtle.   No, no, he did but jest.

    Face. Go to. Go, thank the Doctor. He's your friend
To take it so.

    Dapper.   I thank his worship.

    Face.   So?
Another angel?

    Dapper.   Must I?

140   *Face.*   Must you? 'Slight,
What else is thanks? Will you be trivial? Doctor,
When must he come for his familiar?

    Dapper. Shall I not ha' it with me?

    Subtle.   O, good sir!
There must a world of ceremonies pass:

145 You must be bathed and fumigated first;
Besides, the Queen of Faery does not rise
Till it be noon.

    Face.   Not if she danced tonight.

    Subtle And she must bless it.

    Face.   Did you never see
Her Royal Grace yet?

    Dapper.   Whom?

    Face.   Your aunt of Faery?

150   *Subtle.* Not since she kissed him in the cradle, Captain;
I can resolve you that.

    Face.   Well, see her Grace,
Whate'er it cost you, for a thing that I know.

---

138 GO TO "*come on now.*"
141 TRIVIAL *petty.*
147 DANCED *i.e. in the fairy dances.*
151 RESOLVE *assure.*

It will be somewhat hard to compass; but
However, see her. You are made, believe it,
If you can see her. Her Grace is a lone woman,   155
And very rich, and if she take a fancy
She will do strange things. See her, at any hand.
'Slid, she may hap to leave you all she has!
It is the Doctor's fear.
 Dapper.   How will't be done, then?
 Face. Let me alone; take you no thought. Do you   160
But say to me, "Captain, I'll see her Grace."
 Dapper. Captain, I'll see her Grace.
 Face.   Enough.
     One knocks without.
 Subtle.   Who's there?
Anon! [*Aside to Face.*] Conduct him forth by the back way.
[*To Dapper.*] Sir, against one o'clock prepare yourself.
Till when, you must be fasting; only, take   165
Three drops of vinegar in at your nose,
Two at your mouth, and one at either ear;
Then, bathe your fingers' ends and wash your eyes,
To sharpen your five senses, and cry "hum"
Thrice, and then "buz" as often; and then, come.   170
 Face. Can you remember this?
 Dapper.   I warrant you.
 Face. Well then, away. 'Tis but your bestowing
Some twenty nobles 'mong her Grace's servants;
And put on a clean shirt. You do not know
What grace her Grace may do you in clean linen. [*Exeunt.*] 175

153 COMPASS *arrange.*
155 LONE *unmarried.*
164 AGAINST *for.*
171 WARRANT *guarantee.*

Act I Scene 3

Subtle. [*Answers the door and admits Drugger.*] Come in!
　　　　　　　[*Calling out the door.*]
　　　　　　　　　Good wives, I pray you forbear me now.
Troth, I can do you no good till afternoon.
　　　　　　　[*Closes the door, turning back to Drugger.*]
What is your name, say you? Abel Drugger?
　　Drugger.　　　　　　　　　Yes, sir.
　　Subtle. A seller of tobacco?
　　Drugger.　　　　　Yes, sir.
　　Subtle.　　　　　　Umh!
Free of the Grocers?
　　Drugger.　　Ay, an't please you.
5　　*Subtle.*　　　　　　　Well—
Your business, Abel?
　　Drugger.　　　This, an't please your worship:
I am a young beginner, and am building
Of a new shop, an't like your worship, just
At corner of a street. Here's the plot on 't—
10　And I would know by art, sir, of your worship,
Which way I should make my door, by necromancy.
And where my shelves? And which should be for boxes?
And which for pots? I would be glad to thrive, sir.
And I was wished to your worship by a gentleman,

1 GOOD WIVES *some of the "mutes" of the play. Perhaps those referred to in*
　I.4.1–3.
5 FREE OF THE GROCERS *a full member of the Grocers' Company, a mercantile guild*
　to which admission was limited. Grocers also sold tobacco.
9 PLOT *plan.*
14 WISHED *recommended.*

One Captain Face, that says you know men's planets,   15
And their good angels, and their bad.
    Subtle.   I do,
If I do see 'em—

               [*Enter Face.*]
    Face.   What! my honest Abel?
Thou art well met here.
    Drugger.   Troth, sir, I was speaking,
Just as your worship came here, of your worship.
I pray you, speak for me to Master Doctor.   20
    Face. He shall do anything. Doctor, do you hear,
This is my friend, Abel, an honest fellow,
He lets me have good tobacco, and he does not
Sophisticate it with sack-lees or oil,
Nor washes it in muscadel and grains,   25
Nor buries it in gravel underground,
Wrapped up in greasy leather, or pissed clouts,
But keeps it in fine lily pots that, opened,
Smell like conserve of roses, or French beans.
He has his maple block, his silver tongs,   30
Winchester pipes, and fire of juniper.
A neat, spruce, honest fellow, and no goldsmith.
    Subtle. He's a fortunate fellow, that I am sure on—
    Face. Already, sir, ha' you found it? Lo thee Abel!
    Subtle. And in right way toward riches—

15 PLANETS *fortunes, told by position of stars.*
17 IF I DO SEE 'EM *i.e. the coins, angels. Drugger meant guardian spirits.*
24 SOPHISTICATE *adulterate.*
24–27 SACK-LEES . . . CLOUTS *N.*
28 FINE LILY POTS *vases, jars for storing drugs and tobacco.*
29 CONSERVE OF ROSES *medicinal preparation made from roses.* FRENCH BEANS *broad*
    bean, with a sweet smelling flower.
30–31 MAPLE . . . JUNIPER *N.*
32 GOLDSMITH *usurer; goldsmiths sometimes served as bankers.*

> *Face.*   Sir!

35   *Subtle.*   This summer
He will be of the clothing of his company,
And next spring called to the scarlet. Spend what he can.
> *Face.* What, and so little beard?
> *Subtle.*   Sir, you must think,
He may have a receipt to make hair come.
40   But he'll be wise, preserve his youth, and fine for 't;
His fortune looks for him another way.
> *Face.* 'Slid, Doctor, how canst thou know this so soon?
I'm amused at that.
> *Subtle.*   By a rule, Captain,
In metoposcopy, which I do work by,
45   A certain star i' the forehead, which you see not.
Your chestnut or your olive-colored face
Does never fail, and your long ear doth promise.
I knew 't by certain spots, too, in his teeth,
And on the nail of his mercurial finger.
> *Face.* Which finger's that?
50   *Subtle.*   His little finger. Look.
You were born upon a Wednesday?

---

36 CLOTHING OF HIS COMPANY *wear the livery (uniform) of the (Grocers') company.*
     A much desired honor for tradesmen.
37 SCARLET *elected a sheriff; another high honor in the city.* SPEND . . . CAN *have all*
     the money he is able to spend.
38 SO LITTLE BEARD *so young.*
39 RECEIPT . . . COME *recipe for hair grower.*
40 FINE *the fine Drugger will have to pay for refusing to accept the civic office of*
     Sheriff, since he is to remain young and find fortune by other means.
43 AMUSED *bemused, amazed.*
44 METOPOSCOPY *fortune-telling from the shape of the forehead and details of body*
     structure.
46 CHESTNUT *this complexion was thought jovial, honest, straightforward.*
47 LONG EAR *sign of intelligence.*

Drugger.   Yes, indeed, sir.

Subtle. The thumb, in chiromancy, we give Venus;
The forefinger to Jove; the midst to Saturn;
The ring to Sol; the least to Mercury,
Who was the lord, sir, of his horoscope,   55
His house of life being Libra, which foreshowed
He should be a merchant and should trade with balance.

Face. Why, this is strange! Is't not, honest Nab?

Subtle. There is a ship now coming from Ormus,
That shall yield him such a commodity   60
Of drugs—[*Takes the plan from Drugger.*]
              This is the west, and this the south?

Drugger. Yes, sir.

Subtle.   And those are your two sides?

Drugger.   Ay, sir.

Subtle. Make me your door, then, south; your broad side, west;
And, on the east side of your shop, aloft,
Write Mathlai, Tarmiel, and Baraborat;   65
Upon the north part, Rael, Velel, Thiel.
They are the names of those Mercurial spirits
That do fright flies from boxes.

Drugger.   Yes, sir.

Subtle.   And
Beneath your threshold bury me a loadstone
To draw in gallants that wear spurs; the rest,   70
They'll seem to follow.

52 CHIROMANCY *palm reading.*
55–57 N.
59 ORMUS *Hormuz, center for spice trade on the Persian Gulf.*
60 COMMODITY *supply.*
65–68 N.
69 LOADSTONE *magnet.*
71 SEEM *be seen, i.e. automatically, where one gallant goes others will immediately follow to be in fashion.*

Face.   That's a secret, Nab!

Subtle. And, on your stall, a puppet, with a vice,

And a court-fucus, to call city-dames.

You shall deal much with minerals.

Drugger.   Sir, I have,

At home, already—

75   *Subtle.*   Ay, I know, you've arsenic,

Vitriol, sal-tartar, argaile, alkali,

Cinoper: I know all. This fellow, Captain,

Will come, in time, to be a great distiller,

And give a[s]say—I will not say directly,

80   But very fair—at the philosopher's stone.

Face. Why, how now, Abel! Is this true?

Drugger.   Good Captain,

What must I give?

Face.   Nay, I'll not counsel thee.

Thou hear'st what wealth he says, spend what thou canst,

Th' art like to come to.

Drugger.   I would gi' him a crown.

85   *Face.* A crown! and toward such a fortune? Heart,

Thou shalt rather gi' him thy shop. No gold about thee?

---

72 STALL *table set in front of a store to display wares.* PUPPET WITH A VICE *some type of figure capable of moving by means of a "vice" or device.*

73 COURT-FUCUS *cosmetic, face powder (used in court?).* CALL *attract.* CITY-DAMES *merchants' wives (who would be eager to learn and use court fashions).*

74 MINERALS *drugs, chemicals. Drugger's tobacco store is already evolving into the modern drugstore.*

76 ARGAILE *cream of tartar.*

77 CINOPER *cinnibar, mercuric sulphide.*

78 DISTILLER *chemist, alchemist.*

79 GIVE A[S]SAY *"have a try at."*

83 SPEND . . . CANST *"no matter how much you spend"* (?).

84 CROWN *silver coin worth five shillings, twenty-five new pence.*

85 TOWARD *"on your way to."*

Drugger. Yes, I have a portague I ha' kept this half-year.

Face. Out on thee, Nab! 'Slight, there was such an offer—
Shalt keep 't no longer. I'll gi' it him for thee?

[*Gives coin to Subtle.*]

Doctor, Nab prays your worship to drink this, and swears   90
He will appear more grateful, as your skill
Does raise him in the world.

Drugger.   I would entreat
Another favor of his worship.

Face.   What is't, Nab?

Drugger. But to look over, sir, my almanac,
And cross out my ill days, that I may neither   95
Bargain nor trust upon them.

Face.   That he shall, Nab.
Leave it, it shall be done, 'gainst afternoon.

Subtle. And a direction for his shelves.

Face.   Now, Nab,
Art thou well pleased, Nab?

Drugger.   Thank, sir, both your worships.

Face.   Away!

[*Exit Drugger.*]

Why, now, you smoky persecutor of nature!   100
Now do you see that something's to be done
Beside your beech-coal, and your cor'sive waters,
Your crosslets, crucibles, and cucurbites?
You must have stuff brought home to you to work on!

87 PORTAGUE *Portugese gold piece, worth about sixteen or more crowns.*
94 ALMANAC *horoscope.*
95 ILL DAYS *unlucky times.*
96 BARGAIN NOR TRUST "*buy nor give credit.*"
98 DIRECTION *plan, layout.*
100 SMOKY PERSECUTOR OF NATURE *i.e. alchemist. N.*
102–03 *for the precise meaning of these and other technical terms see Appendix I.*
104 STUFF *raw materials, in two senses:* (1) *crude metals,* (2) *fools who can be conned.*

105 And yet you think I am at no expense
In searching out these veins, then following 'em,
Then trying 'em out. 'Fore God, my intelligence
Costs me more money than my share oft comes to
In these rare works.

    Subtle.   You're pleasant, sir. How now!

105 EXPENSE *i.e. of time and effort.*

Act I Scene 4

                      [Enter Dol Common.]
    Subtle. What says my dainty Dolkin?
    Dol Common.   Yonder fishwife
Will not away. And there's your giantess,
The bawd of Lambeth.
    Subtle.   Heart, I cannot speak with 'em.
    Dol Common. Not afore night I have told 'em, in a voice
5 Thorough the trunk, like one of your familiars.
But I have spied Sir Epicure Mammon—
    Subtle.   Where?
    Dol Common. Coming along, at far end of the lane,
Slow of his feet, but earnest of his tongue
To one that's with him.
    Subtle.   Face, go you and shift.   *[Exit Face.]*
10 Dol, you must presently make ready too—

3 LAMBETH *area south of the Thames, where the brothels were located.* HEART " *God's Heart," mild oath.*
5 THOROUGH *through.* TRUNK *speaking tube.* FAMILIARS *attendant spirits.*
9 SHIFT *change clothing.*

Dol Common. Why, what's the matter?
   Subtle.   O, I did look for him
With the sun's rising, marvel he could sleep!
This is the day I am to perfect for him
The magisterium, our great work, the stone;
And yield it, made, into his hands; of which   15
He has, this month, talked as he were possessed.
And now he's dealing pieces on 't away.
Methinks I see him ent'ring ordinaries,
Dispensing for the pox; and plaguy houses,
Reaching his dose; walking Moorfields for lepers,   20
And off'ring citizens' wives pomander-bracelets
As his preservative, made of the elixir;
Searching the 'spital, to make old bawds young;
And the highways for beggars to make rich.
I see no end of his labors. He will make   25
Nature ashamed of her long sleep, when art,
Who's but a step-dame, shall do more than She
In Her best love to mankind ever could.
If his dream last, he'll turn the age to gold.   [*Exeunt.*]

---

14 MAGISTERIUM *the mastery, or philosopher's stone which reputedly gave alchemists control over metals and the ability to change them to gold.*

17 DEALING *giving.* ON'T *of it.*

18 ORDINARIES *inns.*

19 DISPENSING *N.* POX *smallpox, and the great pox, syphilis.* PLAGUY HOUSES *quarantined homes or hospitals for those sick with plague.*

20 REACHING HIS DOSE *"extending (to the sick) his potion" (?).* MOORFIELDS *open area outside the northern city walls where lepers (anyone affected with serious skin diseases), who were denied entrance to London, could beg.*

21 POMANDER-BRACELETS *perfumed ball worn in a bracelet to protect against infection of plague.*

22 ELIXIR *medicinal form of the philosopher's stone.*

23 'SPITAL *hospital.*

26–27 NATURE . . . STEP-DAME *N.*

Act II Scene 1

[*Enter Sir Epicure Mammon and Surly.*]
   Mammon. Come on, sir. Now you set your foot on shore
In Novo Orbe; here's the rich Peru,
And there within, sir, are the golden mines,
Great Solomon's Ophir! He was sailing to 't
5   Three years, but we have reached it in ten months.
This is the day wherein, to all my friends,
I will pronounce the happy word, "Be Rich."
This day you shall be spectatissimi.
You shall no more deal with the hollow die,
10   Or the frail card; no more be at charge of keeping
The livery-punk for the young heir, that must
Seal, at all hours, in his shirts. No more,
If he deny, ha' him beaten to 't, as he is
That brings him the commodity. No more
15   Shall thirst of satin, or the covetous hunger

2 NOVO ORBE *the new world.* N.
4–5 OPHIR . . . THREE YEARS *N.*
8 SPECTATISSIMI *center of attention, cynosure.*
9 HOLLOW DIE *loaded dice (singular, die).*
10 FRAIL CARD *frail because not "a sure thing" like alchemy. Since the dice are loaded, the cards are probably marked.* CHARGE *expense.*
11–14 LIVERY-PUNK . . . COMMODITY *N.*

Of velvet entrails for a rude-spun cloak,
To be displayed at Madam Augusta's, make
The sons of sword and hazard fall before
The golden calf, and on their knees, whole nights,
Commit idolatry with wine and trumpets,   20
Or go a-feasting after drum and ensign.
No more of this. You shall start up young viceroys,
And have your punks and punketees, my Surly.
And unto thee I speak it first, "Be Rich."
Where is my Subtle there? Within, ho!
   [*Face.*] *within.*   Sir,   25
He'll come to you, by and by.
   Mammon.   That's his fire-drake,
His Lungs, his Zephyrus, he that puffs his coals
Till he firk nature up in her own center.
You are not faithful, sir. This night I'll change
All that is metal in my house to gold.   30
And, early in the morning will I send
To all the plumbers and the pewterers
And buy their tin and lead up; and to Lothbury
For all the copper.
   Surly.   What, and turn that too?
   Mammon. Yes, and I'll purchase Devonshire and Cornwall,   35

16 ENTRAILS *lining.*
17 AUGUSTA'S *probably a brothel.*
17–21 *N.*
26 FIRE-DRAKE *salamander or dragon living in fire, thus an alchemist's assistant who tended the fires of the furnace.*
27 LUNGS . . . ZEPHYRUS *the attendant who worked the bellows, blowing or puffing on the fire.*
28 FIRK . . . UP *excite, energize. See N. to I.4.26.*
29 FAITHFUL *credulous, in sense of believing.*
33 LOTHBURY *London street where metal-workers had their shops.*
35 DEVONSHIRE AND CORNWALL *site of tin and copper mines.*

Act II Scene 1

And make them perfect Indies! You admire now?
   Surly. No, faith.
   Mammon.   But when you see th' effects of the great med'cine,
Of which one part projected on a hundred
Of Mercury, or Venus, or the Moon,
40 Shall turn it to as many of the Sun;
Nay, to a thousand, so *ad infinitum*,
You will believe me.
   Surly.   Yes, when I see 't, I will.
But if my eyes do cozen me so, and I
Giving 'em no occasion, sure I'll have
A whore shall piss 'em out next day.
45   *Mammon.*   Ha! Why?
Do you think I fable with you? I assure you
He that has once the flower of the sun,
The perfect ruby, which we call elixir,
Not only can do that, but by its virtue
50 Can confer honor, love, respect, long life;
Give safety, valure, yea, and victory,
To whom he will. In eight-and-twenty days
I'll make an old man of fourscore a child.
   Surly. No doubt, he's that already.
   Mammon.   Nay, I mean
55 Restore his years, renew him, like an eagle,
To the fifth age; make him get sons and daughters,

36 INDIES *the new world, thought still to be lands of gold.* ADMIRE *wonder, are amazed.*

37 GREAT MED'CINE *philosopher's stone.*

39–40 MERCURY . . . SUN *in alchemy metals had their corresponding planets: Mercury, quicksilver; Venus, copper; Moon, silver; Sun, gold.*

46 FABLE WITH *tell stories to.*

47–48 FLOWER . . . ELIXIR *all terms for the stone. For definitions see Appendix I.*

51 VALURE *valor and wealth.*

56 FIFTH AGE *years between fifty and sixty-five.*

Young giants, as our philosophers have done,
The ancient patriarchs afore the flood,
But taking, once a week, on a knife's point,
The quantity of a grain of mustard of it;   60
Become stout Marses, and beget young Cupids.
   Surly. The decayed vestals of Pickt-hatch would thank you
That keep the fire alive there.
   Mammon.   'Tis the secret
Of nature naturized 'gainst all infections,
Cures all diseases coming of all causes,   65
A month's grief in a day, a year's in twelve;
And, of what age soever, in a month.
Past all the doses of your drugging doctors.
I'll undertake, withal, to fright the plague
Out o' the kingdom in three months.
   Surly.   And I'll   70
Be bound the players shall sing your praises then,
Without their poets.
   Mammon.   Sir, I'll do 't. Meantime,
I'll give away so much unto my man
Shall serve th' whole city with preservative

57–58 PHILOSOPHERS . . . PATRIARCHS *the longevity of such biblical figures as
Noah was said by the alchemists to result from their possession of the stone and
elixir.*

61 CUPIDS *Cupid was born of Mars and Venus.*

62 DECAYED . . . PICKT-HATCH *old whores. Pickt-hatch near Blackfriars was notorious for the trade. "Vestals" is an ironic reference to the Roman vestal virgins.*

64 NATURE NATURIZED *N.*

66 GRIEF *pain, suffering.*

68 DOSES *medicines.*

71 PLAYERS *theaters were closed whenever deaths from plague reached forty a week.
The actors then lost their salaries.*

72 POETS *playwrights.*

73 MAN *servant.*

75 Weekly, each house his dose, and at the rate—
    Surly. As he that built the water-work does with water?
    Mammon. You are incredulous.
    Surly.   Faith, I have a humor,
I would not willingly be gulled. Your stone
Cannot transmute me.
    Mammon.   Pertinax, Surly
80 Will you believe antiquity? Records?
I'll show you a book where Moses, and his sister,
And Solomon have written of the art;
Ay, and a treatise penned by Adam.
    Surly.   How!
    Mammon. O' the philosopher's stone, and in High Dutch.
    Surly. Did Adam write, sir, in High Dutch?
85   *Mammon.*   He did.
Which proves it was the primitive tongue.
    Surly.   What paper?
    Mammon. On cedar board.
    Surly.   Oh that, indeed, they say,
Will last 'gainst worms.
    Mammon.   'Tis like your Irish wood
'Gainst cobwebs. I have a piece of Jason's fleece too,
90 Which was no other than a book of alchemy,
Writ in large sheepskin, a good fat ram-vellum.

76 WATER-WORK *water had only recently begun to be piped into some London houses*
    from the Thames.
77 HUMOR *strong disposition.*
78 GULLED *tricked.*
81–83 MOSES . . . ADAM *N.*
84 HIGH DUTCH *High German, theorized by some to be the language spoken in Eden.*
86 PRIMITIVE TONGUE *first, original language, from which all other languages derive.*
88 IRISH WOOD *supposed impervious to spiders and rot, through the blessing of*
    St. Patrick.
89–103 JASON'S FLEECE . . . DEMOGORGON *N.*

Such was Pythagoras' thigh, Pandora's tub;
And all that fable of Medea's charms
The manner of our work: the bulls, our furnace,
Still breathing fire; our *argent-vive*, the dragon;   95
The dragon's teeth, mercury sublimate,
That keeps the whiteness, hardness, and the biting;
And they are gathered into Jason's helm,
Th' alembic, and then sowed in Mars his field,
And thence sublimed so often, till they are fixed.   100
Both this, th' Hesperian garden, Cadmus' story,
Jove's shower, the boon of Midas, Argus' eyes,
Boccace his Demogorgon, thousands more,
All abstract riddles of our stone—How now!

104 ABSTRACT RIDDLES *allegories.*

Act II Scene 2

[*Enter Face, disguised as Lungs the Alchemist's Assistant.*]
Mammon. Do we succeed? Is our day come? And holds it?
Face. The evening will set red upon you, sir;
You have color for it, crimson: the red ferment
Has done his office. Three hours hence prepare you
To see projection.
Mammon.   Pertinax, my Surly,   5
Again I say to thee, aloud, "Be Rich."
This day thou shalt have ingots, and tomorrow
Give lords th' affront. Is it, my Zephyrus, right?

2–3 RED . . . CRIMSON *red was the climactic color in the sequence leading to the stone.*
5 PROJECTION *changing base metals to gold.*
8 AFFRONT *insult.*

Act II Scene 2

Blushes the bolt's-head?

    Face.   Like a wench with child, sir

10   That were but now discovered to her master.

    Mammon. Excellent witty, Lungs! My only care is
Where to get stuff enough now to project on;
This town will not half serve me.

    Face.   No, sir? Buy
The covering off o' churches.

    Mammon.   That's true.

    Face.   Yes,

15   Let 'em stand bare, as do their auditory.
Or cap 'em new with shingles.

    Mammon.   No, good thatch:
Thatch will lie light upo' the rafters, Lungs.
Lungs, I will manumit thee from the furnace;
I will restore thee thy complexion, Puff,

20   Lost in the embers; and repair this brain, [*Patting his head.*]
Hurt wi' the fume o' the metals.

    Face.   I have blown, sir,
Hard, for your worship; thrown by many a coal
When 't was not beech; weighed those I put in, just,
To keep your heat still even. These bleared eyes

25   Have waked to read your several colors, sir,
Of the pale citron, the green lion, the crow,

---

9 BLUSHES *turns red.* BOLT'S-HEAD *flask with long neck.*

10 DISCOVERED *revealed.*

11 CARE *concern.*

14 COVERING . . . CHURCHES *churches had lead roofs.*

15 AUDITORY *congregation.*

22 THROWN BY *discarded.*

23 JUST *precisely.*

25 SEVERAL COLORS *the sequence of colors the experiment passed through are listed in the following two lines.*

The peacock's tail, the plumèd swan.
    Mammon.   And, lastly,
Thou hast descried the flower, the *sanguis agni*?
    Face. Yes, sir.
    Mammon.   Where's master?
    Face.   At's prayers, sir, he,
Good man, he's doing his devotions,   30
For the success.
    Mammon.   Lungs, I will set a period
To all thy labors; thou shalt be the master
Of my seraglio.
    Face.   Good, sir.
    Mammon.   But do you hear?
I'll geld you, Lungs.
    Face.   Yes, sir.
    Mammon.   For I do mean
To have a list of wives and concubines   35
Equal with Solomon, who had the stone
Alike with me; and I will make me a back
With the elixir, that shall be as tough
As Hercules', to encounter fifty a night.
Th'art sure thou saw'st it blood?
    Face.   Both blood and spirit, sir.   40
    Mammon. I will have all my beds blown up, not stuffed:
Down is too hard. And then mine oval room

---

28 FLOWER *a term for the last stage of the experiment.* SANGUIS AGNI *blood of the lamb, i.e. red, the climactic color.*

31 PERIOD *end.*

37 BACK *because the elixir made all things perfect, sexual potency would be increased by it.*

39 HERCULES' *on one of his adventures the hero impregnated all but one of the fifty daughters of Thestius.*

40 BLOOD *red as blood.* BLOOD AND SPIRIT *color and quality.*

Filled with such pictures as Tiberius took
From Elephantis, and dull Aretine
45 But coldly imitated. Then, my glasses
Cut in more subtle angles, to disperse
And multiply the figures as I walk
Naked between my succubae. My mists
I'll have of perfume, vapored 'bout the room,
50 To loose our selves in; and my baths like pits
To fall into; from whence we will come forth
And roll us dry in gossamer and roses.—
Is it arrived at ruby?—Where I spy
A wealthy citizen, or rich lawyer,
55 Have a sublimed pure wife, unto that fellow
I'll send a thousand pound to be my cuckold.
    Face. And I shall carry it?
    Mammon.   No. I'll ha' no bawds
But fathers and mothers. They will do it best.
Best of all others. And my flatterers
60 Shall be the pure and gravest of divines
That I can get for money. My mere fools,
Eloquent burgesses; and then my poets

43–44 TIBERIUS . . . ELEPHANTIS *N.*
44 DULL ARETINE *N.*
45 COLDLY *uninspiredly.* GLASSES *mirrors. The picture here is of a room of mirrors reflecting Mammon's image from every angle in infinite numbers.*
48 SUCCUBAE *female demons who had intercourse with men. Also, a whore.* MISTS *some variety of incense or a vaporized perfume blown through the air. N.*
50 LOOSE *N.*
53 RUBY *a more intense stage of red, closer to completion.*
55 SUBLIMED *intensely. Sublimation was in alchemy a process of repeated distillation.*
60 DIVINES *clergymen.*
61 MERE *total.*
62 BURGESSES *councilmen.*

The same that writ so subtly of the fart,
Whom I will entertain, still, for that subject.
The few that would give out themselves to be   65
Court and town stallions, and each where belie
Ladies who are known most innocent, for them,
These will I beg to make me eunuchs of,
And they shall fan me with ten ostrich tails
Apiece, made in a plume to gather wind.   70
We will be brave, Puff, now we ha' the med'cine.
My meat shall all come in in Indian shells,
Dishes of agate, set in gold, and studded,
With emeralds, sapphires, hyacinths, and rubies.
The tongues of carps, dormice, and camels' heels,   75
Boiled i' the spirit of Sol, and dissolved pearl
(Apicius' diet, 'gainst the epilepsy)
And I will eat these broths with spoons of amber,
Headed with diamond and carbuncle.
My foot-boy shall eat pheasants, calvered salmons,   80
Knots, godwits, lampreys. I myself will have
The beards of barbels served instead of salads;
Oiled mushrooms; and the swelling unctuous paps

63 SUBTLY *intricately, elaborately.* WRIT . . . FART *N.*
64 ENTERTAIN *employ.*
66 EACH WHERE *everywhere.*
67 FOR THEM *in connection with them (i.e. those particular braggarts).*
71 BRAVE *dashing, bold, magnificent.* PUFF *another reference to Face's function as bellows tender.*
74 HYACINTH *originally a rare blue stone; now zircon.*
76 SPIRIT OF SOL *distillate of gold.*
77 APICIUS *N.* 'GAINST *to prevent.*
79 CARBUNCLE *precious red stone, e.g. ruby.*
80 CALVERED *sliced fresh, even alive, and pickled.*
81 KNOTS, GODWITS *small wildfowl, considered delicacies.*
82 BARBELS *carplike fish; a fleshy "beard" hangs from its mouth.*

Of a fat pregnant sow, newly cut off,
85 Dressed with an exquisite and poignant sauce;
For which, I'll say unto my cook, "There's gold,
Go forth and be a knight."

    Face.   Sir, I'll go look
A little how it heightens.   *[Exit.]*

    Mammon.   Do. My shirts
I'll have of taffeta-sarsnet, soft and light
90 As cobwebs; and for all my other raiment
It shall be such as might provoke the Persian,
Were he to teach the world riot anew.
My gloves of fishes' and birds' skins, perfumed
With gums of paradise, and Eastern air—

95   *Surly.* And do you think to have the stone with this?
    Mammon. No, I do think t' have all this with the stone.
    Surly. Why, I have heard he must be *homo frugi*,
A pious, holy, and religious man,
One free from mortal sin, a very virgin.

100   *Mammon.* That makes it, sir, he is so. But I buy it.
My venture brings it me. He, honest wretch,
A notable, superstitious, good soul,
Has worn his knees bare and his slippers bald
With prayer and fasting for it. And, sir, let him
105 Do it alone, for me, still. Here he comes.
Not a profane word afore him! 'Tis poison.

88 IT HEIGHTENS *i.e. the experiment develops.*
89 TAFFETA-SARSNET *thin, silky material.*
91 PERSIAN *oriental potentates were famed for luxury.*
92 RIOT *riotous living, luxury.*
94 GUMS OF PARADISE *essences from the East, where Eden was located.*
97 HOMO FRUGI *a temperate man.*
97–99 *See Appendix I for the tradition that the alchemist must be morally perfect to find the stone.*
102 NOTABLE *outstanding.*

Act II Scene 3

[*Enter Subtle.*]

Mammon. Good morrow, father.

Subtle.   Gentle son, good morrow,
And to your friend there. What is he is with you?

Mammon. An heretic, that I did bring along
In hope, sir, to convert him.

Subtle.   Son, I doubt
You're covetous, that thus you meet your time   5
I' the just point, prevent your day, at morning.
This argues something worthy of a fear
Of importune and carnal appetite.
Take heed you do not cause the blessing leave you
With your ungoverned haste. I should be sorry   10
To see my labors, now e'en at perfection,
Got by long watching and large patience,
Not prosper where my love and zeal hath placed 'em.
Which (heaven I call to witness, with yourself,
To whom I have poured my thoughts) in all my ends,   15
Have looked no way but unto public good,
To pious uses, and dear charity,
No[w] grown a prodigy with men. Wherein
If you, my son, should now prevaricate,

4 DOUBT *suspect.*

6 I' . . . POINT *so precisely.* PREVENT *come before (i.e. in the morning of the day on which the experiment will be completed).*

7 ARGUES *shows, suggests.*

15 ENDS *aims.*

18 PRODIGY *abnormality.*

19 PREVARICATE *swerve aside (from the holy way of the alchemist).*

20   And to your own particular lusts employ
So great and catholic a bliss, be sure
A curse will follow, yea, and overtake
Your subtle and most secret ways.

    Mammon.   I know, sir;
You shall not need to fear me. I but come
To ha' you confute this gentleman.

25   *Surly.*   Who is,
Indeed, sir, somewhat costive of belief
Toward your stone; would not be gulled.

    Subtle.   Well, son,
All that I can convince him in is this,
The work is done: bright Sol is in his robe.

30   We have a med'cine of the triple soul,
The glorified spirit. Thanks be to heaven,
And make us worthy of it!

                         [Calling out.]
                         Ulen Spiegel!

    Face. [From within.] Anon, sir.

    Subtle.   Look well to the register,
And let your heat still lessen by degrees,
To the aludels.

    Face. [Within.] Yes, sir.

35   *Subtle.*   Did you look
O' the bolt's-head yet?

    Face. [Within.]   Which? On D, sir?

21 CATHOLIC *universal.*

26 COSTIVE *constipated, i.e. reluctant.*

29 SOL . . . ROBE " *The essence of gold is ascendant, ready to work projection.*"

30–31 TRIPLE . . . SPIRIT "*most refined and potent quality.*" N.

32 ULEN SPIEGEL *literally,* "*Owl Glass*" *or mirror.* N.

33 ANON *at once.* REGISTER *this and the many other specialized alchemical terms found
in this scene are glossed in Appendix I. Subtle, though using the terms correctly,
is spouting them to impress and confuse his listeners.*

   Subtle.   Ay,
What's the complexion?
   Face. [*Within.*]   Whitish.
   Subtle.   Infuse vinegar,
To draw his volatile substance and his tincture,
And let the water in glass E be filtered
And put into the gripe's egg. Lute him well   40
And leave him closed *in balneo.*
   Face. [*Within.*]   I will, sir.
   Surly. What a brave language here is! next to canting!
   Subtle. I have another work you never saw, son,
That three days since passed the philosopher's wheel,
In the lent heat of Athanor, and's become   45
Sulphur o' nature.
   Mammon.   But 'tis for me?
   Subtle.   What need you?
You have enough in that is perfect.
   Mammon.   O, but—
   Subtle. Why, this is covetise!
   Mammon.   No, I assure you,
I shall employ it all in pious uses,
Founding of colleges and grammar schools,   50
Marrying young virgins, building hospitals,
And, now and then, a church.
                   [*Enter Face.*]
   Subtle.   How now?
   Face.   Sir, please you,

---

42 NEXT TO CANTING "*Almost as 'brave' as the jargon of thieves.*"
43 WORK *experiment.*
45 LENT *slow, soft.*
47 IS PERFECT (*which*) *is completed.*
50 COLLEGES *foundations, not just institutes of higher education as now.*
51 MARRYING *i.e. by providing dowries.*

Shall I not change the filter?

   Subtle.   Marry, yes.

And bring me the complexion of glass B.   *[Exit Face.]*

   Mammon. Ha' you another?

55   *Subtle.*   Yes, son, were I assured

Your piety were firm, we would not want

The means to glorify it. But I hope the best.

I mean to tinct C in sand-heat tomorrow,

And give him imbibition.

   Mammon.   Of white oil?

60   *Subtle.* No, sir, of red. F is come over the helm too,

I thank my Maker, in St. Mary's bath,

And shows lac virginis. Blessèd be heaven!

I sent you of his feces there calcined.

Out of that calx I' ha' won the salt of mercury.

65   *Mammon.* By pouring on your rectified water?

   Subtle. Yes, and reverberating in Athanor.

                  [Enter Face.]

How now! what color says it?

   Face.   The ground black, sir.

   Mammon. That's your crow's head?

   Surly.   Your cockscomb's, is 't not?

   Subtle. No, 'tis not perfect. Would it were the crow.

That work wants something.

70   *Surly. [Aside.]*   O, I looked for this.

The hay is a-pitching.—

   Subtle.   Are you sure you loosed 'em

I' their own menstrue?

   Face.   Yes, sir, and then married 'em,

---

68 COCKSCOMB'S *i.e. of a fool.*

71 HAY IS A-PITCHING *a net or "hay" was thrown over a rabbit hole to catch the rabbit. In thieves' language a rabbit or "cony" was the victim of a swindle, and con games were known as "cony-catching."*

And put 'em in a bolt's-head nipped to digestion,
According as you bade me, when I set
The liquor of Mars to circulation   75
In the same heat.
    Subtle.   The process then was right.
    Face. Yes, by the token, sir; the retort brake,
And what was saved was put into the pelican,
And signed with Hermes' seal.
    Subtle.   I think 't was so.
We should have a new amalgama.
    Surly. [*Aside.*]   O, this ferret   80
Is rank as any polecat.—
    Subtle.   But I care not.
Let him e'en die; we have enough beside
In embrion. H has his white shirt on?
    Face.   Yes, sir,
He's ripe for inceration: he stands warm
In his ash-fire. I would not you should let   85
Any die now, if I might counsel, sir,
For luck's sake to the rest. It is not good.
    Mammon. He says right.
    Surly. [*Aside.*]   Ay, are you bolted?
    Face.   Nay, I know 't, sir,
I've seen th' ill fortune. What is some three ounces
Of fresh materials?
    Mammon.   Is 't no more?
    Face.   No more, sir,   90
Of gold t' amalgam with some six of mercury.

77 TOKEN *signs, outward appearance.*
80 FERRET *ferrets were put into burrows to drive rabbits out into the net.*
81 RANK *bad smelling.*
83 EMBRION *beginning.*
88 BOLTED *driven out of the hole (like the rabbit into the net).*

   Mammon. Away, here's money. What will serve?

   Face. [*Pointing to Subtle.*]   Ask him, sir.

   Mammon. How much?

   Subtle.   Give him nine pound; you may gi' him ten.

   Surly. [*Aside.*] Yes, twenty, and be cozened, do.

   Mammon. [*Gives money.*]   There 't is.

95   *Subtle.* This needs not but that you will have it so

To see conclusions of all. For two

Of our inferior works are at fixation,

A third is in ascension. [*To Face.*] Go your ways.

Ha' you set the oil of Luna in kemia?

   Face. Yes, sir.

   Subtle.   And the philosopher's vinegar?

100   *Face.*   Ay.   [*Exit.*]

   Surly. We shall have a salad!

   Mammon.   When do you make projection?

   Subtle. Son, be not hasty; I exalt our med'cine,

By hanging him in *balneo vaporoso*,

And giving him solution; then congeal him;

105 And then dissolve him; then again congeal him.

For look, how oft I iterate the work,

So many times I add unto his virtue.

As, if at first one ounce convert a hundred,

After his second loose he'll turn a thousand;

110 His third solution, ten; his fourth, a hundred.

After his fifth, a thousand thousand ounces

Of any imperfect metal into pure

96–99 FOR . . . KEMIA *N.*

102–07 EXALT . . . VIRTUE *N.*

106 ITERATE *repeat.*

107 VIRTUE *strength, power.*

108–14 *the stone or med'cine increased in power each time it was refined by distillation.*

Silver or gold, in all examinations
As good as any of the natural mine.
Get you your stuff here against afternoon,   115
Your brass, your pewter, and your andirons.
   Mammon. Not those of iron?
   Subtle.   Yes. You may bring them too.
We'll change all metals.
   Surly.   I believe you in that.
   Mammon. Then I may send my spits?
   Subtle.   Yes, and your racks.
   Surly. And dripping-pans, and pot-hangers, and hooks?   120
Shall he not?
   Subtle.   If he please.
   Surly.   To be an ass.
   Subtle. How, sir!
   Mammon.   This gent'man, you must bear withal.
I told you he had no faith.
   Surly.   And little hope, sir,
But much less charity should I gull myself.
   Subtle. Why, what have you observed, sir, in our art,   125
Seems so impossible?
   Surly.   But your whole work, no more.
That you should hatch gold in a furnace, sir,
As they do eggs in Egypt!
   Subtle.   Sir, do you
Believe that eggs are hatched so?
   Surly.   If I should?
   Subtle. Why, I think that the greater miracle.   130
No egg but differs from a chicken more

---

119 RACKS *brackets supporting spits.*
122 BEAR WITHAL *put up with, endure.*
126 BUT *only.*
128 EGGS IN EGYPT *i.e. in an incubator or some artificially warm place.*

Than metals in themselves.

    Surly.   That cannot be.
The egg's ordained by nature to that end,
And is a chicken *in potentia*.

135   *Subtle*. The same we say of lead and other metals,
Which would be gold if they had time.

    Mammon.   And that
Our art doth further.

    Subtle.   Ay, for 'twere absurd
To think that nature in the earth bred gold
Perfect, i' the instant. Something went before.
There must be remote matter.

140   *Surly*.   Ay, what is that?

    Subtle. Marry, we say—

    Mammon.   Ay, now it heats: stand, Father.
Pound him to dust—

    Subtle.   It is, of the one part,
A humid exhalation, which we call
Materia liquida, or the unctuous water;

145 On th' other part, a certain crass and viscous
Portion of earth; both which, concorporate,
Do make the elementary matter of gold;
Which is not yet *propria materia*,
But common to all metals and all stones.

150 For, where it is forsaken of that moisture,
And hath more dryness, it becomes a stone;
Where it retains more of the humid fatness,
It turns to sulphur, or to quicksilver,
Who are the parents of all other metals.

135–37 LEAD . . . FURTHER *N*.
140 REMOTE MATTER matter before it took form in metals.
141 HEATS (*i.e. the argument*) *intensifies*.
142–70 *N*.

Nor can this remote matter suddenly   155
Progress so from extreme unto extreme,
As to grow gold, and leap o'er all the means.
Nature doth first beget th' imperfect; then
Proceeds She to the perfect. Of that airy
And oily water, mercury is engend'red;   160
Sulphur o' the fat and earthy part; the one,
Which is the last, supplying the place of male,
The other of the female, in all metals.
Some do believe hermaphrodeity,
That both do act and suffer. But these two   165
Make the rest ductile, malleable, extensive.
And even in gold they are; for we do find
Seeds of them by our fire, and gold in them,
And can produce the species of each metal
More perfect thence than nature doth in earth.   170
Beside, who doth not see in daily practice
Art can beget bees, hornets, beetles, wasps,
Out of the carcasses and dung of creatures;
Yea, scorpions of an herb, being rightly placed?
And these are living creatures, far more perfect   175
And excellent than metals.
    Mammon.   Well said, Father!
Nay, if he take you in hand, sir, with an argument,
He'll bray you in a mortar.
    Surly.   Pray you, sir, stay.
Rather than I'll be brayed, sir, I'll believe

157 MEANS *intermediary stages.*
171–74 *the reference here is to the belief that insects could be spontaneously generated*
    from carrion. That the eggs had previously been laid in the rotting matter was
    not known.
174 RIGHTLY *in the prescribed, ritual, fashion.*
178 BRAY *grind to bits with a pestle.*

75

180 That alchemy is a pretty kind of game,
Somewhat like tricks o' the cards, to cheat a man
With charming.

  Subtle.   Sir?

  Surly.   What else are all your terms,
Whereon no one o' your writers 'grees with other?
Of your elixir, your lac virginis,

185 Your stone, your med'cine, and your chrysosperm,
Your sal, your sulphur, and your mercury,
Your oil of height, your tree of life, your blood,
Your marchesite, your tutie, your magnesia,
Your toad, your crow, your dragon, and your panther,

190 Your sun, your moon, your firmament, your adrop,
Your lato, azoch, zernich, chibrit, heautarit,
And then your red man, and your white woman,
With all your broths, your menstrues, and materials
Of piss, and egg-shells, women's terms, man's blood,

195 Hair o' the head, burnt clouts, chalk, merds, and clay,
Poulder of bones, scalings of iron, glass,
And worlds of other strange ingredients,
Would burst a man to name?

  Subtle.   And all these, named,
Intending but one thing; which art our writers

180 PRETTY . . . GAME *clever swindle.*
182 CHARMING *entrancing by magic.*
183 'GREES *agrees. Since alchemy was not a true science its terms were never defined accurately.*
184–93 *the terms in this catalogue are glossed in Appendix I.*
193 MATERIALS *the raw materials used in alchemical experiments.*
195 CLOUTS *clods, lumps of earth.*
196 POULDER *powder.*
198 BURST *because they are so many(?) or so grotesque(?).*
199 INTENDING *meaning.*
199–200 ART . . . ART *N.*

Used to obscure their art.

   Mammon.   Sir, so I told him: 200
Because the simple idiot should not learn it
And make it vulgar.

   Subtle.   Was not all the knowledge
Of the Egyptians writ in mystic symbols?
Speak not the Scriptures oft in parables?
Are not the choicest fables of the poets,   205
That were the fountains and first springs of wisdom,
Wrapped in perplexèd allegories?

   Mammon.   I urged that
And cleared to him that Sisyphus was damned
To roll the ceaseless stone, only because
He would have made ours common.

                       Dol is seen.

                     Who is this?   210

   Subtle. God's precious—What do you mean? Go in good lady,
Let me intreat you.

          [Dol disappears. Subtle calls out.]
           Where's this varlet?

   Face. [Entering.]   Sir?

   Subtle. You very knave! Do you use me thus?

   Face.   Wherein, sir?

   Subtle. Go in and see, you traitor. Go!

                      [Exit Face.]
              Who is it, sir?

202 VULGAR *ordinary, commonplace.*

203 EGYPTIANS . . . SYMBOLS *Egyptian hieroglyphs could not be read at this time.*

204 SCRIPTURES *see Mark 4:12.*

207 PERPLEXÈD *difficult.*

208 CLEARED *explained.* SISYPHUS *N.*

210 COMMON *ordinary, commonplace. Mares points out that this is a theatrical cue for Dol to appear.*

211 GOD'S PRECIOUS *"by God's precious body."*

213 VERY *absolute.* USE *treat.*

Subtle. Nothing, sir. Nothing.

215   *Mammon.*   What's the matter, good sir?

I have not seen you thus distemp'red. Who is 't?

Subtle. All arts have still had, sir, their adversaries;

But ours the most ignorant—

Face returns.

                  What now?

Face. 'T was not my fault, sir; she would speak with you.

Subtle. Would she, sir! Follow me.   [*Exit.*]

Mammon.   Stay, Lungs.

220   *Face.*   I dare not, sir.

Mammon. Stay, man; what is she?

Face.   A lord's sister, sir.

Mammon. How! 'Pray thee stay?

Face. [*Starting.*]   She's mad, sir, and sent hither—

He'll be mad too.

Mammon.   I warrant thee.—Why sent hither?

Face. Sir, to be cured.

Subtle. [*From offstage.*] Why, rascal!

Face. [*Calling.*]   Lo, you. Here, sir!

He goes out.

225   *Mammon.* 'Fore God, a Bradamante, a brave piece.

Surly. Heart, this is a bawdy-house! I'll be burnt else.

Mammon. O, by this light, no! Do not wrong him. He's

Too scrupulous that way. It is his vice.

No, he's a rare physician, do him right,

230 An excellent Paracelsian, and has done

217 STILL *always.*

222 PRAY THEE "*do I have to beg you to.*"

223 WARRANT *license (i.e. to stay).* "*Warrant*" *also carries the sense of* "*protect.*"

225 BRADAMANTE *heroine from romance (female knight in Ariosto's* Orlando Furioso). BRAVE *gallant, handsome.*

226 BURNT *i.e. as a heretic, unbeliever.*

230–33 PARACELSIAN . . . RECIPES *N.*

Strange cures with mineral physic. He deals all
With spirits, he. He will not hear a word
Of Galen or his tedious recipes.

Face again.

How now, Lungs!

   Face.   Softly, sir, speak softly. I meant
To ha' told your worship all. This must not hear.   235

   Mammon. No, he will not be gulled; let him alone.

   Face. Y' are very right, sir; she is a most rare scholar,
And is gone mad with studying Broughton's works.
If you but name a word touching the Hebrew,
She falls into her fit, and will discourse   240
So learnedly of genealogies,
As you would run mad, too, to hear her, sir.

   Mammon. How might one do t' have conference with her, Lungs?

   Face. O, divers have run mad upon the conference.
I do not know, sir; I am sent in haste   245
To fetch a vial.

   Surly.   Be not gulled, Sir Mammon.

   Mammon. Wherein? Pray ye, be patient.

   Surly.   Yes, as you are,
And trust confederate knaves, and bawds, and whores.

   Mammon. You are too foul, believe it. Come here, Ulen.
One word.

   Face.   I dare not, in good faith. [*Leaving.*]

   Mammon.   Stay, knave.   250

   Face. He's extreme angry that you saw her, sir.

---

235 THIS *i.e. Surly.*
238–41 BROUGHTON'S . . . GENEALOGIES *N.*
243 DO *manage.* CONFERENCE *conversation.*
244 DIVERS *different (persons).*
248 CONFEDERATE *banded together, i.e. conspiring.*

Act II Scene 3

    Mammon. Drink that. [*Gives him gold.*]
                     What is she when she's out of her fit?
    Face. O, the most affablest creature, sir! so merry!
So pleasant! She'll mount you up, like quicksilver
255 Over the helm; and circulate like oil,
A very vegetal; discourse of state,
Of mathematics, bawdry, anything—
    Mammon. Is she no way accessible? No means,
No trick to give a man a taste of her—wit—
Or so?—Ulen?
260   *Face.* [*Rushing off.*] I'll come to you again, sir.
    Mammon. Surly, I did not think one o' your breeding
Would traduce personages of worth.
    Surly. [*Bowing.*]   Sir Epicure,
Your friend to use; yet, still, loath to be gulled.
I do not like your philosophical bawds.
265 Their stone is lechery enough to pay for,
Without this bait.
    Mammon.   'Heart, you abuse yourself.
I know the lady, and her friends, and means,
The original of this disaster. Her brother
Has told me all.
    Surly.   And yet you ne'er saw her
Till now?
270   *Mammon.* O yes, but I forgot. I have, believe it,

254–55 *a specific description of the art of whoring, using the terms of alchemical experiment. Dol is a volatile gas under heat.*
256 VEGETAL *Latin* vegetus: *active, lively.* DISCOURSE OF STATE *discuss politics.*
263 YOUR . . . USE *"(I am) yours for any purpose."*
265 LECHERY *ignorance, as well as lust.*
266 ABUSE *wrong.*
267 MEANS *wealth.*
268 ORIGINAL *source.*

One o' the treacherou'st memories, I do think,
Of all mankind.

   Surly.   What call you her brother?

   Mammon.   My lord—
He wi' not have his name known, now I think on't.

   Surly. A very treacherous memory!

   Mammon.   O' my faith—

   Surly. Tut, if you ha' it not about you, pass it   275
Till we meet next.

   Mammon.   Nay, by this hand, 'tis true.
He's one I honor, and my noble friend,
And I respect his house.

   Surly.   Heart! can it be
That a grave sir, a rich, that has no need,
A wise sir, too, at other times, should thus   280
With his own oaths and arguments make hard means
To gull himself? And this be your elixir,
Your lapis mineralis, and your lunary,
Give me your honest trick, yet, at primero,
Or gleek; and take your lutum sapientis,   285
Your menstruum simplex. I'll have gold before you,
And with less danger of the quicksilver,
Or the hot sulphur.

              [*Enter Face. Speaks*] *to Surly.*

   Face.   Here's one from Captain Face, sir,

275 PASS *forget.*

281 MAKE HARD MEANS *seek out difficult ways.*

282 AND *if.*

283 LUNARY *an herb, but here probably "silver."*

284–85 PRIMERO OR GLEEK *card games. Surly is a gambler, and apparently one who "tricks" or cheats. See II.1.9–10.*

287–88 QUICKSILVER . . . SULPHUR *these two basic materials of alchemy were also used to treat venereal disease.*

288 ONE *i.e. a messenger.*

Desires you meet him i' the Temple church,
290 Some half-hour hence, and upon earnest business.

                   He whispers Mammon.

Sir, if you please to quit us now, and come
Again within two hours, you shall have
My master busy examining o' the works,
And I will steal you in unto the party,
That you may see her converse. [*To Surly.*]
295   Sir, shall I say
You'll meet the Captain's worship?
   Surly.   Sir, I will.
[*Aside.*] But, by attorney, and to a second purpose.
Now I am sure it is a bawdy-house;
I'll swear it, were the marshal here to thank me:
300 The naming this commander doth confirm it.
Don Face! Why he's the most authentic dealer
I' these commodities! The superintendent
To all the quainter traffickers in town.
He is their visitor and does appoint
305 Who lies with whom, and at what hour, what price,
Which gown, and in what smock, what fall, what tire.
Him will I prove, by a third person, to find
The subtleties of this dark labyrinth;
Which if I do discover, dear Sir Mammon,

289 TEMPLE CHURCH *church in the Temple, law chambers near Blackfriars, used for
business appointments.*
297 ATTORNEY *a representative; not in this case another person but Surly in disguise
as a Spaniard.* A SECOND PURPOSE *another end.*
303 QUAINTER TRAFFICKERS *more cunning traders. "Quaint" carries a pun on the
female parts.*
304 VISITOR *official inspector.*
306 FALL *flat collar.* TIRE *headdress, or attire.*
307 PROVE *test.*
308 SUBTLETIES *intricate workings, ins and outs.*

You'll give your poor friend leave, though no philosopher,　　310
To laugh; for you that are, 't is thought, shall weep.
 Face. Sir, he does pray you'll not forget.
 Surly.   I will not, sir.
Sir Epicure, I shall leave you?   [*Exit.*]
 Mammon.   I follow you straight.
 Face. But do so, good sir, to avoid suspicion.
This gent'man has a parlous head.
 Mammon.   But wilt thou, Ulen,　　315
Be constant to thy promise?
 Face.   As my life, sir.
 Mammon. And wilt thou insinuate what I am? and praise me?
And say I am a noble fellow?
 Face.   O, what else, sir?
And that you'll make her royal with the stone,
An empress; and yourself king of Bantam.　　320
 Mammon. Wilt thou do this?
 Face.   Will I, sir?
 Mammon.   Lungs, my Lungs!
I love thee.
 Face. Send your stuff, sir, that my master
May busy himself about projection.
 Mammon. Th' hast witched me, rogue. Take, go.
     [*Gives him money.*]
 Face.   Your jack, and
  all, sir.

---

315 PARLOUS HEAD *perilous, i.e. dangerously clever mind.*
320 BANTAM *capital of a Mohammedan empire in Indonesia, thought to be fabulously
 rich.*
324 WITCHED *bewitched.*
324–26 JACK, WEIGHTS *the jack was a machine run by weights, like a clock, which
 turned the spit.*

325   *Mammon.* Thou art a villain—I will send my jack,
And the weights too. Slave, I could bite thine ear.
Away, thou dost not care for me.
    Face.   Not I, sir?
    Mammon. Come, I was born to make thee, my good weasel,
Set thee on a bench, and ha' thee twirl a chain
With the best lord's vermin of 'em all.
330   *Face.*   Away, sir.
    Mammon. A count, nay, a count palatine—
    Face.   Good sir, go.
    Mammon. Shall not advance thee better, no, nor faster.   [*Exit.*]

325–26 VILLAIN . . . SLAVE . . . EAR *terms and acts of hostility which express good
nature when used between close friends.*
328 MAKE THEE "*raise you up in the world.*"
329–30 BENCH . . . VERMIN *N.*
330 LORD'S VERMIN *the ermine worn by a lord; also "a parasite" (?).*
331 COUNT PALATINE *a count of a palatinate, having the powers of a king.*

Act II Scene 4

                   [*Enter Subtle and Dol.*]
    Subtle. Has he bit? Has he bit?
    Face.   And swallowed, too, my Subtle.
I ha' given him line, and now he plays, i' faith.
    Subtle. And shall we twitch him?
    Face.   Through both the gills.
A wench is a rare bait, with which a man
5 No sooner's taken, but he straight firks mad.

5 FIRKS MAD *goes wild.*

Subtle. Dol, my Lord What's-um's sister, you must now
Bear yourself statelich.
   Dol Common.   O, let me alone.
I'll not forget my race, I warrant you.
I'll keep my distance, laugh and talk aloud,
Have all the tricks of a proud scurvy lady,   10
And be as rude's her woman.
   Face.   Well said, Sanguine!
   Subtle. But will he send his andirons?
   Face.   His jack too,
And's iron shoeing-horn; I ha' spoke to him. Well,
I must not lose my wary gamester yonder.
   Subtle. O, Monsieur Caution, that will not be gulled?   15
   Face. Ay, if I can strike a fine hook into him, now.
The Temple-church, there I have cast mine angle.
Well, pray for me. I'll about it.   *One knocks.*
   Subtle.   What, more gudgeons!
Dol, scout, scout! Stay, Face, you must go to the door;
'Pray God it be my Anabaptist. Who is 't, Dol? [*Dol looks out.*] 20
   Dol Common. I know him not. He looks like a gold-end-man.
   Subtle. Gods so! 'tis he he said he would send. What call you him?
The sanctified elder, that should deal
For Mammon's jack and andirons? Let him in.
Stay, help me off, first, with my gown. Away,   25
Madam, to your withdrawing chamber. Now,   [*Exit Dol.*]
In a new tune, new gesture, but old language.
This fellow is sent from one negotiates with me

---

7 STATELICH *in a stately manner; i.e. befitting a sister of a great lord.*
11 WOMAN *personal servant.* SANGUINE *the sanguinary humor is active and cheerful.*
17 ANGLE *hook.*
18 GUDGEONS *fish (to be caught).*
20 ANABAPTIST *N.*
21 GOLD-END-MAN *peddler buying odd pieces of gold jewelry.*

About the stone too, for the holy brethren
30 Of Amsterdam, the exiled saints, that hope
To raise their discipline by it. I must use him
In some strange fashion now, to make him admire me.
                        [*Face opens the door.*]

30 AMSTERDAM *a center for Anabaptists driven out of Germany.*
31 RAISE THEIR DISCIPLINE *"improve the status or power of their church."*
32 STRANGE *haughty, distant.*

Act II Scene 5

                    [*Enter Ananias.*]
  Subtle. Where is my drudge?
  Face.   Sir!
  Subtle.   Take away the recipient,
And rectify your menstrue from the phlegma.
Then pour it o' the Sol, in the cucurbite,
And let 'em macerate together.
    Face.   Yes, sir.
And save the ground?
5   *Subtle.*   No. *Terra damnata*
Must not have entrance in the work. [*Turning to Ananias.*] Who are
    you?
    Ananias. A faithful brother, if it please you.
    Subtle.   What's that?

  1 RECIPIENT *this and the many other alchemical terms in this scene are explained in
    Appendix I. What Face and Subtle do here is to provide an outline of how
    alchemists worked, steadily refining their materials until they arrived at essential
    gold.*
  5 TERRA DAMNATA *inferior materials, the ground or residue left after distillation.*

A Lullianist? a Ripley? *Filius artis*?
Can you sublime and dulcify? Calcine?
Know you the sapor pontic? Sapor styptic?   10
Or what is homogene, or heterogene?
   Ananias. I understand no heathen language, truly.
   Subtle. Heathen, you Knipperdoling! Is *ars sacra*,
Or chrysopoeia, or spagyrica,
Or the pamphysic, or panarchic knowledge   15
A heathen language?
   Ananias.   Heathen Greek, I take it.
   Subtle. How! Heathen Greek?
   Ananias.   All's heathen but the Hebrew.
   Subtle. Sirrah, my varlet, stand you forth and speak to him
Like a philosopher. Answer i' the language.
Name the vexations, and the martyrizations   20
Of metals in the work.
   Face.   Sir, putrefaction,
Solution, ablution, sublimation,
Cohobation, calcination, ceration, and
Fixation.
   Subtle. This is heathen Greek to you now?
And when comes vivification?
   Face.   After mortification.   25
   Subtle. What's cohobation?
   Face.   'Tis the pouring on

---

  8 LULLIANIST . . . ARTIS *N*.

13 KNIPPERDOLING *Bernt Knipperdolinck helped to lead an Anabaptist rising in
    Munster in 1534.* ARS SACRA *the sacred art, alchemy.*

14 CHRYSOPOEIA *making gold.*

15 PAMPHYSIC, PANARCHIC KNOWLEDGE *universal knowledge, a unified field theory
    covering all nature.*

17 BUT THE HEBREW *i.e. because the Old Testament was written in Hebrew, and the
    Anabaptists considered this the only book of value.*

21 THE WORK *alchemy.*

Act II Scene 5

Your aqua regis, and then drawing him off,
To the trine circle of the seven spheres.
    Subtle. What's the proper passion of metals?
    Face.   Malleation.
    Subtle. What's your *ultimum supplicium auri*?
30   *Face.*   Antimonium.
    Subtle. This's heathen Greek to you? And what's your mercury?
    Face. A very fugitive, he will be gone, sir.
    Subtle. How know you him?
    Face.   By his viscosity,
His oleosity, and his suscitability.
    Subtle. How do you sublime him?
35   *Face.*   With the calce of egg-shells,
White marble, talc.
    Subtle.   Your magisterium now?
What's that?
    Face.   Shifting, sir, your elements,
Dry into cold, cold into moist, moist in-
To hot, hot into dry.
    Subtle.   This's heathen Greek to you, still?
Your lapis philosophicus?
40   *Face.*   'Tis a stone, and not
A stone; a spirit, a soul, and a body,

28 TRINE . . . SPHERES *N.*

29 PROPER PASSION *distinguishing quality, i.e. that quality appropriate to a particular substance.*

30 ULTIMUM . . . AURI *"the final punishment of gold"—antimony "punishes" gold by making it immalleable.*

32 FUGITIVE *i.e. difficult to locate.*

36 MAGISTERIUM *the mastery, i.e. the stone.*

37–39 ELEMENTS . . . DRY *N.*

40–44 *the meaning of all this elaborate language is that the stone is superior to natural things.*

Which if you do dissolve, it is dissolved;
If you coagulate, it is coagulated;
If you make it to fly, it flieth.

 Subtle.   Enough.   *[Exit Face.]*
This's heathen Greek to you? What are you, sir?   45
 Ananias. Please you, a servant of the exiled Brethren,
That deal with widows' and with orphans' goods,
And make a just account unto the Saints:
A deacon.
 Subtle. O, you are sent from Master Wholesome,
Your teacher?
 Ananias. From Tribulation Wholesome,   50
Our very zealous pastor.
 Subtle.   Good. I have
Some orphans' goods to come here.
 Ananias.   Of what kind, sir?
 Subtle. Pewter, and brass, andirons and kitchen-ware,
Metals that we must use our med'cine on,
Wherein the Brethren may have a penn-orth,   55
For ready money.
 Ananias. Were the orphans' parents
Sincere professors?
 Subtle. Why do you ask?
 Ananias.   Because
We then are to deal justly, and give, in truth,
Their utmost value.
 Subtle.   'Slid, you'd cozen else
An if their parents were not of the faithful?   60
I will not trust you, now I think on't,

47 DEAL *trade in. N.*
55 PENN'ORTH *penny's worth, i.e. a little share.*
57 PROFESSORS *believers, i.e. who professed the Anabaptist faith.*

Till I ha' talked with your pastor. Ha' you brought money
To buy more coals?

    Ananias.   No, surely.

    Subtle.   No? How so?

    Ananias. The Brethren bid me say unto you, sir,

65 Surely, they will not venter any more
Till they may see projection.

    Subtle.   How!

    Ananias.   You've had
For the instruments, as bricks, and loam, and glasses,
Already thirty pound; and for materials,
They say, some ninety more. And they have heard, since,

70 That one at Heidelberg made it of an egg
And a small paper of pin-dust.

    Subtle.   What's your name?

    Ananias. My name is Ananias.

    Subtle.   Out! The varlet
That cozened the apostles! Hence, away!
Flee, mischief! Had your holy consistory

75 No name to send me of another sound
Than wicked Ananias? Send your elders
Hither, to make atonement for you, quickly.
And gi' me satisfaction, or out goes
The fire, and down th' alembics, and the furnace,

80 Piger Henricus, or what not. Thou wretch,
Both sericon and bufo shall be lost,
Tell 'em. All hope of rooting out the bishops,
Or th' anti-Christian hierarchy shall perish,

71 PIN-DUST *metal shavings from making pins.*
73 APOSTLES *see Acts 5:1–11.*
74 CONSISTORY *assembly, governing body.*
82–83 BISHOPS . . . HIERARCHY *N.*

If they stay threescore minutes. The aqueity,
Terreity, and sulphureity   85
Shall run together again, and all be annulled,
Thou wicked Ananias! [*Exit Ananias.*] This will fetch 'em,
And make 'em haste towards their gulling more.
A man must deal like a rough nurse, and fright
Those that are froward to an appetite.   90

84 STAY *wait, delay.*
84–85 AQUEITY . . . SULPHUREITY *moisture, earthiness, "sulphurosity." See N. to*
    lines 37–39.
90 FROWARD *difficult, hard to manage.*

Act II Scene 6

[*Enter Face, dressed as captain, and Abel Drugger.*]
Face. He's busy with his spirits, but we'll upon him.
Subtle. How now! What mates, what Bayards, ha' we here?
Face. I told you he would be furious. Sir, here's Nab
Has brought yo' another piece of gold to look on.
                    [*Aside to Drugger.*]
—We must appease him. Give it me—and prays you   5
You would devise—what is it, Nab?
Drugger.   A sign, sir.
Face. Ay, a good lucky one, a thriving sign, Doctor.
Subtle. I was devising now.
Face. [*Aside to Subtle.*]—'Slight, do not say so;
He will repent he ga' you any more—

1 SPIRITS *N.*
2 MATES *low fellows.* BAYARDS *Bayard was a name for a horse, and "bold as*
  Bayard" meant "foolhardy."

91

10 What say you to his constellation, Doctor?
     The Balance?
       Subtle.   No, that way is stale and common.
     A townsman born in Taurus gives the bull,
     Or the bull's head; in Aries, the ram.
     A poor device! No, I will have his name
15 Formed in some mystic character, whose radii,
     Striking the senses of the passers-by
     Shall, by a virtual influence, breed affections,
     That may result upon the party owns it:
     As thus—
       Face.   Nab!
       Subtle.   He first shall have a bell, that's Abel;
20 And by it standing one whose name is Dee,
     In a rug gown; there's D and Rug, that's Drug;
     And right anenst him a dog snarling "er";
     There's Drugger, Abel Drugger. That's his sign.
     And here's now mystery and hieroglyphic!
       Face. Abel, thou art made.
25   *Drugger.* [*Bows.*]   Sir, I do thank his worship.
       Face. Six o' thy legs more will not do it, Nab.
     He has brought you a pipe of tobacco, Doctor.
       Drugger.   Yes, sir.

10 WHAT . . . CONSTELLATION *"How about using his zodiacal sign"?*

11 BALANCE *Libra, the scales, appropriate for merchants.*

15 MYSTIC CHARACTER *symbolic letters.* RADII *emanations, rays.*

17 VIRTUAL *Latin* virtu: *force, power.* AFFECTIONS *desires, i.e. for tobacco.*

18 RESULT . . . IT *the rays of force attracted by the symbols from the stars and focused on the prospective customer will come to rest ("result") on the owner of the sign.*

20 DEE *N.*

21 RUG *coarse wool.*

22 ANENST *next.* ER *"grrr."*

24 HIEROGLYPHIC *N.*

26 LEGS *bows.*

I have another thing I would impart—
   Face. Out with it, Nab.
   Drugger.   Sir, there is lodged, hard by me,
A rich young widow—
   Face.   Good! a bona roba?   30
   Drugger. But nineteen at the most.
   Face.   Very good, Abel.
Drugger. Marry, she's not in fashion yet; she wears
A hood, but 't stands a cop.
   Face.   No matter, Abel.
   Drugger. And I do now and then give her a fucus—
   Face. What! dost thou deal, Nab?
   Subtle.   I did tell you, Captain.   35
   Drugger. And physic too sometime, sir; for which she trusts me
With all her mind. She's come up here of purpose
To learn the fashion.
   Face.   Good.—[*Aside.*] His match too.—On, Nab.
   Drugger. And she does strangely long to know her fortune.
   Face. God's lid, Nab, send her to the Doctor, hither.   40
   Drugger. Yes, I have spoke to her of his worship already;
But she's afraid it will be blown abroad
And hurt her marriage.
   Face.   Hurt it? 'Tis the way

29 HARD BY *near.*

30 BONA ROBA *literally, well-dressed; slang for whore.*

33 HOOD . . . A COP *the hood was out of fashion—in favor of hats—but she wears it in some special way on her head, "a cop."*

34 FUCUS *cosmetics, makeup.*

35 DEAL *trade (in materials other than tobacco). Deal has some of the modern suggestion of crookedness.*

36 PHYSIC *medicine; perhaps more specifically "laxative" here.*

38 MATCH *equal. ("She is about as smart as Drugger if she is doing business with him.")*

42 BLOWN ABROAD *noised about, made known.*

To heal it, if 'twere hurt; to make it more
45   Followed and sought. Nab, thou shalt tell her this.
She'll be more known, more talked of; and your widows
Are ne'er of any price till they be famous;
Their honor is their multitude of suitors.
Send her! It may be thy good fortune. [*Drugger shakes his head.*]
    What?
Thou dost not know?

50   *Drugger*.   No, sir, she'll never marry
Under a knight. Her brother has made a vow.
   Face. What, and dost thou despair, my little Nab,
Knowing what the Doctor has set down for thee,
And seeing so many o' the city dubbed?
55   One glass o' thy water with a madam I know
Will have it done, Nab. What's her brother? A knight?
   Drugger. No, sir, a gentleman, newly warm in's land, sir,
Scarce cold in his one-and-twenty, that does govern
His sister here; and is a man himself
60   Of some three thousand a year, and is come up
To learn to quarrel and to live by his wits,
And will go down again and die i' the country.
   Face. How! To quarrel?
   Drugger.   Yes, sir, to carry quarrels
As gallants do, and manage 'em by line.
65   *Face*. 'Slid, Nab! The Doctor is the only man
In Christendom for him. He has made a table,

53 SET DOWN *predicted; i.e. that he will be rich and famous.*
54 "*Seeing that so many rich merchants have already been knighted.*"
55 WATER *urine (for a witch to use to make a love potion to make Dame Pliant love Drugger).*
57 NEWLY WARM *just come of age and inherited his property.*
61 QUARREL . . . WITS *N.*
64 BY LINE *by exact rules.*
66 TABLE *diagram.*

With mathematical demonstrations,
Touching the art of quarrels. He will give him
An instrument to quarrel by. Go, bring 'em both,
Him and his sister. And, for thee, with her   70
The Doctor happ'ly may persuade. Go to!
'Shalt give his worship a new damask suit
Upon the premises.
    Subtle.   O, good Captain!
    Face.   He shall,
He is the honestest fellow, Doctor. Stay not,
No offers, bring the damask, and the parties.   75
    Drugger. I'll try my power, sir.
    Face.   And thy will too, Nab.
    Subtle. 'Tis good tobacco this! What is't an ounce?
    Face. He'll send you a pound, Doctor.
    Subtle.   O no.
    Face.   He will do't.
It is the goodest soul. Abel, about it.
Thou shalt know more anon. Away, be gone.   80
               [Face pushes Abel out.]
A miserable rogue, and lives with cheese,
And has the worms. That was the cause, indeed,
Why he came now. He dealt with me in private
To get a med'cine for 'em.
    Subtle.   And shall, sir. This works.
    Face. A wife, a wife for one on's, my dear Subtle.   85
We'll e'en draw lots, and he that fails shall have

69 INSTRUMENT *means, but also with the suggestion of some kind of bogus scientific apparatus* (?).
73 PREMISES *beginnings, i.e. the scheme that has only been started.*
84 THIS WORKS "*the plan goes well.*"
85 ON *of.*

The more in goods the other has in tail.
   Subtle. Rather the less. For she may be so light
She may want grains.
   Face.   Ay, or be such a burden
90 A man would scarce endure her for the whole.
   Subtle. Faith, best let's see her first, and then determine.
   Face. Content. But Dol must ha' no breath on't.
   Subtle.   Mum.
Away! You to your Surly yonder, catch him.
   Face. Pray God I ha' not stayed too long.
   Subtle.   I fear it.   [*Exeunt.*]

87 IN TAIL *the sexual pun is clear, but in law an estate* in tail, *or entailed, could not be disposed of but must pass to a designated heir.*
88 LIGHT *promiscuous.*
89 WANT GRAINS *lack weight (to make up the value of the goods against which she is weighed).*

Act III Scene 1

[*Tribulation Wholesome and Ananias in the street outside the house.*]

   Tribulation. These chastisements are common to the Saints,
And such rebukes we of the Separation
Must bear, with willing shoulders, as the trials
Sent forth to tempt our frailties.

   Ananias.   In pure zeal,
I do not like the man: he is a heathen,   5
And speaks the language of Canaan, truly.

   Tribulation. I think him a profane person indeed.

   Ananias.   He bears
The visible mark of the Beast in his forehead.
And for his stone, it is a work of darkness,
And with philosophy blinds the eyes of man.   10

   Tribulation. Good brother, we must bend unto all means
That may give furtherance to the holy cause.

   Ananias. Which his cannot: the sanctified cause
Should have a sanctified course.

   Tribulation.   Not always necessary.

---

2 SEPARATION *those marked off by God as His chosen people.*

4 ZEAL *the standard term used by Puritans to denote their dedication to the Lord.*

6 CANAAN *N.*

8 MARK OF THE BEAST *the sign of damnation, of being a worshiper of false Gods. See Revelation (19:20), a favorite source of Puritan imagery.*

11 BEND *yield.*

Act III Scene 1

15 The children of perdition are oft times
    Made instruments even of the greatest works.
    Beside, we should give somewhat to man's nature,
    The place he lives in, still about the fire,
    And fume of metals, that intoxicate
20 The brain of man, and make him prone to passion.
    Where have you greater atheists than your cooks?
    Or more profane, or choleric, than your glass-men?
    More anti-Christian than your bell-founders?
    What makes the Devil so devilish, I would ask you,
25 Sathan, our common enemy, but his being
    Perpetually about the fire, and boiling
    Brimstone and ars'nic? We must give, I say,
    Unto the motives, and the stirrers up
    Of humors in the blood. It may be so,
30 When as the work is done, the stone is made,
    This heat of his may turn into a zeal,
    And stand up for the beauteous discipline
    Against the menstruous cloth and rag of Rome.
    We must await his calling, and the coming
35 Of the good spirit. You did fault t' upbraid him
    With the Brethren's blessing of Heidelberg, weighing
    What need we have to hasten on the work,
    For the restoring of the silenced Saints,

---

17 GIVE . . . NATURE *"take into account somewhat the disposition of the alchemist."*
22 CHOLERIC *angry.* GLASS-MEN *glass blowers (who worked around hot fires).*
23 FOUNDERS *casters.*
29 HUMORS *dispositions, strong tendencies.*
32 BEAUTEOUS DISCIPLINE *i.e. Puritanism.*
33 MENSTRUOUS . . . ROME *N.*
36 BLESSING *the successful alchemy referred to in II.5.70.* WEIGHING *considering.*
38 SILENCED *nonconforming clergy were excommunicated in England after 1604 and forbidden to preach.*

98

Which ne'er will be but by the philosopher's stone.
And so a learned elder, one of Scotland,   40
Assured me; *aurum potabile* being
The only med'cine for the civil magistrate,
T' incline him to a feeling of the cause,
And must be daily used in the disease.

   Ananias. I have not edified more, truly, by man,   45
Not since the beautiful light first shone on me,
And I am sad my zeal hath so offended.

   Tribulation. Let us call on him then.

   Ananias.   The motion's good,
And of the spirit; I will knock first. [*Knocks.*] Peace be within!

41 AURUM POTABILE *drinkable gold; thought to be a sovereign medicine. What is
meant here is a bribe to the civil authorities to be lenient with the Puritans.*
48 MOTION *conception, motive.*

Act III Scene 2

[*Subtle opens the door to them.*]
   Subtle. O, are you come? 'Twas time. Your threescore minutes
Were at the last thread, you see, and down had gone
Furnus acediae, turris circulatorius:
Limbec, bolt's-head, retort, and pelican
Had all been cinders. [*Seeing Ananias.*] Wicked Ananias!   5
Art *thou* returned? Nay then, it goes down yet.

   Tribulation. Sir, be appeased, he is come to humble
Himself in spirit, and to ask your patience
If too much zeal hath carried him aside

3 FURNUS *for this and other specialized alchemical terms in this scene, see Appendix I.*

From the due path.

10   *Subtle.*   Why, this doth qualify!

Tribulation. The Brethren had no purpose, verily,

To give you the least grievance, but are ready

To lend their willing hands to any project

The spirit and you direct.

Subtle.   This qualifies more!

15   *Tribulation.* And for the orphans' goods, let them be valued,

Or what is needful else to the holy work,

It shall be numb'red; here, by me, the Saints

Thrown down their purse before you.

Subtle.   This qualifies most!

Why, thus it should be; now you understand.

20   Have I discoursed so unto you of our stone?

And of the good that it shall bring your cause?

Showed you (beside the main of hiring forces

Abroad, drawing the Hollanders, your friends,

From th' Indies, to serve you, with all their fleet)

25   That even the med'cinal use shall make you a faction

And party in the realm? As, put the case,

That some great man in state, he have the gout,

Why, you but send three drops of your elixir,

You help him straight: there you have made a friend.

30   Another has the palsy or the dropsy,

He takes of your incombustible stuff,

---

10 DUE *proper.*

14 SPIRIT *the holy spirit; the light within the elect.*

22 MAIN *chief point.*

23 HOLLANDERS *N.*

25 MED'CINAL USE *use of gold as the med'cine or elixir, described by Mammon II.1.
63–70.*

25–26 MAKE . . . PARTY *attract powerful friends.*

27 STATE *political office.*

31 INCOMBUSTIBLE *i.e. of such purity that it will not decay or burn.*

He's young again: there you have made a friend.
A lady that is past the feat of body,
Though not of mind, and hath her face decayed
Beyond all cure of paintings, you restore   35
With the oil of talc: there you have made a friend,
And all her friends. A lord that is a leper,
A knight that has the bone-ache, or a squire
That hath both these, you make 'em smooth and sound
With a bare fricace of your med'cine; still   40
You increase your friends.
    Tribulation.   Ay, 'tis very pregnant.
    Subtle. And then the turning of this lawyer's pewter
To plate at Christmas—
    Ananias.   "Christ-tide," I pray you.
    Subtle. Yet, Ananias!
    Ananias.   I have done.
    Subtle.   Or changing
His parcel-gilt to massy gold. You cannot   45
But raise you friends. With all to be of power
To pay an army in the field, to buy
The King of France out of his realms, or Spain
Out of his Indies. What can you not do
Against lords spiritual or temporal   50

33–34 FEAT . . . MIND "*still capable of thinking of sex but past the performance of it.*"

36 OIL OF TALC *a cosmetic powder; also a form of the elixir.*

38 BONE-ACHE *syphilis; "ache" was pronounced "aitch."*

40 BARE FRICACE *mere rubbing.*

41 PREGNANT *true, filled with possibility.*

43 PLATE *silver or gold dishes.* CHRIST-TIDE "*Christ's time*"; *Puritans objected to* "*Christmas*" *because it contained the hated word "mass."*

45 PARCEL-GILT *gilded silver, the usual form of gold work.*

50 LORDS . . . TEMPORAL *rulers of church and state.*

That shall oppone you?

    Tribulation.   Verily, 'tis true.

We may be temporal lords, ourselves, I take it.

    Subtle. You may be anything, and leave off to make

Long-winded exercises, or suck up

55 Your "ha" and "hum" in a tune. I not deny

But such as are not graced in a state

May, for their ends, be adverse in religion,

And get a tune to call the flock together.

For, to say sooth, a tune does much with women

60 And other phlegmatic people; it is your bell.

    Ananias. Bells are profane; a tune may be religious.

    Subtle. No warning with you? Then farewell my patience.

'Slight, it shall down; I will not be thus tortured.

    Tribulation. I pray you, sir.

    Subtle.   All shall perish. I have spoke it.

65   *Tribulation.* Let me find grace, sir, in your eyes; the man

He stands corrected: neither did his zeal,

But as yourself, allow a tune somewhere,

Which now, being to'ard the stone, we shall not need.

---

51 OPPONE *oppose.*

54 EXERCISES *prayers or sermons. Puritans were noted for the length of their speeches and prayers.*

54–55 SUCK . . . TUNE *an exaggerated, extended sucking in of breath when singing hymns or chanting. A style apparently affected by Puritans.*

56 SUCH . . . GRACED *"those out of power."*

58 TUNE *i.e. program, political and religious platform; ways of doing things which identify and unite a social group.*

60 BELL *i.e. to call the people together.*

61 PROFANE *because associated with traditional churches.*

66–68 *"Like you, he only permitted the use of tunes, and these will no longer be needed now that we will have the stone" (?).*

68 TO'ARD *toward, near to (making).*

Subtle. No, nor your holy vizard to win widows
To give you legacies; or make zealous wives   70
To rob their husbands for the common cause;
Nor take the start of bonds broke but one day,
And say they were forfeited by Providence.
Nor shall you need o'er-night to eat huge meals,
To celebrate your next day's fast the better,   75
The whilst the Brethren and the Sisters humbled,
Abate the stiffness of the flesh. Nor cast
Before your hungry hearers scrupulous bones:
As whether a Christian may hawk or hunt,
Or whether matrons of the holy assembly   80
May lay their hair out, or wear doublets,
Or have that idol, Starch, about their linen.
    Ananias. It is, indeed, an idol.
    Tribulation.   Mind him not, sir.
                    [*Blessing Ananias.*]
I do command thee, spirit of zeal, but trouble,
To peace within him! Pray you sir, go on.   85
    Subtle. Nor shall you need to libel 'gainst the prelates,
And shorten so your ears against the hearing
Of the next wire-drawn grace. Nor, of necessity,
Rail against plays to please the alderman
Whose daily custard you devour. Nor lie   90
With zealous rage till you are hoarse. Not one

69 HOLY VIZARD *mask of piety.*
72 TAKE . . . DAY "*collect the sureties on loans only a day overdue.*"
73 PROVIDENCE *Puritans believed in predestination and thus attributed everything, including their own prosperity, to the will of God.*
74 O'ER-NIGHT *during the night.*
77 STIFFNESS *bodily pride, with a sexual pun. Some Puritan sects were accused of orgies and using women in common.*
78–97 SCRUPULOUS BONES *petty points of doctrine, detailed in the following lines.* N.

Of these so singular arts. Nor call yourselves
By names of "Tribulation," "Persecution,"
"Restraint," "Long-patience," and such like affected
95   By the whole family, or wood, of you,
Only for glory, and to catch the ear
Of the disciple.
     Tribulation. Truly, sir, they are
Ways that the godly Brethren have invented
For propagation of the glorious cause,
100 As very notable means, and whereby, also,
Themselves grow soon and profitably famous.
     Subtle. O, but the stone, all's idle to't! Nothing!
The art of angels, nature's miracle,
The divine secret that doth fly in clouds
105 From east to west, and whose tradition
Is not from men, but spirits!
     Ananias.   I hate traditions;
I do not trust them—
     Tribulation.   Peace!
     Ananias.   They are Popish, all!
I will not peace! I will not—
     Tribulation.   Ananias!
     Ananias. Please the profane to grieve the godly. I may not.
110 *Subtle.* Well, Ananias, thou shalt overcome.
     Tribulation. It is an ignorant zeal that haunts him, sir.
But truly, else, a very faithful brother,

92 SINGULAR ARTS *extraordinary practices.*
95 WOOD *collection; the word also meant "crazy."*
102 IDLE TO'T *empty, useless, compared to it.*
103–06 ART . . . SPIRITS *N.*
106 HATE TRADITIONS *the Puritans considered traditions, religious and social, as willful errors which blocked the pure truths revealed plainly to them in the Bible by their own inner light.*

A botcher, and a man by revelation
That hath a competent knowledge of the truth.
   Subtle. Has he a competent sum, there i' the bag,   115
To buy the goods within? I am made guardian
And must for charity and conscience' sake,
Now see the most be made for my poor orphans,
Though I desire the Brethren, too, good gainers.
There they are within. When you have viewed and bought 'em, 120
And ta'en the inventory of what they are,
They are ready for projection; there's no more
To do: cast on the med'cine, so much silver
As there is tin there, so much gold as brass,
I'll gi' it you in by weight.
   Tribulation.   But how long time,   125
Sir, must the Saints expect yet?
   Subtle.   Let me see,
How's the moon now? Eight, nine, ten days hence,
He will be silver potate; then, three days
Before he citronize: some fifteen days
The magisterium will be perfected.   130
   Ananias. About the second day of the third week
In the ninth month?
   Subtle.   Yes, my good Ananias.
   Tribulation. What will the orphans' goods arise to, think you?
   Subtle. Some hundred marks; as much as filled three cars,

113 BOTCHER *tailor who mended clothes.*
113–14 REVELATION . . . TRUTH *N.*
114 COMPETENT *sufficient.*
125 GI' . . . WEIGHT *i.e. change the iron to an equal weight of gold.*
126 EXPECT *wait.*
127 MOON *projection required the heavens to be in a favorable position.*
132 NINTH MONTH *N.*
133 ARISE *amount.*
134 HUNDRED MARKS *about ninety-eight pounds.* CARS *carts.*

135 Unladed now; you'll make six millions of 'em.
But I must ha' more coals laid in.

    Tribulation.   How?

    Subtle.   Another load,

And then we ha' finished. We must now increase
Our fire to *ignis ardens*; we are past
Fimus equinus, balnei, cineris,

140 And all those lenter heats. If the holy purse
Should with this draught fall low, and that the Saints
Do need a present sum, I have [a] trick
To melt the pewter you shall buy now, instantly,
And with a tincture make you as good Dutch dollars
As any are in Holland.

145   *Tribulation.*   Can you so?

    Subtle. Ay, and shall bide the third examination.

    Ananias. It will be joyful tidings to the Brethren.

    Subtle. But you must carry it secret.

    Tribulation.   Ay, but stay;

This act of coining, is it lawful?

    Ananias.   Lawful?

150 We know no magistrate. Or, if we did,
This's foreign coin.

    Subtle.   It is no coining, sir.

It is but casting.

    Tribulation.   Ha! you distinguish well.

---

140 LENTER *gentler.*

142 PRESENT SUM *ready cash.*

144 TINCTURE *some wash or coloring agent to make the pewter look like silver coins.*

146 BIDE . . . EXAMINATION *endure three assays* (?). *Endure the most severe test* (?).

149 COINING *counterfeiting.*

150 KNOW NO MAGISTRATE *"recognize no civil authority." Anabaptists felt that only God and conscience could properly rule them.*

152 CASTING *a nice bit of verbal juggling of the sort some Puritans were adept at.*

Casting of money may be lawful.

   Ananias.   'Tis, sir.

   Tribulation. Truly, I take it so.

   Subtle.   There is no scruple,

Sir, to be made of it; believe Ananias;   155

This case of conscience he is studied in.

   Tribulation. I'll make a question of it to the Brethren.

   Ananias. The Brethren shall approve it lawful, doubt not.

Where shall't be done?

   Subtle.   For that we'll talk anon.

                 Knock without.

There's some to speak with me. Go in, I pray you,   160

And view the parcels. That's the inventory.

I'll come to you straight.   *[Exeunt Tribulation and Ananias.]*

            Who is it? Face! *[He conjures.]* Appear!

157 QUESTION *topic of discussion.*
162 STRAIGHT *straightway.*

Act III Scene 3

             [Enter Face.]

   Subtle. How now? Good prize?

   Face.   Good pox! Yond' costive cheater

Never came on.

   Subtle.   How then?

   Face.   I ha' walked the round

1 COSTIVE CHEATER *unbelieving gambler, i.e. Surly.*
2 CAME ON *showed up.* ROUND *around the aisles (of the circular Temple Church, where Face was to meet Surly).*

Till now, and no such thing.

    Subtle.   And ha' you quit him?

    Face. Quit him? And hell would quit him too, he were happy.

5 'Slight! would you have me stalk like a mill-jade,

All day, for one that will not yield us grains?

I know him of old.

    Subtle.   O, but to ha' gulled him

Had been a mast'ry.

    Face.   Let him go, black boy,

And turn thee that some fresh news may possess thee.

10 A noble count, a don of Spain, my dear

Delicious compeer and my party-bawd,

Who is come hither, private, for his conscience

And brought munition with him, six great slops,

Bigger than three Dutch hoys, beside round trunks,

15 Furnished with pistolets, and pieces of eight,

Will straight be here, my rogue, to have thy bath—

That is the color—and to make his batt'ry

---

3 QUIT HIM *given up on him.*

4 "*I have certainly given up on him, and if he could avoid going to hell he would be a happy man.*"

5 MILL-JADE *a horse who walked in circles pushing the arm which turned a grindstone.*

6 GRAINS *flour produced by the mill; also grains of gold, money.*

8 BLACK BOY *see Subtle's* "*complexion of the Roman wash*," *I.1.29; but perhaps only a reference to Subtle's sooty occupation as alchemist.*

11 PARTY-BAWD *fellow pimp.*

12 PRIVATE *incognito.* CONSCIENCE *religious convictions.*

13 MUNITION *provisions, i.e. supplies of money and clothes.* SLOPS *fashionable large trousers.*

14 HOYS *small boats.*

15 PISTOLETS . . . EIGHT *gold coins.*

16 BATH *some special medical treatment (?).*

17 COLOR *pretext.* BATTR'Y *assault.*

Upon our Dol, our castle, our cinque port,
Our Dover pier, our what thou wilt. Where is she?
She must prepare perfumes, delicate linen,   20
The bath in chief, a banquet, and her wit,
For she must milk his epididymis.
Where is the doxy?
    Subtle.   I'll send her to thee;
And but dispatch my brace of little John Leydens
And come again myself.
    Face.   Are they within then?   25
    Subtle. Numb'ring the sum.
    Face.   How much?
    Subtle.   A hundred marks, boy.
                                      [*Exit.*]

    Face. Why, this's a lucky day! Ten pounds of Mammon!
Three o' my clerk! A portague o' my grocer!
This o' the Brethren! Beside reversions
And states to come i' the widow, and my count!   30
My share today will not be bought for forty—
               [*Enter Dol.*]
    Dol Common.   What?
    Face. Pounds, dainty Dorothy! Art thou so near?
    Dol Common. Yes. Say, lord general, how fares our camp?
    Face. As with the few that had entrenched themselves

18–19 CINQUE PORT . . . PIER *the five ports of southeast England, including Dover, which were specially defended because most vulnerable to invasion.*
21 BATH IN CHIEF *"especially a bath"; bathing is obviously a part of the elaborate treatment in a fancy brothel.*
22 EPIDIDYMIS *tube carrying sperm from the testes.*
24 JOHN LEYDEN *Anabaptist leader.*
29 REVERSION *legal term for a right to something at some future date.*
30 STATES *estates, inheritances.*
31 SHARE *i.e. of the booty.*
33 *N.*

35 Safe, by their discipline, against a world, Dol,
And laughed within those trenches, and grew fat
With thinking on the bootys, Dol, brought in
Daily by their small parties. This dear hour
A doughty don is taken with my Dol,
40 And thou mayst make his ransom what thou wilt,
My Dousabel; he shall be brought here, fettered
With thy fair looks before he sees thee; and thrown
In a down-bed, as dark as any dungeon;
Where thou shalt keep him waking with thy drum,
45 Thy drum, my Dol, thy drum, till he be tame
As the poor blackbirds were i' the great frost,
Or bees are with a basin; and so hive him
I' the swan-skin coverlid and cambric sheets,
Till he work honey and wax, my little God's-gift.
    Dol Common. What is he, General?
50 *Face.*   An *adalantado*,
A grandee, girl. Was not my Dapper here yet?
    Dol Common. No.
    Face.   Nor my Drugger?
    Dol Common.   Neither.
    Face.   A pox on 'em,
They are so long a furnishing! Such stinkards
Would not be seen upon these festival days.

38 SMALL PARTIES *raiders.*

41 DOUSABEL *literally "sweet and beautiful," but the name suggests a heroine of romance and fits in with the extended fairy tale Face is constructing.*

46 FROST *the Thames froze over in an unusually hard winter of 1607–08.*

47 BEES . . . BASIN *banging pots together was believed to make bees settle.*

48 SWAN-SKIN COVERLID *silky quilt.*

49 GOD'S-GIFT *the Greek meaning of* Dorothea.

50 ADALANTADO *governor.*

53 A FURNISHING *bringing the goods promised.*

54 FESTIVAL *festal, i.e. days of particular importance and enjoyment.*

[*Enter Subtle.*]

How now! ha' you done?

 Subtle.   Done. They are gone. The sum   55
Is here in bank, my Face. I would we knew
Another chapman now would buy 'em outright.

 Face. 'Slid, Nab shall do't, against he ha' the widow,
To furnish household.

 Subtle.   Excellent, well thought on.
Pray God he come.

 Face.   I pray he keep away   60
Till our new business be o'erpast.

 Subtle.   But, Face,
How cam'st thou by this secret don?

 [*Face.*]   A spirit
Brought me th'intelligence in a paper, here, [*Shows a note.*]
As I was conjuring, yonder, in my circle
For Surly; I ha' my flies abroad. Your bath   65
Is famous, Subtle, by my means. Sweet Dol,
You must go tune your virginal, no losing
O' the least time. And—do you hear?—good action.
Firk like a flounder; kiss like a scallop, close;
And tickle him with thy mother-tongue. His great   70

56 IN BANK *safely locked away.*

57 CHAPMAN *merchant.* 'EM *i.e. Mammon's ironwork.*

58 AGAINST *in preparation for the time.*

64 CONJURING . . . CIRCLE *literally, walking around the church, which Face compares to the charmed circle from which a magician invokes spirits.*

65 FLIES *familiars, spirits who do the magician's bidding.*

67 VIRGINAL *early form of piano; with an obvious pun.*

67–68 NO . . . TIME *"don't waste any time."*

69 FIRK *act lively; see II.1.28 for use of same word in connection with alchemy. The terms of whoring and alchemy frequently coincide.*

Verdugoship has not a jot of language;
So much the easier to be cozened, my Dolly.
He will come here in a hired coach, obscure,
And our own coachman, whom I have sent as a guide,
No creature else—

                    One knocks.
                Who's that?

75   *Subtle.*   It i' not he?

      Face. O no, not yet this hour.

      Subtle.   Who is't?

      Dol Common. [*Looking out.*]   Dapper,
Your clerk.

      Face.   God's will then, Queen of Faery,
On with your tire [*Exit Dol.*] and, Doctor, with your robes.
Let's dispatch him, for God's sake.

      Subtle.   'Twill be long.

80   *Face.* I warrant you, take but the cues I give you,
It shall be brief enough. [*Looking out the window.*]
                    'Slight, here are more!
Abel, and, I think, the angry boy, the heir,
That fain would quarrel.

      Subtle.   And the widow?

      Face.   No,
Not that I see. Away! [*Subtle hurries off. Face opens the door.*]
                O, sir, you are welcome.

71 VERDUGOSHIP *Spanish, the hangman; used here with mock solemnity.* HAS . . .
   LANGUAGE *speaks no English.*

73 OBSCURE *secretly.*

78 TIRE *clothing, costume.*

82 ANGRY BOY *quarrelsome young man of fashion.*

Act III Scene 4

[*Enter Dapper.*]

Face. The Doctor is within a-moving for you.
I have had the most ado to win him to it!
He swears you'll be the dearling o' the dice;
He never heard her Highness dote till now, he says.
Your aunt has giv'n you the most gracious words   5
That can be thought on.

    Dapper.   Shall I see her Grace?

    Face. See her, and kiss her too.

                [*Enter Abel Drugger, and Kastril.*]

                      What, honest Nab?

Hast brought the damask?

    Drugger.   No, sir; here's tobacco.

    Face. 'Tis well done, Nab; thou'lt bring the damask too?

    Drugger. Yes. Here's the gentleman, Captain, Master Kastril,   10
I have brought to see the Doctor.

    Face.   Where's the widow?

    Drugger. Sir, as he likes, his sister, he says, shall come.

    Face. O, is it so? 'Good time. Is your name Kastril, sir?

    Kastril. Ay, and the best o' the Kastrils, I'd be sorry else,
By fifteen hundred a year. Where is this Doctor?   15
My mad tobacco-boy here tells me of one
That can do things. Has he any skill?

---

1 A-MOVING *conjuring* (to get the fly promised earlier).

2 ADO *difficulty.*

6 ON *of.*

12 AS HE LIKES *if he likes* (the Doctor's work).

14 SORRY *i.e. poorer.*

16 MAD *reckless, wild. Kastril is such a bumpkin that he takes Drugger for a gallant.*

    Face.   Wherein, sir?

    Kastril. To carry a business, manage a quarrel fairly,
Upon fit terms.

    Face.   It seems, sir, you're but young

20 About the town, that can make that a question.

    Kastril. Sir, not so young but I have heard some speech
Of the angry boys, and seen 'em take tobacco,
And in his shop; and I can take it too.
And I would fain be one of 'em, and go down
And practise i' the country.

25   *Face.*   Sir, for the duello,
The Doctor, I assure you, shall inform you
To the least shadow of a hair; and show you
An instrument he has of his own making,
Wherewith, no sooner shall you make report

30 Of any quarrel, but he will take the height on't
Most instantly, and tell in what degree
Of safety it lies in, or mortality.
And how it may be borne, whether in a right line
Or a half circle; or may else be cast

35 Into an angle blunt, if not acute:
All this he will demonstrate. And then, rules
To give and take the lie by.

    Kastril.   How! to take it?

    Face. Yes, in oblique he'll show you, or in circle,

22 TAKE TOBACCO *smoking and snuff were new and fashionable, and so had to be used with style.*

25 PRACTISE *i.e. swagger and smoke.*

26–27 INFORM . . . HAIR *"teach you the finest points."*

28 INSTRUMENT *chart or book; handy guide.*

29 MAKE REPORT *describe.*

30–35 N.

37 GIVE . . . LIE *"call a man a liar or be called one." The most deadly insult to honor.*

38–39 OBLIQUE . . . DIAMETER N.

But never in diameter. The whole town
Study his theorems and dispute them ordinarily   40
At the eating academies.
    Kastril.   But does he teach
Living by the wits too?
    Face.   Anything whatever.
You cannot think that subtlety but he reads it.
He made me a captain. I was a stark pimp,
Just o' your standing, 'fore I met with him—   45
It's not two months since. I'll tell you his method.
First, he will enter you at some ordinary.
    Kastril. No, I'll not come there. You shall pardon me.
    Face.   For why, sir?
    Kastril. There's gaming there, and tricks.
    Face.   Why, would you be
A gallant and not game?
    Kastril.   Ay, 'twill spend a man.   50
    Face. Spend you? It will repair you when you are spent.
How do they live by their wits, there, that have vented
Six times your fortunes?
    Kastril.   What, three thousand a year!
    Face. Ay, forty thousand.
    Kastril.   Are there such?
    Face.   Ay, sir.
And gallants, yet. Here's a young gentleman [*Brings Dapper forward.*]   55
Is born to nothing—forty marks a year,

41 EATING ACADEMIES *rather a grand name for the inns where young men gathered to
eat, drink, and gamble. Also called "ordinaries."*

43 THINK *imagine.* READS *understands.*

47 ENTER *introduce.*

50 SPEND *ruin(financially).*

53 THREE THOUSAND *this is not six times the amount Kastril has just said he has.
Either he cannot figure, or his real income is only five hundred a year.*

Act III Scene 4

Which I count nothing. He's to be initiated,
And have a fly o' the Doctor. He will win you
By unresistible luck, within this fortnight,
60 Enough to buy a barony. They will set him
Upmost, at the groom-porter's, all the Christmas!
And for the whole year through at every place
Where there is play, present him with the chair,
The best attendance, the best drink, sometimes
65 Two glasses of Canary, and pay nothing;
The purest linen and the sharpest knife,
The partridge next his trencher, and, somewhere,
The dainty bed, in private, with the Dainty.
You shall ha' your ordinaries bid for him,
70 As playhouses for a poet; and the master
Pray him aloud to name what dish he affects,
Which must be butter'd shrimps; and those that drink
To no mouth else will drink to his, as being
The goodly president mouth of all the board.
  Kastril. Do you not gull one?
75 *Face.*   'Ods my life! Do you think it?
You shall have a cast commander (can but get
In credit with a glover, or a spurier,
For some two pair, of either's ware, aforehand)

61 UPMOST *i.e. in the seat of honor.* GROOM-PORTER *official in charge of gambling in the royal court.* CHRISTMAS *festival season at which gambling was heavy at court.*
64 ATTENDANCE *service.*
65 CANARY *fine sweet wine.*
70 PLAYHOUSES . . . POET *the repertory companies of actors commissioned playwrights to write plays for them.*
71 AFFECTS *fancies.*
72–73 DRINK . . . MOUTH *toast.*
76 CATT COMMANDER *discharged officer.*
77 IN CREDIT *charge (the officer has very little credit).*

Will by most swift posts dealing with him,
Arrive at competent means to keep himself,   80
His punk, and naked boy, in excellent fashion.
And be admired for 't.
    Kastril.   Will the Doctor teach this?
    Face. He will do more, sir. When your land is gone
(As men of spirit hate to keep earth long)
In a vacation, when small money is stirring,   85
And ordinaries suspended till the term,
He'll show a perspective, where on one side
You shall behold the faces and the persons
Of all sufficient young heirs in town,
Whose bonds are current for commodity;   90
On th' other side, the merchants' forms, and others,
That without help of any second broker
(Who would expect a share) will trust such parcels;
In the third square, the very street and sign
Where the commodity dwells, and does but wait   95
To be delivered, be it pepper, soap,
Hops, or tobacco, oatmeal, woad, or cheeses.
All which you may so handle to enjoy
To your own use, and never stand obliged.
    Kastril. I' faith! Is he such a fellow?
    Face.   Why, Nab here knows him.   100
And then for making matches for rich widows,

---

79 BY . . . POSTS *swiftly.*
81 BOY *N.*
85–86 *There was little activity in the vacations between the sessions of the courts, the*
    terms.
87 PERSPECTIVE *a magical crystal ball, or a mirror showing the future.*
89 SUFFICIENT *self-sufficient, those who have come into their estates.*
90 CURRENT *outstanding.*
90–99 COMMODITY *N.*

Young gentlewomen, heirs, the fortunat'st man!
He's sent to, far and near, all over England,
To have his counsel, and to know their fortunes.
    Kastril. God's will, my suster shall see him.
105   *Face.*   I'll tell you, sir,
What he did tell me of Nab. It's a strange thing
(By the way, you must eat no cheese, Nab, it breeds melancholy,
And that same melancholy breeds worms) but pass it:
He told me honest Nab here was ne'er at tavern
But once in's life.
110   *Drugger.*   Truth, and no more I was not.
    Face. And then he was so sick—
    Drugger.   Could he tell you that too?
    Face. How should I know it?
    Drugger.   In troth, we had been a-shooting,
And had a piece of fat ram-mutton to supper,
That lay so heavy o' my stomach—
    Face.   And he has no head
115 To bear any wine; for, what with the noise o' the fiddlers,
And care of his shop, for he dares keep no servants—
    Drugger. My head did so ache—
    Face.   As he was fain to be brought
    home,
The Doctor told me. And then a good old woman—
    Drugger. Yes, faith, she dwells in Seacoal-lane, did cure me
120 With sodden ale, and pellitory o' the wall:

102 FORTUNAT'ST *most fortune-bringing.*
105 SUSTER *sister; Kastril has a broad country accent.*
107 CHEESE *thought to make a man melancholy, depressed, or even mad.*
108 PASS IT *"let that go"; with a pun on "pass."*
115 FIDDLERS *musicians in the inn.*
116 CARE *concern; the shop was untended while Drugger was out.*
120 SODDEN *boiled.* PELLITORY O' THE WALL *bush which grows at foot of walls.*

Cost me but twopence. I had another sickness
Was worse than that.

    Face.   Ay, that was with the grief
Thou took'st for being 'sessed at eighteenpence
For the waterwork.

    Drugger.   In truth, and it was like
T' have cost me almost my life.

    Face.   Thy hair went off?   125

    Drugger. Yes, sir; 'twas done for spite.

    Face.   Nay, so says the Doctor.

    Kastril. Pray thee, tobacco-boy, go fetch my suster;
I'll see this learned boy before I go,
And so shall she.

    Face.   Sir, he is busy now,
But if you have a sister to fetch hither,   130
Perhaps your own pains may command her sooner;
And he, by that time, will be free.

    Kastril.   I go.   [*Exit.*]

    Face. Drugger, she's thine: the damask.   [*Exit Drugger.*]

                   [*Aside.*]—Subtle and I
Must wrestle for her—Come on, Master Dapper.
You see how I turn clients here away   135
To give your cause dispatch. Ha' you performed
The ceremonies were enjoined you?

    Dapper.   Yes, o' the vinegar,
And the clean shirt.

---

123 'SESSED *assessed.*

124 WATERWORK *the new pump supplying water to houses in town from the river Thames.*

126 SPITE *Drugger thinks the assessment for water was much too high because someone disliked him.*

131 PAINS *efforts.*

137 ENJOINED *prescribed for.*

    Face.   'Tis well; that shirt may do you
More worship than you think. Your aunt's afire,
140 But that she will not show it, t' have a sight on you.
Ha' you provided for her Grace's servants?
    Dapper. Yes, here are six-score Edward shillings.
    Face.   Good.
    Dapper. And an old Harry's sovereign.
    Face.   Very good!
    Dapper. And three James' shillings, and an Elizabeth groat,
Just twenty nobles.
145   *Face.*   O, you are too just.
I would you had had the other noble in Mary's.
    Dapper. I have some Philip and Mary's.
    Face.   Ay, those same
Are best of all. Where are they? Hark, the Doctor.

142–47 SHILLINGS *N.*

145 TOO JUST *too exact; i.e.* "*you should have brought a bit more to show
generosity.*"

Act III Scene 5

                [*Enter*] *Subtle disguised like a Priest of Faery.*
    Subtle. Is yet her Grace's cousin come?
    Face.   He is come.
    Subtle. And is he fasting?
    Face.   Yes.
    Subtle.   And hath cried "hum"?
    Face. Thrice, you must answer.
    Dapper.   Thrice.
    Subtle.   And as oft "buz"?

SD PRIEST OF FAERY *N.*

Face. If you have, say.
Dapper.   I have.
Subtle.   Then, to her coz.
Hoping that he hath vinegared his senses,   5
As he was bid, the Faery Queen dispenses,
By me, this robe, the petticoat of Fortune;
Which that he straight put on, she doth importune.
                    [*They wrap him in a petticoat.*]
And though to Fortune near be her petticoat,
Yet nearer is her smock, the Queen doth note;   10
And, therefore, even of that a piece she hath sent,
Which, being a child, to wrap him in was rent;
And prays him for a scarf he now will wear it,
With as much love as then her Grace did tear it,
About his eyes, to show he is fortunate.   15
                    They blind him with a rag.
And, trusting unto her to make his state,
He'll throw away all worldly pelf about him,
Which that he will perform, she doth not doubt him.
    Face. She need not doubt him, sir. Alas, he has nothing
But what he will part withal as willingly   20
Upon her Grace's word—throw away your purse—
                    [*Dapper empties his pockets.*]
As she would ask it—handkerchiefs and all—
She cannot bid that thing but he'll obey.
If you have a ring about you, cast it off,

---

9 FORTUNE *used in joking way to refer to her private parts.*
10 SMOCK *undergarment.*
12 RENT *torn (as swaddling for "child").*
15 "*Fortune is blind.*"
16 STATE *fortune.*
17 WORLDLY PELF *trash of this world; i.e. money.*

25   Or a silver seal at your wrist; her Grace will send
                  He throws away, as they bid him.
    Her faeries here to search you; therefore deal
    Directly with her Highness. If they find
    That you conceal a mite you are undone.
        Dapper. Truly, there's all.
        Face.   All what?
        Dapper.   My money, truly.
30   *Face.* Keep nothing that is transitory about you.
    [*Aside.*] Bid Dol play music.—Look, the elves are come
              Dol enters with a cittern. They pinch him.
    To pinch you, if you tell not truth. Advise you.
        Dapper. O! I have a paper with a spur-ryal in't.
        Face.   Ti, ti,
    They knew't, they say.
        Subtle.   Ti, ti, ti, ti, he has more yet.
        Face. Ti, ti-ti-ti. I' the tother pocket? [*They search him.*]
35   *Subtle.*   Titi, titi, titi, titi.
    They must pinch him or he will never confess, they say.
        Dapper. O, O!
        Face.   Nay, pray you, hold; he is her Grace's nephew.
    Ti, ti, ti? What care you? Good faith, you shall care.
    Deal plainly, sir, and shame the faeries. Show
    You are an innocent.
40   *Dapper.*   By this good light, I ha' nothing.

    25 SEAL *a charm.*
    27 DIRECTLY *straightforwardly.*
    30 TRANSITORY *i.e. the things of this world which do not endure.*
    SD CITTERN *a lutelike instrument.*
    32 ADVISE YOU *be advised; take heed.*
    33 SPUR-RYAL *"royal" or "rose noble" stamped with a blazing sun resembling a spur rowel. Worth about eighty new pence.*
    39 *Compare the old saying, "Tell truth and shame the devil."*
    40 INNOCENT (1) *sinless man;* (2) *fool.*

Subtle. Ti ti, ti ti to ta. He does equivocate, she says—
Ti, ti do ti, ti ti do, ti da—and swears by the light when he is blinded.

Dapper. By this good dark, I ha' nothing but a half-crown
Of gold about my wrist, that my love gave me,
And a leaden heart I wore sin' she forsook me.   45

Face. I thought 'twas something. And would you incur
Your aunt's displeasure for these trifles? Come,
I had rather you had thrown away twenty half-crowns.

     [Removes the bracelet.]
You may wear your leaden heart still—

    [Dol gestures from the window.]
          How now?

  [Dapper is pushed aside so he cannot hear.]

Subtle. What news, Dol?

Dol Common.   Yonder's your knight, Sir Mammon.   50

Face. God's lid, we never thought of him till now.
Where is he?

Dol Common. Here, hard by. He's at the door.

Subtle. [*To Face.*] And you are not ready now! Dol, get his suit.

          [Exit Dol.]
He must not be sent back.

Face.   O, by no means.
What shall we do with this same puffin here,   55
Now he's o' the spit?

Subtle.   Why, lay him back awhile
With some device. [*Goes to Dapper.*]

    Ti, ti ti, ti ti ti. [*Calls out.*]

        Would her Grace speak with me?

---

45 SIN' *since.*
53 SUIT *i.e. the costume of Lungs, the alchemist's assistant.*
55 PUFFIN *silly-looking bird, thought to be half fish, half bird.*
56 O' THE SPIT *spitted; in process of being "roasted."*
56–57 LAY . . . DEVICE *"put him aside with some trick."*

I come! [*Whispers urgently.*] Help, Dol!

    Face.   Who's there? Sir Epicure!

    He speaks through the keyhole, the other knocking.

My master's i' the way. Please you to walk

60 Three or four turns, but till his back be turned,

And I am for you. [*Aside.*] Quickly, Dol!

  [*Dol enters and begins dressing Face as Lungs. Subtle turns to Dapper.*]

    Subtle.   Her Grace

Commends her kindly to you, Master Dapper.

    Dapper. I long to see her Grace.

    Subtle.   She, now, is set

At dinner in her bed, and she has sent you

65 From her own private trencher, a dead mouse

And a piece of gingerbread, to be merry withal

And stay your stomach, lest you faint with fasting.

Yet if you could hold out till she saw you, she says,

It would be better for you.

    Face.   Sir, he shall

70 Hold out, and 'twere this two hours, for her Highness;

I can assure you that. We will not lose

All we ha' done—

    Subtle.   He must nor see, nor speak

To anybody, till then.

    Face.   For that we'll put, sir,

A stay in's mouth.

    Subtle.   Of what?

    Face.   Of gingerbread.

75 Make you it fit. He that hath pleased her Grace

61 FOR *ready for.*

67 STAY YOUR STOMACH *ease your appetite.*

70 AND . . . THIS "*even if it were as long as.*"

74 STAY *gag.*

75 MAKE . . . FIT "*you put it in.*"

Thus far, shall not now crinkle for a little.

[*To Dapper.*] Gape, sir, and let him fit you. [*They gag him.*]

   Subtle. [*Aside.*]   Where shall we now

Bestow him?

   Dol Common. I' the privy.

   Subtle. [*Taking Dapper by the hand.*] Come along, sir,

I now must show you Fortune's privy lodgings.

   Face. Are they perfumed, and his bath ready?

   Subtle.   All.   80

Only the fumigation's somewhat strong.

                     [*Dol and Subtle lead Dapper off.*]

   Face. [*Speaks through the door.*] Sir Epicure, I am yours, sir, by and

   by.

76 CRINKLE . . . LITTLE *shrink back from a trifle.*
82 BY AND BY *at once.*

Act IV Scene 1

[*Face, dressed as Lungs, opens the door to Mammon.*]

Face. O, sir, y' are come i' the only finest time—

Mammon. Where's Master?

Face. Now preparing for projection, sir.
Your stuff will be all changed shortly.

Mammon. Into gold?

Face. To gold and silver, sir.

Mammon. Silver I care not for.

Face. Yes, sir, a little to give beggars.

5   *Mammon.* Where's the lady?

Face. At hand, here. I ha' told her such brave things o' you,
Touching your bounty and your noble spirit—

Mammon. Hast thou?

Face. As she is almost in her fit to see you.
But, good sir, no divinity i' your conference,
For fear of putting her in rage—

10   *Mammon.* I warrant thee.

Face. Six men will not hold her down. And then,
If the old man should hear or see you—

Mammon. Fear not.

Face. The very house, sir, would run mad. You know it,
How scrupulous he is, and violent,

15   'Gainst the least act of sin. Physic, or mathematics,

1 THE ONLY FINEST *absolutely the best.*
9 NO . . . CONFERENCE *"no talk of theology."*
10 RAGE *madness.*
15 PHYSIC *medicine.*

Poetry, state, or bawdry, as I told you,
She will endure, and never startle; but
No word of controversy.

   Mammon.   I am schooled, good Ulen.

   Face. And you must praise her house, remember that,
And her nobility.

   Mammon.   Let me alone: 20
No herald, no, nor antiquary, Lungs,
Shall do it better. Go.

   Face. [*Leaving. Aside.*] Why, this is yet
A kind of modern happiness, to have
Dol Common for a great lady.

   Mammon. [*Alone.*]   Now, Epicure,
Heighten thyself, talk to her all in gold;   25
Rain her as many showers as Jove did drops
Unto his Danaë; show the god a miser
Compared with Mammon. What! the stone will do't.
She shall feel gold, taste gold, hear gold, sleep gold;
Nay, we will *concumbere* gold. I will be puissant   30
And mighty in my talk to her!

           [*Enter Face with Dol.*]
               Here she comes.

   Face. [*Aside.*] To him, Dol, suckle him.—This is the noble knight

---

16 STATE *politics.*

19 HOUSE *noble family* (*Dol is pretending to be the sister of a great lord*).

20 LET ME ALONE "*leave it to me.*"

21 HERALD *an official concerned with coats of arms and family trees of the nobility.*
ANTIQUARY *historian.*

23 MODERN *trivial—the best days, "the golden age," were thought to be past and the
world steadily degenerating, so anything modern was worthless.*

26 JOVE *who came to the imprisoned girl Danaë and loved her in the form of a shower
of gold.*

30 CONCUMBERE *couple (sexually).*

I told your ladyship—

    Mammon.   Madame, with your pardon,

I kiss your vesture. [*Bows low and takes her hem.*]

    Dol Common.   Sir, I were uncivil

35   If I would suffer that; my lip to you, sir. [*Kisses him.*]

    Mammon. I hope my lord your brother be in health, lady?

    Dol Common. My lord, my brother is, though I no lady, sir.

    Face. [*Aside.*] Well said, my guinea bird.

    Mammon.   Right noble madame—

    Face. [*Aside.*] O, we shall have most fierce idolatry.

    Mammon. 'Tis your perogative.

40   *Dol Common.*   Rather your courtesy.

    Mammon. Were there nought else t' enlarge your virtues to me,

These answers speak your breeding and your blood.

    Dol Common. Blood we boast none, sir; a poor baron's daughter.

    Mammon. Poor! and gat you? Profane not. Had your father

45   Slept all the happy remnant of his life

After the act, lien but there still, and panted,

He'd done enough to make himself, his issue,

And his posterity noble.

    Dol Common.   Sir, although

We may be said to want the gilt and trappings,

50   The dress of honor, yet we strive to keep

The seeds and the materials.

    Mammon.   I do see

The old ingredient, virtue, was not lost,

---

38 GUINEA BIRD *slang for whore.*

40 PEROGATIVE *right (i.e. to be called "lady").*

41 ENLARGE *make known.*

43 BARON *one of the lower orders of nobility.*

50 DRESS *outward appearance.*

51 SEEDS . . . MATERIALS *i.e. the essential elements; the terms are again taken from alchemy.*

Nor the drug, money, used to make your compound.
There is a strange nobility i' your eye,
This lip, that chin! Methinks you do resemble   55
One o' the Austriac princes.
    Face. [*Aside.*]   Very like.
Her father was an Irish costermonger.
    Mammon. The house of Valois, just, had such a nose.
And such a forehead, yet, the Medici
Of Florence boast.
    Dol Common.   Troth, and I have been lik'ned   60
To all these princes.
    Face. [*Aside.*]   I'll be sworn, I heard it.
    Mammon. I know not how! it is not any one,
But e'en the very choice of all their features.
    Face. [*Aside.*] I'll in, and laugh.   [*Exit.*]
    Mammon.   A certain touch, or air,
That sparkles a divinity beyond   65
An earthly beauty!
    Dol Common.   O, you play the courtier.
    Mammon. Good lady, gi' me leave—
    Dol Common.   In faith, I may not
To mock me, sir.
    Mammon.   To burn i' this sweet flame:
The phoenix never knew a nobler death.
    Dol Common. Nay, now you court the courtier, and destroy   70
What you would build. This art, sir, i' your words,

---

56 AUSTRIAC *Habsburg, the royal house of Austria, noted for a prominent lower lip.*
57 COSTERMONGER *fruit seller on the street.*
58 VALOIS *the royal house of France.*
59 MEDICI *the great ruling family of Florence.*
68 SWEET FLAME *i.e. love.*
69 PHOENIX *N.*
70 COURT THE COURTIER *outgo the courtier (in praise and manners).*

Calls your whole faith in question.

    Mammon.   By my soul—

    Dol Common. Nay, oaths are made o' the same air, sir.

    Mammon.   Nature

Never bestowed upon mortality

75 A more unblamed, a more harmonious feature;

She played the step-dame in all faces else.

Sweet madam, le' me be particular—

    Dol Common. Particular, sir? I pray you, know your distance.

    Mammon. In no ill sense, sweet lady, but to ask

80 How your fair graces pass the hours? I see

Y' are lodged here, i' the house of a rare man,

An excellent artist; but, what's that to you?

    Dol Common. Yes, sir, I study here the mathematics,

And distillation.

    Mammon.   O, I cry your pardon.

85 He's a divine instructor! can extract

The souls of all things by his art; call all

The virtues and the miracles of the sun

Into a temperate furnace; teach dull nature

What her own forces are. A man the Emp'ror

90 Has courted above Kelley; sent his medals

And chains t' invite him.

    Dol Common.   Ay, and for his physic, sir—

    Mammon. Above the art of Aesculapius,

---

75 UNBLAMED *unblemished.*

76 STEP-DAME *stepmother; i.e. grudging in what she gave.*

77 PARTICULAR *Mammon means "more precise," but Dol chooses to take the meaning as "intimate."*

84 DISTILLATION *alchemy.*

85–89 N.

89–91 EMP'ROR . . . KELLEY . . . HIM N.

92–93 AESCULAPIUS . . . THUNDERER *Aesculapius, a great physician who restored Hippolytus to life, was killed by Jove lest men should become immortal.*

That drew the envy of the Thunderer!
I know all this, and more.
   Dol Common.   Troth, I am taken, sir,
Whole, with these studies that contemplate nature.   95
   Mammon. It is a noble humor. But this form
Was not intended to so dark a use!
Had you been crooked, foul, of some coarse mold,
A cloister had done well; but such a feature
That might stand up the glory of a kingdom,   100
To live recluse! is a mere solecism,
Though in a nunnery. It must not be.
I muse my lord your brother will permit it!
You should spend half my land first, were I he.
Does not this diamond better on my finger   105
Than i' the quarry?
   Dol Common.   Yes.
   Mammon.   Why, you are like it.
You were created, lady, for the light!
Here, you shall wear it; take it, the first pledge
                [*Gives her the ring.*]
Of what I speak; to bind you to believe me.
   Dol Common. In chains of adamant?
   Mammon.   Yes, the strongest bands.   110
And take a secret too. Here, by your side
Doth stand, this hour, the happiest man in Europe.
   Dol Common. You are contented, sir?
   Mammon.   Nay, in true being
The envy of princes and the fear of states.
   Dol Common. Say you so, Sir Epicure?

95 WHOLE *entirely.*
101 MERE SOLECISM *absolute impropriety.*
110 ADAMANT *the strongest iron.*

Act IV Scene 1

　　Mammon.　　　　　　　　　　Yes, and thou shalt prove
115　　　it,
　　Daughter of honor. I have cast mine eye
　　Upon thy form, and I will rear this beauty
　　Above all styles.
　　　　Dol Common. You mean no treason, sir!
　　　　Mammon. No, I will take away that jealousy.
120　I am the lord of the philosopher's stone,
　　And thou the lady.
　　　　Dol Common. How, sir! ha' you that?
　　　　Mammon. I am the master of the mast'ry.
　　This day, the good old wretch, here, o' the house
　　Has made it for us. Now, he's at projection.
125　Think, therefore, thy first wish now; let me hear it,
　　And it shall rain into thy lap, no shower
　　But floods of gold, whole cataracts, a deluge,
　　To get a nation on thee.
　　　　Dol Common.　　　　You are pleased, sir,
　　To work on the ambition of our sex.
130　　*Mammon.* I'm pleased the glory of her sex should know
　　This nook, here, of the Friars is no climate
　　For her to live obscurely in, to learn
　　Physic and surgery for the constable's wife
　　Of some odd hundred in Essex; but come forth,
135　And taste the air of palaces; eat, drink

115 PROVE *test, try.*
118 STYLES *types, i.e. above all other kinds of beauty.*
119 JEALOUSY *suspicion.*
122 MAST'RY *the master work, the stone.*
128 GET A NATION *beget multitudes. Mammon is overreaching Jove's impregnation of Danaë in a mere shower of gold, which begot only one son, Perseus.*
131 FRIARS *Blackfriars, where Lovewit's house is.*
133–34 CONSTABLE'S . . . ESSEX *N.*

The toils of emp'rics and their boasted practice;
Tincture of pearl, and coral, gold, and amber;
Be seen at feasts, and triumphs; have it asked,
What miracle she is? set all the eyes
Of court a-fire, like a burning glass,   140
And work 'em into cinders, when the jewels
Of twenty states adorn thee, and the light
Strikes out the stars; that, when thy name is mentioned
Queens may look pale; and, we but showing our love,
Nero's Poppaea may be lost in story!   145
Thus, will we have it.
    Dol Common.   I could well consent, sir.
But in a monarchy, how will this be?
The prince will soon take notice, and both seize
You and your stone, it being a wealth unfit
For any private subject.
    Mammon.   If he knew it.   150
    Dol Common. Youself do boast it, sir.
    Mammon.   To thee, my life.
    Dol Common. O, but beware, sir! you may come to end
The remnant of your days in a loath'd prison,
By speaking of it.
    Mammon.   'Tis no idle fear!
We'll therefore go with all, my girl, and live   155
In a free state, where we will eat our mullets

---

136 EMP'RICS *empirics, practical scientists or technicians. Mammon sees himself as the
entrepreneur, the idea man, who knows how to use and organize the work or
"practice" of others.*

140 BURNING *magnifying.*

145 NERO'S POPPAEA *wife of the Roman emperor Nero, for whom he murdered his
mother and first wife.* LOST IN STORY *either, "her story forgotten (because our love
is so much greater)," or, "become only a story (in contrast to the actuality we live)."*

154 IDLE FEAR *mere anxiety.* N.

156 FREE STATE *republic, like Venice or Switzerland.*

Soused in high-country wines, sup pheasants' eggs,
And have our cockles boiled in silver shells,
Our shrimps to swim again, as when they lived,
160 In a rare butter made of dolphins' milk,
Whose cream does look like opals; and with these
Delicate meats set ourselves high for pleasure,
And take us down again, and then renew
Our youth and strength with drinking the elixir;
165 And so enjoy a perpetuity
Of life and lust. And thou shalt ha' thy wardrobe
Richer than Nature's, still, to change thyself,
And vary oft'ner, for thy pride, than she,
Or Art, her wise and almost-equal servant.

[*Enter Face.*]

170   *Face.* Sir, you are too loud. I hear you, every word,
Into the laboratory. Some fitter place!
The garden, or great chamber above. [*Aside to Mammon.*] How like
    you her?

    Mammon. Excellent, Lungs! There's for thee.

[*Gives him gold.*]

  Face.   But do you hear,
Good sir, beware, no mention of the Rabbins.
    Mammon. We think not on 'em.
    Face.   O, it is well, sir.

[*Exeunt Mammon and Dol.*]
175   Subtle!

---

162 HIGH FOR PLEASURE *sexually excited, but also intent on and ready for any sensual delight.*

169 SERVANT *art is the servant of nature because it does not create new laws but merely follows nature's.*

174 RABBINS *rabbinical scholars whose biblical commentaries dealt with the kind of theological questions which will drive Dol into her fits.*

Act IV Scene 2

[*Enter Subtle.*]

Face. Dost thou not laugh?

Subtle.   Yes. Are they gone?

Face.   All's clear.

Subtle. The widow is come.

Face.   And your quarreling disciple?

Subtle. Ay.

Face.   I must to my captainship again then.

Subtle. Stay, bring 'em in first.

Face.   So I meant. What is she?
A bonnibel?

Subtle.   I know not.

Face.   We'll draw lots;   5
You'll stand to that?

Subtle.   What else?

Face.   O, for a suit
To fall now like a curtain, flap!

Subtle.   To th' door, man.

Face. You'll ha' the first kiss, cause I am not ready.

[*Going to the door.*]

Subtle. [*Aside.*] Yes, and perhaps hit you through both the nostrils.

Face. [*Opens door.*] Who would you speak with?

---

5 BONNIBEL *beauty.*

6 SUIT *i.e. his captain's costume; the many quick changes required of him are becoming exhausting.*

7 CURTAIN *N.*

9 HIT . . . NOSTRILS *some slangy saying meaning roughly, "get the better of you" (?).*

Act IV Scene 2

> *Kastril.* Where's the Captain?
>
> 10 *Face.* Gone, sir,
> About some business.
>
> *Kastril.* Gone!
>
> *Face.* He'll return straight.
> But Master Doctor, his lieutenant, is here. [*Exit.*]
>
> [*Enter Kastril and Dame Pliant.*]
>
> *Subtle.* Come near, my worshipful boy, my *terrae fili*,
> That is, my boy of land; make thy approaches.
> 15 Welcome; I know thy lusts and thy desires,
> And I will serve and satisfy 'em. Begin,
> Charge me from thence, or thence, or in this line;
> Here is my center: ground thy quarrel.
>
> *Kastril.* You lie.
>
> *Subtle.* How, child of wrath and anger! the loud lie?
> For what, my sudden boy?
>
> 20 *Kastril.* Nay, that look you to,
> I am aforehand.
>
> *Subtle.* O, this's no true grammar,
> And as ill logic! You must render causes, child:
> Your first and second intentions, know your canons
> And your divisions, moods, degrees, and differences,
> 25 Your predicaments, substance, and accident,
> Series extern, and intern, with their causes

---

13 TERRAE FILI "*son of the soil*"; *can mean* "*boob*" *also, as well as Subtle's transla-
tion,* "*landed.*"

15 LUSTS *wishes.*

17 "*Attack me from there, or there, or from this direction.*"

18 CENTER *i.e. the position I will occupy.* GROUND *explain, give the basis of.*
YOU LIE *not a very subtle beginning. The rules dictated beginning in a more circum-
spect way.*

21 I AM AFOREHAND "*I got there first.*" GRAMMAR *proper procedure.*

23–28 N.

Efficient, material, formal, final,
And ha' your elements perfect—
    Kastril.   What, is this
The angry tongue he talks in?
    Subtle.   That false precept
Of being aforehand has deceived a number,   30
And made 'em enter quarrels oftentimes
Before they were aware; and afterward
Against their wills.
    Kastril.   How must I do then, sir?
    Subtle. I cry this lady mercy. She should first
                 [*Turning to Dame Pliant.*]
Have been saluted. I do call you lady   35
Because you are to be one ere't be long,
My soft and buxom widow. *He kisses her.*
    Kastril.   Is she, i' faith?
    Subtle. Yes, or my art is an egregious liar.
    Kastril. How know you?
    Subtle.   By inspection on her forehead,
And subtlety of her lip, which must be tasted   40
Often, to make a judgment. *He kisses her again.*
                 'Slight, she melts
Like a myrobolane! Here is yet a line, [*Looking at her forehead.*]
In *rivo frontis*, tells me he is no knight.
    Dame Pliant. What is he then, sir?
    Subtle.   Let me see your hand.
O, your *linea fortunae* makes it plain;   45
And stella, here, in *monte veneris*;
But, most of all, *junctura annularis*.

40 SUBTLETY *exquisiteness.*
42 MYROBOLANE *plum-like delicacy from the East.*
43–47 RIVO FRONTIS, ETC. *N.*
43 HE . . . KNIGHT *"the man (she will marry) is of higher rank than a knight."*

He is a soldier, or a man of art, lady,
But shall have some great honor shortly.
 Dame Pliant.   Brother,
He's a rare man, believe me!
50 *Kastril*.   Hold your peace.
     [*Enter Face as Captain*.]
Here comes the tother rare man. 'Save you, Captain.
 Face. Good master Kastril. Is this your sister?
 Kastril.   Ay, sir.
Please you to kuss her, and be proud to know her?
 Face. I shall be proud to know you, lady.
      [*Kisses her*.]
 Dame Pliant.   Brother,
He calls me lady, too.
55 *Kastril*.   Ay, peace. I heard it.
    [*Face and Subtle speak aside*.]
 Face. The Count is come.
 Subtle.   Where is he?
 Face.   At the door.
 Subtle. Why, you must entertain him.
 Face.   What'll you do
With these the while?
 Subtle. Why, have 'em up, and show 'em
Some fustian book, or the dark glass.
 Face.   'Fore God,
60 She is a delicate dabchick! I must have her.   [*Exit*.]
 Subtle. Must you! Ay, if your fortune will, you must.
   [*Turning back to Kastril and Dame Pliant*.]
Come, sir, the Captain will come to us presently.

---

48 SOLDIER . . . ART *i.e. either Captain Face or Doctor Subtle*.
59 FUSTIAN *cloth used as substitute for silk; thus, as an adjective the word came to
mean "pretentious" or "false."* DARK GLASS *the crystal ball used by mediums*.
60 DABCHICK *small water fowl; i.e. soft and cuddly*.

I'll ha' you to my chamber of demonstrations,
Where I'll show you both the grammar and logic
And rhetoric of quarreling; my whole method   65
Drawn out in tables; and my instrument,
That hath the several scale upon't, shall make you
Able to quarrel at a straw's-breadth by moonlight.
And, lady, I'll have you look in a glass,
Some half an hour, but to clear your eyesight,   70
Against you see your fortune; which is greater
Than I may judge upon the sudden, trust me.

                                        [*Exeunt.*]

64–65 GRAMMAR ... RHETORIC *the three divisions of the* trivium, *the basis of education in lower schools.*

66 TABLES *diagrams.*

67 SEVERAL *different, separate.*

68 AT ... MOONLIGHT "*over how wide a straw is, even when the light is dim.*"

71 AGAINST *for the time.*

72 UPON THE SUDDEN *in so short a time.*

Act IV Scene 3

                         [*Enter Face.*]

Face. Where are you, Doctor?
Subtle. [*Within.*]   I'll come to you presently.
Face. I will ha' this same widow, now I ha' seen her,
On any composition.

                    [*Enter Subtle.*]
Subtle.   What do you say?
Face. Ha' you disposed of them?
Subtle.   I ha' sent 'em up.

3 COMPOSITION *arrangement, terms.*

5   *Face.* Subtle, in troth, I needs must have this widow.

    Subtle. Is that the matter?

    Face.   Nay, but hear me.

    Subtle.   Go to.

If you rebel once, Dol shall know it all.

Therefore be quiet and obey your chance.

    Face. Nay, thou art so violent now—do but conceive,

Thou art old, and canst not serve—

10   *Subtle.*   Who? Cannot I?

'Slight, I will serve her with thee, for a—

    Face.   Nay,

But understand; I'll gi' you composition.

    Subtle. I will not treat with thee; what, sell my fortune?

'Tis better than my birthright. Do not murmur.

15 Win her and carry her. If you grumble, Dol

Knows it directly.

    Face.   Well, sir, I am silent.

Will you go help to fetch in Don, in state?

    Subtle. I follow you, sir. [*Exit Face.*] We must keep Face in awe,

Or he will overlook us like a tyrant.

               [*Enter Face with*] *Surly like a Spaniard.*

20 Brain of a tailor! Who comes here? Don John!

    Surly. Señores, beso las manos, à vuestras mercedes.

---

  6 MATTER *central issue.*

  8 OBEY . . . CHANCE *accept the luck of the draw.*

10 SERVE *service (as a bull a cow).*

12 COMPOSITION *equal valve (in trade).*

13 TREAT *deal.*

14 MURMUR *grumble.*

17 IN STATE *in a ceremonial fashion.*

19 OVERLOOK *be haughty with.*

20 TAILOR *Surly's clothes are fantastically elaborate.* DON JOHN *Don Juan, i.e. the lover.*

21 *"Gentlemen, I kiss your honors' hands."*

Subtle. Would you had stooped a little, and kissed our *anos.*

Face. Peace, Subtle.

Subtle.   Stab me, I shall never hold, man.

He looks in that deep ruff like a head in a platter,

Served in by a short cloak upon two trestles.   25

Face. Or what do you say to a collar of brawn, cut down

Beneath the souse, and wrigglèd with a knife?

Subtle. 'Slud, he does look too fat to be a Spaniard.

Face. Perhaps some Fleming or some Hollander got him

In d'Alva's time, Count Egmont's bastard.

Subtle.   Don,   30

Your scurvy, yellow, Madrid face is welcome.

Surly. Gratia.

Subtle.   He speaks out of a fortification.

'Pray God he ha' no squibs in those deep sets.

Surly. Por diós, Señores, muy linda casa!

Subtle. What says he?

Face.   Praises the house, I think;   35

I know no more but's action.

Subtle.   Yes, the *casa,*

My precious Diego, will prove fair enough

To cozen you in. Do you mark? You shall

Be cozened, Diego.

Face.   Cozened, do you see,

My worthy Donzel, cozened.

23 HOLD *keep quiet.*
24 DEEP RUFF *elaborate folded collar.*
26 COLLAR OF BRAWN *pig's neck.*
27 SOUSE *ears.* WRIGGLÈD *cut in ripples (i.e. like a ruff).*
30 ALVA . . . EGMONT *the Duke of Alva led the Spanish armies in the Netherlands, where he executed the Dutch patriot Egmont in 1568.*
33 SQUIBS *rockets.* DEEP SETS *the deep folds in the ruff.*
34 *"By God, a most pleasant house, gentlemen."*
36 *"I only understand his gestures."*

40   *Surly.*   *Entiendo.*

Subtle. Do you intend it? So do we, dear Don.
Have you brought pistolets? or portagues?
My solemn Don? [*To Face.*] Dost thou feel any?
                      He feels his pockets.

Face.   Full.

Subtle. You shall be emptied, Don, pumped and drawn
Dry, as they say.

45   *Face.*   Milked, in troth, sweet Don.

Subtle. See all the monsters; the great lion of all, Don.

Surly. *Con licencia, se puede ver à està señora?*

Subtle. What talks he now?

Face.   O' the *señora.*

Subtle.   O, Don
That is the lioness, which you shall see
Also, my Don.

50   *Face.*   'Slid, Subtle, how shall we do?

Subtle. For what?

Face.   Why, Dol's employed, you know.

Subtle.   That's true.
'Fore heav'n I know not. He must stay, that's all.

Face. Stay? That he must not by no means.

Subtle.   No? Why?

Face. Unless you'll mar all. 'Slight, he'll suspect it.

55   And then he will not pay, not half so well.
This is a travelled punk-master, and does know
All the delays; a notable hot rascal,

40 ENTIENDO "*I understand,*" *which Surly does, of course.*
46 MONSTERS . . . LION *N.*
47 "*With your permission, can this lady be seen?*"
52 STAY *wait.*
56 TRAVELLED PUNK-MASTER *experienced whoremaster.*
57 NOTABLE *notorious.*

And looks, already, rampant.

    Subtle.   'Sdeath, and Mammon

Must not be troubled.

    Face.   Mammon! in no case.

    Subtle. What shall we do then?

    Face.   Think; you must be sudden.   60

    Surly. Entiendo, que la señora es tan hermosa, que codicio tan
à verla, como la bien aventuranza de mi vida.

    Face. Mi vida? 'Slid, Subtle, he puts me in mind o' the widow.

What dost thou say to draw her to it, ha?

And tell her it is her fortune. All our venter   65

Now lies upon't. It is but one man more,

Which on's chance to have her; and, beside,

There is no maidenhead to be feared or lost.

What dost thou think on't, Subtle?

    Subtle.   Who, I? Why—

    Face. The credit of our house too is engaged.   70

    Subtle. You made me an offer for my share erewhile.

What wilt thou gi' me, i'faith?

    Face.   O, by that light,

I'll not buy now. You know your doom to me:

"E'en take your lot, obey your chance, sir; win her

And wear her, out, for me."

58 RAMPANT *heraldic term for animal standing up on its hind legs.*

60 SUDDEN *quick.*

61–62 " *The lady is so lovely, I understand, that it will be the great good fortune of
my life to see her.*"

66–67 IT . . . HER " *She will only have been had by one more man (being already a
widow), no matter which of us gets her.*"

68 FEARED *concerned about.*

70 ENGAGED *involved.*

73 DOOM *judgment, sentence.*

74–75 WIN . . . WEAR *proverbial expression, which Face transforms into a sexual
meaning,* " *wear her out.*"

75   *Subtle.*   'Slight, I'll not work her then.
        Face. It is the common cause; therefore bethink you.
        Dol else must know it, as you said.
            Subtle.   I care not.
        Surly. Señores, por qué se tarda tanto?
        Subtle. Faith, I am not fit, I am old.
            Face.   That's now no reason, sir.
80   *Surly. Puede ser de hazer burla de mi amor?*
        Face. You hear the Don too? By this air, I call
        And loose the hinges. Dol!
            Subtle.   A plague of hell—
        Face. Will you then do?
            Subtle.   Y'are a terrible rogue!
        I'll think of this. Will you, sir, call the widow?
85   *Face.* Yes, and I'll take her, too, with all her faults,
        Now I do think on't better.
            Subtle.   With all my heart, sir;
        Am I discharged o' the lot?
            Face.   As you please.
            Subtle.   Hands!
                        [*They shake hands.*]
        Face. Remember now, that upon any change
        You never claim her.
            Subtle.   Much good joy, and health to you, sir.
90   Marry a whore? Fate, let me wed a witch first.

75 WORK *persuade (to entertain Surly).*
78 "*Gentlemen, why so much delay?*"
79 FIT *able (sexually).*
80 "*Perhaps you make a joke of my love?*"
82 LOOSE THE HINGES "*let everything go to pieces.*"
87 DISCHARGED O' THE LOT "*freed from having to take part in the gamble.*"
88 CHANGE *i.e. of mind, or of events.*

Surly. Por estas honradas barbas—
Subtle. He swears by his beard.
Dispatch, and call the brother, too. [*Exit Face.*]
Surly. *Tengo dúda, Señores,*
Que no me hágan alguna trayción.
Subtle. How, issue on? Yes, *presto, Señor.* Please you
Enthratha the *chambratha*, worthy Don,   95
Where if it please the Fates, in your *bathada,*
You shall be soaked, and stroked, and tubbed, and rubbed,
And scrubbed, and fubbed, dear Don, before you go.
You shall, in faith, my scurvy baboon Don,
Be currièd, clawed, and flawed, and tawed, indeed.   100
I will the heartilier go about it now,
And make the widow a punk, so much the sooner,
To be revenged on this impetuous Face:
The quickly doing of it is the grace.
[*Subtle leads Surly off.*]

91 "*By this honorable beard.*"
92 DISPATCH *hurry up.*
92–93 "*I am afraid, gentlemen, that you are tricking me.*"
98 FUBBED *cheated.*
100 FLAWED *skinned.* TAWED *tanned, beaten.*

Act IV Scene 4

[*Enter Face, with Kastril and Dame Pliant.*]
Face. Come, lady. [*To Kastril.*] I knew the Doctor would not leave
Till he had found the very nick of her fortune.
Kastril. To be a countess, say you?

1 LEAVE *leave off, quit.*
2 VERY NICK *exact point.*

Act IV Scene 4

  [*Face.*]   A Spanish countess, sir.
  Dame Pliant. Why, is that better than an English countess?
5 *Face.* Better? 'Slight, make you that a question, lady?
  Kastril. Nay, she is a fool, Captain, you must pardon her.
  Face. Ask from your courtier, to your inns-of-court-man,
  To your mere milliner: they will tell you, all,
  Your Spanish jennet is the best horse; your Spanish
10 Stoop is the best garb; your Spanish beard
  Is the best cut; your Spanish ruffs are the best
  Wear; your Spanish pavin the best dance;
  Your Spanish titillation in a glove
  The best perfume; and for your Spanish pike,
15 And Spanish blade, let your poor Captain speak.
  Here comes the Doctor.
        [*Enter Subtle.*]
  Subtle.   My most honored lady,
  For so I am now to style you, having found
        [*He holds up a horoscope.*]
  By this my scheme, you are to undergo
  An honorable fortune, very shortly.
  What will you say now, if some—
20 *Face.*   I ha' told her all, sir.
  And her right worshipful brother, here, that she shall be

  7 INNS-OF-COURT-MAN *lawyer.*
  9 JENNET *small Spanish horse.*
  10 STOOP *bow (?).* GARB *style (?).*
  12 PAVIN *elaborate formal dance.*
  13 TITILLATION *perfume—gloves were soaked in perfumed oils to fix the scent.*
  14 PIKE *type of spear used by infantry. The Spanish were the most famous soldiers in Europe.*
  15 BLADE *sword—the best came from Toledo.* CAPTAIN SPEAK *as an English soldier, a Captain would probably have campaigned helping the Protestant Dutch against the Spanish in Holland.*
  18 UNDERGO *receive (but with an obvious pun).*

A countess; do not delay 'em, sir. A Spanish countess.

    Subtle. Still, my scarce-worshipful Captain, you can keep
No secret! Well, since he has told you, madam,
Do you forgive him, and I do.

    Kastril.   She shall do that, sir.   25
I'll look to't; 'tis my charge.

    Subtle.   Well, then. Nought rests
But that she fit her love, now, to her fortune.

    Dame Pliant. Truly, I shall never brook a Spaniard.

    Subtle.   No?

    Dame Pliant. Never sin' eighty-eight could I abide 'em,
And that was some three year afore I was born, in truth.   30

    Subtle. Come, you must love him, or be miserable:
Choose which you will.

    Face.   By this good rush, persuade her.
She will cry strawberries else, within this twelvemonth.

    Subtle. Nay, shads and mackerel, which is worse.

    Face.   Indeed, sir?

    Kastril. God's lid, you shall love him, or I'll kick you.

    Dame Pliant.   Why,   35
I'll do as you will ha' me, brother.

    Kastril.   Do,
Or by this hand I'll maul you.

    Face.   Nay, good sir,
Be not so fierce.

    Subtle.   No, my enragèd child;

---

26 CHARGE *responsibility.* RESTS *remains.*

27 *"But that she love the noble whom fortune has given her."*

29 EIGHTY-EIGHT *the year, 1588, the Spanish Armada tried to invade England.*

32 RUSH *floors were still covered with rushes.*

33 CRY STRAWBERRIES *be calling out and selling strawberries in the street, i.e. be poor.*

34 SHADS *selling fish; i.e. become a fishwife or shrew.*

She will be ruled. What, when she comes to taste
40 The pleasures of a countess! to be courted—
    Face. And kissed and ruffflèd!
    Subtle.   Ay, behind the hangings.
    Face. And then come forth in pomp!
    Subtle.   And know her state!
    Face. Of keeping all th' idolators o' the chamber
Barer to her than at their prayers!
    Subtle.   Is served
Upon the knee!
45   *Face.*   And has her pages, ushers,
Footmen, and coaches—
    Subtle.   Her six mares—
    Face.   Nay, eight!
    Subtle. To hurry her through London, to th' Exchange,
Bet'lem, the China-houses—
    Face.   Yes, and have
The citizens gape at her, and praise her tires!
50 And my lord's goose-turd bands, that rides with her!
    Kastril. Most brave! By this hand, you are not my suster
If you refuse.
    Dame Pliant. I will not refuse, brother.

39 BE RULED *accept your control.*
41 HANGINGS *curtains or wall tapestries.*
42 STATE *position.*
43 IDOLATORS O' THE CHAMBER *courtiers (whose elaborate manners keep them always bowing down).*
44 BARER *i.e. with caps off.*
47 EXCHANGE *the New Exchange in the Strand, a center of fashionable women's shops.*
48 BET'LEM *Bedlam, Bethlehem Hospital, the London madhouse. One of the amusements of the town was to go and look at the madmen.* CHINA-HOUSES *shops selling china and other fine goods from the Orient.*
49 TIRES *dresses.*
50 GOOSE-TURD BANDS *collar in the latest, most fashionable color, goose-turd green.*

[*Enter Surly.*]

Surly. Qué es esto, Señores, que non se venga?
Esta tardanza me mata!

   Face.   It is the count come!
The Doctor knew he would be here, by his art.   55

   Subtle. En gallanta madama, Don! gallantissima!

   Surly. Por todos los dioses, la mas acabada
Hermosura, que he visto en mi vida!

   Face. Is't not a gallant language that they speak?

   Kastril. An admirable language! Is't not French?   60

   Face. No, Spanish, sir.

   Kastril.   It goes like law French,
And that, they say, is the courtliest language.

   Face.   List, sir.

   Surly. El sol ha perdido su lumbre, con el
Resplandor que trae esta dama! Válgame dios!

   Face. H'admires your sister.

   Kastril.   Must not she make curtsy?   65

   Subtle. 'Ods will, she must go to him, man, and kiss him!
It is the Spanish fashion for the women
To make first court.

   Face.   'Tis true he tells you, sir;
His art knows all.

   Surly.   *Por qué no se acude?*

   Kastril. He speaks to her, I think?

   Face.   That he does, sir.   70

53–54 "*How is it, gentlemen, that she does not come? The wait is killing me.*"
56 "*A fine lady, Don, most fine.*"
57–58 "*By all the gods, the most perfect lady I have ever seen.*"
61–62 LAW FRENCH . . . COURTLIEST *a corrupt Norman French used in the law courts until the seventeenth century.*
63–64 "*The sun has lost its light to the splendor of this Lady! God bless me!*"
69 "*Why does she not approach?*"

Surly. *Por el amor de diós, qué es esto, que se tarda?*

Kastril. Nay, see: she will not understand him! Gull, Noddy!

Dame Pliant. What say you, brother?

Kastril.   Ass, my suster,
Go kuss him, as the cunning man would ha' you;
I'll thrust a pin i' your buttocks else.

75 *Face.*   O, no, sir.

Surly. *Señora mia, mi persona muy indigna esta*
Allegar a tanta hermosura.

Face. Does he not use her bravely?

Kastril.   Bravely, i' faith!

Face. Nay, he will use her better.

Kastril.   Do you think so?

80 *Surly.* *Señora, si sera servida, entremos.*

[*Exits with Dame Pliant.*]

Kastril. Where does he carry her?

Face.   Into the garden, sir;
Take you no thought. I must interpret for her. [*Leaving.*]

Subtle. [*To Face as he leaves.*] Give Dol the word.

[*To Kastril.*] Come, my fierce child, advance,
We'll to our quarrelling lesson again.

Kastril.   Agreed.

85 I love a Spanish boy, with all my heart.

Subtle. Nay, and by this means, sir, you shall be brother
To a great count.

Kastril.   Ay, I knew that, at first.
This match will advance the house of the Kastrils.

Subtle. 'Pray God your sister prove but pliant.

Kastril.   Why,

71 "*For the love of God, why does she wait?*"
76–77 "*My lady, I am not worthy the achievement of such beauty.*"
80 "*Lady, if you will, let us enter.*"

Her name is so, by her other husband.

    Subtle.   How!   90

    Kastril. The Widow Pliant. Knew you not that?

    Subtle.   No, faith, sir.

Yet, by the erection of her figure, I guessed it.

Come, let's go practise.

    Kastril.   Yes, but do you think, Doctor,

I e'er shall quarrel well?

    Subtle.   I warrant you.   [*Exeunt.*]

92 ERECTION . . . FIGURE *casting her horoscope (with an obvious pun).*

Act IV Scene 5

[*Enter Dol,*] *in her fit of talking.*

    Dol Common. For, after Alexander's death—

    Mammon. [*Following.*]   Good lady—

    Dol Common. That Perdiccas and Antigonus were slain,

The two that stood, Seleuc' and Ptolemy—

    Mammon. Madam—

    Dol Common.   Made up the two legs, and the fourth beast.

That was Gog-north and Egypt-south: which after   5

Was called Gog-iron-leg and South-iron-leg—

    Mammon.   Lady—

    Dol Common. And then Gog-hornèd. So was Egypt, too.

Then Egypt-clay-leg, and Gog-clay-leg—

    Mammon.   Sweet madam—

1 ALEXANDER *Alexander the Great, the Macedonian king who extended the Greek empire over all the known world.*

2–3 PERDICCAS . . . PTOLEMY *N.*

4–16 TWO LEGS . . . JAVAN *N.*

Act IV Scene 5

   Dol Common. And last Gog-dust, and Egypt-dust, which fall
10 In the last link of the fourth chain. And these
Be stars in story, which none see, or look at—
   Mammon. What shall I do?
   Dol Common.   For, as he says, except
We call the rabbins, and the heathen Greeks—
   Mammon. Dear lady—
   Dol Common.   To come from Salem, and from Athens,
And teach the people of Great Britain—
              [Enter Face, dressed as Lungs.]
15   *Face.*   What's the matter, sir?
   Dol Common. To speak the tongue of Eber and Javan—
   Mammon.   O,
She's in her fit.
   Dol Common. We shall know nothing—
   Face.   Death, sir,
We are undone!
   Dol Common. Where, then, a learned linguist
Shall see the ancient used communion
Of vowels and consonants—
20   *Face.*   My master will hear!
   Dol Common. A wisdom which Pythagoras held most high—
   Mammon. Sweet honorable lady.
   Dol Common.   To comprise
All sounds of voices, in few marks of letters—
   Face. Nay, you must never hope to lay her now.

18–23 LINGUIST . . . LETTERS *a primal tongue spoken in Eden was sought by the
learned as a key to all understanding. (See II.1.83–86). The absence of vowels
referred to here suggests a middle-Eastern language such as Hebrew.*

21 PYTHAGORAS *Greek philosopher and mathematician, thought by the Renaissance to
be one of the original magi or possessors of the secrets of the universe.*

24 LAY *quiet—but with another meaning as well.*

They [Dol, Face, and Mammon] speak together.

Dol Common. And so we may arrive by Talmud skill,   25
And profane Greek, to raise the building up
Of Helen's house, against the Ishmaelite,
King of Thogarma, and his habergions
Brimstony, blue, and fiery; and the force
Of King Abaddon, and the beast of Cittim: 30
Which Rabbi David Kimchi, Onkelos,
And Aben Ezra do interpret Rome.

  Face. How did you put her into't?

  Mammon.   Alas, I talked
Of a fifth monarchy I would erect
With the philosopher's stone, by chance, and she   35
Falls on the other four straight.

  Face.   Out of Broughton!
I told you so. 'Slid, stop her mouth.

  Mammon.   Is't best?

  Face. She'll never leave else. If the old man hear her,
We are but feces, ashes.

  Subtle. [*Within.*]   What's to do there?

  Face. O, we are lost. Now she hears him, she is quiet.   40

SD *in the Folio, Dol's following speech is printed parallel to the words of the other characters.*

25 TALMUD *the body of Jewish civil and religious law.*

26 PROFANE *i.e. because the Greeks were pagans.*

27 HELEN'S HOUSE *i.e. the Kingdom of God. "Helen" should be "Heber," but Dol is mixing Greek and Hebrew grandly.* ISHMAELITE *the sons of Ishmael, i.e. any pagan non-believer.*

28 THOGARMA *rulers of a biblical kingdom (Ezekiel 38: 6).* HABERGIONS *habergouns (?) armor.*

30 ABADDON . . . CITTIM *Broughton uses these names for the Pope.*

31–32 DAVID . . . EZRA *commentators on the Bible.*

32 INTEPRET ROME *"understand to mean the Roman Catholic church, or the Pope."*

34 FIFTH MONARCHY *the Kingdom of God on earth,* N.

38 LEAVE *leave off, stop ranting.*

Act IV Scene 5

Upon Subtle's entry they disperse.

                                    [*Exit Face and Dol.*]

Mammon. Where shall I hide me? [*Turns his back and hides.*]

Subtle.   How! What sight is here!

Close deeds of darkness, and that shun the light!

Bring him again. Who is he? What, my son! [*Turns Mammon around.*]

O, I have lived too long.

Mammon.   Nay, good, dear father,

There was no' unchaste purpose.

45   *Subtle.*   Not? and flee me

When I come in?

Mammon.   That was my error.

Subtle.   Error?

Guilt, guilt, my son. Give it the right name. No marvel

If I found check in our great work within,

When such affairs as these were managing!

Mammon. Why, have you so?

50   *Subtle.*   It has stood still this half hour,

And all the rest of our less works gone back.

Where is the instrument of wickedness,

My lewd false drudge?

Mammon.   Nay, good sir, blame not him.

Believe me, 'twas against his will, or knowledge.

I saw her by chance.

55   *Subtle.*   Will you commit more sin,

T'excuse a varlet?

Mammon.   By my hope, 'tis true, sir.

42 CLOSE *secret.*

43 BRING HIM AGAIN *bring him back.*

48 CHECK *impediment.*

49 MANAGING *going on.*

53 LEWD *ignorant.*

Subtle. Nay, then I wonder less, if you, for whom
The blessing was prepared, would so tempt heaven,
And lose your fortunes.

Mammon.   Why, sir?

Subtle.   This'll retard
The work, a month at least.

Mammon.   Why, if it do,   60
What remedy? But think it not, good father;
Our purposes were honest.

Subtle.   As they were,
So the reward will prove. How now! Ay me. *A great crack*
God and all saints be good to us.—   *and noise within.*

       [*Enter Face.*]
        What's that?

Face. O sir, we are defeated! All the works   65
Are flown *in fumo*, every glass is burst.
Furnace and all rent down, as if a bolt
Of thunder had been driven through the house.
Retorts, receivers, pelicans, bolt-heads,
All struck in shivers!   *Subtle falls down,*

 [*To Mammon.*] Help, good sir! Alas, *as in a swoon.* 70
Coldness and death invades him. Nay, Sir Mammon,
Do the fair offices of a man! You stand
As you were readier to depart than he.   *One knocks.*
Who's there? [*Looking out.*] My lord her brother is come.

Mammon.   Ha, Lungs!

Face. His coach is at the door. Avoid his sight,   75
For he's as furious as his sister is mad.

Mammon. Alas!

Face.   My brain is quite undone with the fume, sir,

62–63 AS . . . PROVE *N.*
66 IN FUMO *vaporized.*
72 FAIR OFFICES *good duties.*

I ne'er must hope to be mine own man again.
    Mammon. Is all lost, Lungs? Will nothing be preserved
Of all our cost?
80   *Face.*   Faith, very little, sir.
A peck of coals, or so, which is cold comfort, sir.
    Mammon. O, my voluptuous mind! I am justly punished.
    Face. And so am I, sir.
    Mammon.   Cast from all my hopes—
    Face. Nay, certainties, sir.
    Mammon.   By mine own base affections.
                       Subtle seems to come to himself.
    Subtle. O, the curst fruits of vice and lust!
85   *Mammon.*   Good father,
It was my sin. Forgive it.
    Subtle.   Hangs my roof
Over us still, and will not fall, O Justice,
Upon us, for this wicked man!
    Face. [*To Mammon.*]   Nay, look, sir,
You grieve him now with staying in his sight.
90   Good sir, the nobleman will come too, and take you,
And that may breed a tragedy.
    Mammon.   I'll go.
    Face. Ay, and repent at home, sir. It may be
For some good penance you may ha' it yet;
A hundred pound to the box at Bet'lem—
    Mammon.   Yes.
    Face. For the restoring such as ha' their wits.
95   *Mammon.*   I'll do't.

78 MINE OWN MAN *i.e. in his right senses.*
84 AFFECTIONS *passions, lusts.*
88 FOR *because of.*
94 BOX *poor box—for charitable gifts to the madmen. An appropriate penance for Mammon.*

Face. I'll send one to you to receive it.

Mammon.   Do.
Is no projection left?

Face.   All flown, or stinks, sir.

Mammon. Will nought be saved that's good for med'cine, think'st
   thou?

Face. I cannot tell, sir. There will be, perhaps,
Something about the scraping of the shards,   100
Will cure the itch.—[*Aside.*] though not your itch of mind, sir.—
It shall be saved for you, and sent home. Good sir,
This way, for fear the lord should meet you.

                                              [*Exit Mammon.*]

Subtle. [*Rising.*]   Face!

Face. Ay.

Subtle.   Is he gone?

Face.   Yes, and as heavily
As all the gold he hoped for were in his blood.   105
Let us be light though.

Subtle. [*Dancing.*]   Ay, as balls, and bound
And hit our heads against the roof for joy:
There's so much of our care now cast away.

Face. Now to our Don.

Subtle.   Yes, your young widow by this time
Is made a countess, Face; she's been in travail   110
Of a young heir for you.

Face.   Good, sir.

Subtle.   Off with your case,

98 MED'CINE *the elixir (which would probably require less of the essence than would
   go into the stone).*

106 LIGHT *joyous.*

108 CARE *worry (about having to produce gold for Mammon at the end of the
   experiment).*

110 TRAVAIL *labor—i.e. satisfying the Don.*

111 CASE *disguise (the costume of Lungs).*

157

And greet her kindly, as a bridegroom should,
After these common hazards.

    Face.   Very well, sir.
Will you go fetch Don Diego off the while?

115   *Subtle.* And fetch him over too, if you'll be pleased, sir.
Would Dol were in her place to pick his pockets now.

    Face. Why, you can do it as well, if you would set to't.
I pray you prove your virtue.

    Subtle.   For your sake, sir.   [*Exeunt.*]

115 FETCH HIM OVER "*take*" *him.*
118 VIRTUE *not moral virtue, but in the older sense of "special ability" or "particular power."*

Act IV Scene 6

[*Enter Surly and Dame Pliant.*]
   Surly. Lady, you see into what hands you are fall'n;
'Mongst what a nest of villains! and how near
Your honor was t'have catched a certain clap,
Through your credulity, had I but been

5   So punctually forward, as place, time,
And other circumstance would ha' made a man;
For y'are a handsome woman; would you were wise too!
I am a gentleman, come here disguised,
Only to find the knaveries of this citadel,

10 And where I might have wronged your honor, and have not,
I claim some interest in your love. You are,

3 CLAP *blow, harm—the word also already meant gonorrhea.*
5 PUNCTUALLY FORWARD *instantly bold—but also "with point forward."*

They say, a widow, rich; and I am a bachelor,
Worth nought. Your fortunes may make me a man,
As mine ha' preserved you a woman. Think upon it,
And whether I have deserved you or no.

  Dame Pliant.   I will, sir.   15
  Surly. And for these household-rogues, let me alone
To treat with them.

        [Enter Subtle.]
  Subtle.   How doth my noble Diego,
And my dear madam Countess? Hath the Count
Been courteous, lady? liberal? and open?
Donzel, methinks you look melancholic   20
After your coitum, and scurvy! Truly,
I do not like the dulness of your eye;
It hath a heavy cast, 'tis upsee Dutch,
And says you are a lumpish whore-master.
Be lighter; I will make your pockets so.   25
       He falls to picking of them.
  Surly. Will you, Don Bawd and Pick-purse?
[Hits him.]   How now? Reel
  you?
Stand up, sir; you shall find, since I am so heavy,
I'll gi' you equal weight.
  Subtle.   Help! Murder!
  Surly.   No, sir.
There's no such thing intended. A good cart
And a clean whip shall ease you of that fear.   30
I am the Spanish Don that should be cozened.

---

20 MELANCHOLIC *the post-coital sadness, or* triste.
23 UPSEE DUTCH *"in the Dutch style." Heavy and phlegmatic.*
29–30 CART . . . WHIP *i.e. to be hauled through the streets in a cart and whipped.*
  Standard punishment for minor crimes.

Act IV Scene 6

Do you see? Cozened? Where's your Captain Face?
That parcel-broker, and whole-bawd, all rascal?
                    [Enter Face as Captain.]

  Face. How, Surly!

  Surly.   O, make your approach, good Captain.
35 I've found from whence your copper rings and spoons
Come, now, wherewith you cheat abroad in taverns.
'Twas here you learned t'annoint your boot with brimstone,
Then rub men's gold on't, for a kind of touch,
And say 'twas naught, when you had changed the color,
40 That you might ha't for nothing. And this Doctor,
Your sooty, smoky-beardèd compeer, he
Will close you so much gold in a bolt's-head,
And, on a turn, convey i' the stead another
With sublimed mercury, that shall burst i' the heat,
45 And fly out all in fumo! Then weeps Mammon;
Then swoons his worship. Or he is the Faustus
That casteth figures and can conjure, cures
Plagues, piles, and pox, by the Ephemerides,
And holds intelligence with all the bawds *[Face slips out.]*
50 And midwives of three shires; while you send in—
Captain!—What, is he gone?—damsels with child,
Wives that are barren, or the waiting-maid

---

33 PARCEL-BROKER *part-time go-between; an intermediary in any business.*
36 CHEAT *by pretending the copper is gold.*
37–39 *N.*
42 CLOSE *enclose. N.*
46 FAUSTUS *magician. N.*
47 FIGURES *horoscopes.*
48 EPHEMERIDES *celestial almanac showing the positions of heavenly bodies at different times.*
49 HOLDS INTELLIGENCE *exchanges information.*
49–53 BAWDS . . . SICKNESS *N.*

With the green sickness. [*Holds Subtle as he tries to leave.*]

　　　　　　　　　—Nay, sir, you must tarry,

Though he be 'scaped, and answer by the ears, sir.

54 EARS *clipping pieces off the ears was a standard punishment.*

Act IV Scene 7

　　　　　　　　[*Enter Face with Kastril.*]

Face. Why, now's the time, if ever you will quarrel

Well, as they say, and be a true-born child.

The Doctor and your sister both are abused.

　　Kastril. Where is he? Which is he? He is a slave,

Whate'er he is, and the son of a whore. [*To Surly.*] Are you　　5

The man, sir, I would know?

　　Surly.　　　　　　　　I should be loath, sir,

To confess so much.

　　Kastril.　　　　Then you lie i' your throat.

　　Surly.　　　　　　　　　　　How?

　　Face. [*To Kastril.*] A very arrant rogue, sir, and a cheater,

Employed here by another conjurer

That does not love the Doctor, and would cross him,　　10

If he knew how—

　　Surly.　　　　Sir, you are abused.

　　Kastril.　　　　　　　　You lie,

And 'tis no matter.

　　Face.　　　　Well said, sir! He is

2 CHILD *knight errant—cf. Childe Harold.*

7 I' YOUR THROAT *absolutely—the worst kind of lie.*

10 CROSS *thwart, harm.*

12 'TIS NO MATTER *a softening phrase used after directly accusing someone of outright lying in order to avoid giving a deadly insult. It is "well said," but this is scarcely the effect Kastril is trying for.*

Act IV Scene 7

The impudent'st rascal—

Surly.　　　　　　　　You are indeed. Will you hear me, sir?

Face. By no means. Bid him be gone.

Kastril.　　　　　　　　　　Begone, sir, quickly.

15　*Surly.* This's strange! Lady, do you inform your brother.

Face. There is not such a foist in all the town.

The Doctor had him presently; and finds yet

The Spanish Count will come here. [*Aside.*] Bear up, Subtle.

Subtle. Yes, sir, he must appear within this hour.

20　*Face.* And yet this rogue would come in a disguise,

By the temptation of another spirit,

To trouble our art, though he could not hurt it.

Kastril.　　　　　　　　　　　　Ay,

I know—[*Dame Pliant whispers in her brother's ear.*]

　　　Away, you talk like a foolish mauther.

Surly. Sir, all is truth she says.

Face.　　　　　　　Do not believe him, sir.

25　He is the lying'st swabber! Come your ways, sir.

Surly. You are valiant out of company.

Kastril.　　　　　　　　　　Yes, how then, sir?

　　　　　　　[*Enter Drugger.*]

Face. Nay, here's an honest fellow too that knows him

And all his tricks. [*Aside to Drugger.*] Make good what I say, Abel;

This cheater would ha' cozened thee o' the widow.—

16　FOIST *cheat—one who changes dice.*

17　HAD HIM PRESENTLY "*had his number right away.*"

18　BEAR UP "*get into the act.*" Subtle, *for the first time, seems to be bewildered or frightened.*

21–22　SPIRIT . . . IT *N.*

23　MAUTHER *dialect for* "*young girl.*"

25　SWABBER *low fellow—or deck swabber.*

26　OUT OF COMPANY "*because there are others to back you up.*"

He owes this honest Drugger, here, seven pound   30
He has had on him in two-penny'orths of tobacco.

   Drugger. Yes, sir. And h' has damned himself three terms to pay
    me.

   Face. And what does he owe for lotium?

   Drugger.   Thirty shillings, sir;
And for six syringes.

   Surly.   Hydra of villainy!

   Face. [*To Kastril.*] Nay, sir, you must quarrel him out o' the
    house.

          Kastril. I will.   35
Sir, if you get not out o' doors, you lie,
And you are a pimp.

   Surly.   Why, this is madness, sir,
Not valor in you. I must laugh at this.

   Kastril. It is my humor; you are a pimp and a trig,
And an Amadis de Gaul, or a Don Quixote.   40

   Drugger. Or a knight o' the curious coxcomb. Do you see?

                [*Enter Ananias.*]

   Ananias. Peace to the household!

   Kastril.   I'll keep peace for no man.

   Ananias. Casting of dollars is concluded lawful.

   Kastril. Is he the constable?

---

32 AND . . . ME "*and has sworn falsely to pay his bill for a year (three terms of court).*"

33 LOTIUM *old urine, used as a hair-dressing.*

34 SYRINGES *i.e. for squirting lotium, or other medicines, perhaps for treating venereal disease.* HYDRA *a monster which grew two heads for every one cut off.*

39 HUMOR *penchant.* TRIG *dandy, fop.*

40 AMADIS . . . QUIXOTE *heroes of famous Spanish romances—to Kastril they are only the names of "foreigners."*

41 CURIOUS COXCOMB *a reference to Surly's strange elaborate hat, mentioned again at line 55.*

Subtle.   Peace, Ananias.

Face. [*To Kastril.*]   No, sir.

45   *Kastril.* [*To Surly.*] Then you are an otter, and a shad, a whit,

A very tim.

Surly.   You'll hear me, sir?

Kastril.   I will not.

Ananias. What is the motive?

Subtle.   Zeal in the young gentleman,

Against his Spanish slops—

Ananias.   They are profane,

Lewd, superstitious, and idolatrous breeches.

Surly. New rascals!

Kastril.   Will you be gone, sir?

50   *Ananias.*   Avoid, Sathan,

Thou art not of the light. That ruff of pride

About thy neck betrays thee, and is the same

With that which the unclean birds, in seventy-seven,

Were seen to prank it with on divers coasts.

55   Thou look'st like Antichrist in that lewd hat.

Surly. I must give way.

Kastril.   Be gone, sir.

Surly.   But I'll take

A course with you—

Ananias.   Depart, proud Spanish fiend!

Surly. Captain and Doctor—

Ananias.   Child of perdition!

---

45 WHIT *pimp* (?).

46 TIM *meaning unknown. Perhaps Kastril is using any words which come to mind;
certainly he is not bright enough to find very good insults.*

53 UNCLEAN . . . SEVEN *N.*

54 PRANK *swagger.* COASTS *places.*

57 COURSE *another turn* (?).

Kastril.   Hence, sir!

                                         [*Exit Surly.*]

Did I not quarrel bravely?

   Face.   Yes, indeed, sir.

   Kastril. Nay, and I give my mind to't, I shall do't.   60

   Face. O, you must follow, sir, and threaten him tame.

He'll turn again else.

   Kastril.   I'll re-turn him then.   [*Exit.*]

   Face. Drugger, this rogue prevented us for thee.

We had determined that thou should'st ha' come

In a Spanish suit, and ha' carried her so; and he,   65

A brokerly slave, goes, puts it on himself.

Hast brought the damask?

   Drugger.   Yes, sir.

   Face.   Thou must borrow

A Spanish suit. Hast thou no credit with the players?

   Drugger. Yes, sir; did you never see me play the Fool?

   Face. I know not, Nab. [*Aside.*] Thou shalt, if I can help it.—   70

Hieronimo's old cloak, ruff, and hat will serve;

I'll tell thee more when thou bring'st 'em.

                                         [*Exit Drugger.*]

    Subtle hath whispered with [Ananias] this while.

   Ananias.   Sir, I know

The Spaniard hates the Brethren, and hath spies

---

60 "*If I really try, I shall (quarrel) well.*"

63 PREVENTED *anticipated (what we had planned for you).*

66 BROKERLY *interfering (like a broker or intermediary).*

68 PLAYERS *the actors, who had stocks of costumes.*

69 FOOL *the actor Robert Armin, who played the fool's parts for the King's Men (Shakespeare's company and the first producers of* The Alchemist), *was presumably playing Drugger.*

71 HIERONIMO *the Spanish hero of the popular old play, Kyd's* The Spanish Tragedy *(1587). Johnson was said to have played this part when he was a young actor.*

Upon their actions; and that this was one
75   I make no scruple. But the Holy Synod
Have been in prayer, and meditation, for it.
And 'tis revealed no less to them than me,
That casting of money is most lawful.
    Subtle.   True.
But here I cannot do it; if the house
80   Should chance to be suspected, all would out.
And we be locked up in the Tower forever,
To make gold there for th' state; never come out;
And then are you defeated.
    Ananias.   I will tell
This to the Elders and the weaker Brethren,
85   That the whole company of the Separation
May join in humble prayer again.
    Subtle.   And fasting.
    Ananias. Yea, for some fitter place. [*Blesses them.*] The peace of
       mind
Rest with these walls.
    Subtle.   Thanks, courteous Ananias.
                               [*Exit Ananias.*]

    Face. What did he come for?
    Subtle.   About casting dollars,
90   Presently, out of hand. And so I told him
A Spanish minister came here to spy
Against the faithful—
    Face.   I conceive. Come, Subtle,
Thou art so down upon the least disaster!

---

75 MAKE NO SCRUPLE "*don't doubt in the slightest.*" SYNOD *governing body of some
    Protestant churches.*

80 OUT *be known.*

81 TOWER *the Tower of London, where important state prisoners were kept.*

92 CONCEIVE *understand.*

How wouldst thou ha' done, if I had not helped thee out?

   Subtle. I thank thee, Face, for the angry boy, i' faith.   95

   Face. Who would ha' looked it should ha' been that rascal
Surly? He had dyed his beard and all. Well, sir,
Heres damask come to make you a suit.

   Subtle.   Where's Drugger?

   Face. He is gone to borrow me a Spanish habit;
I'll be the count now.

   Subtle.   But where's the widow?   100

   Face. Within, with my lord's sister; Madam Dol
Is entertaining her.

   Subtle.   By your favor, Face,
Now she is honest, I will stand again.

   Face. You will not offer it?

   Subtle.   Why?

   Face.   Stand to your word,
Or—here comes Dol!—she knows—

   Subtle.   Y'are tyrannous still.   105

                      [Enter Dol.]

   Face. Strict for my right. How now, Dol? Hast told her
The Spanish Count will come?

   Dol Common.   Yes, but another is come
You little looked for!

   Face.   Who's that?

   Dol Common.   Your master;
The master of the house.

   Subtle.   How, Dol!

   Face.   She lies.
This is some trick. Come, leave your quiblins, Dorothy.   110

---

96 LOOKED *expected.*

103 HONEST *chaste; i.e. not dishonored.* STAND *i.e. for her hand; re-enter the lottery.*

110 QUIBLINS *tricks.*

  Dol Common. Look out and see.

      [*Face looks out the window.*]

  Subtle.   Art thou in earnest?

  Dol Common.   'Slight,

Forty o' the neighbors are about him, talking.

  Face. 'Tis he, by this good day.

  Dol Common.   'Twill prove ill day

For some on us.

  Face. We are undone, and taken.

  Dol Common. Lost, I'm afraid.

115 *Subtle.*   You said he would not come

While there died one a week within the liberties.

  Face. No: 'twas within the walls.

  Subtle.   Was't so? Cry you mercy;

I thought the liberties. What shall we do now, Face?

  Face. Be silent: not a word if he call or knock.

120 I'll into mine old shape again, and meet him,

Of Jeremy the butler. In the meantime,

Do you two pack up all the goods and purchase

That we can carry i' the two trunks. I'll keep him

Off for today, if I cannot longer; and then

125 At night I'll ship you both away to Ratcliff

Where we'll meet tomorrow, and there we'll share.

Let Mammon's brass and pewter keep the cellar;

We'll have another time for that. But, Dol,

'Pray thee, go heat a little water, quickly;

116 DIED *i.e. from the plague.* LIBERTIES *areas, of which Blackfriars was one, which, because they were originally controlled by the church, were under the authority of the Crown but not the city.*

117 WALLS *London wall, marking the boundaries of the square mile of the City of London.* CRY YOU MERCY *"beg your pardon."*

122 PURCHASE *winnings.*

125 RATCLIFF *an area down the Thames.*

127 KEEP *stay in.*

Subtle must shave me. All my captain's beard   130
Must off, to make me appear smooth Jeremy.
You'll do't?

    Subtle. Yes, I'll shave you as well as I can.

    Face. And not cut my throat, but trim me?

    Subtle.   You shall see, sir.

                [*They hurry off together.*]

131 SMOOTH "*plausible*," *as well as smooth-shaven.*
133 TRIM "*cheat*," *as well as barber.*

Act V Scene 1

[*In the street. Lovewit talking to his neighbors.*]
Lovewit. Has there been such resort, say you?
1 Neighbor.   Daily, sir.
2 Neighbor. And nightly, too.
3 Neighbor.   Ay, some as brave as lords.
4 Neighbor. Ladies, and gentlewomen.
5 Neighbor.   Citizens' wives.
1 Neighbor. And knights.
6 Neighbor.   In coaches.
2 Neighbor.   Yes, and oyster-women.
1 Neighbor. Beside other gallants.
3 Neighbor.   Sailors' wives.
5   *4 Neighbor.*   Tobacco men.
5 Neighbor. Another Pimlico!
Lovewit.   What should my knave advance
To draw this company? He hung out no banners
Of a strange calf with five legs to be seen?
Or a huge lobster with six claws?
6 Neighbor.   No, sir.
3 Neighbor. We had gone in then, sir.
10   *Lovewit.*   He has no gift

6 PIMLICO *place of entertainment, near Hogsden.* KNAVE *servant.*

Of teaching i' the nose, that e'er I knew of!
You saw no bills set up that promised cure
Of agues or the tooth-ache?
   2 Neighbor.   No such thing, sir.
   Lovewit. Nor heard a drum struck, for baboons or puppets?
   5 Neighbor. Neither, sir.
   Lovewit.   What device should he bring forth now?   15
I love a teeming wit as I love my nourishment.
'Pray God he ha' not kept such open house
That he hath sold my hangings, and my bedding;
I left him nothing else. If he have eat 'em,
A plague o' the moth, say I! Sure he has got   20
Some bawdy pictures to call all this ging:
The Friar and the Nun; or the new motion
Of the knight's courser covering the parson's mare;
The boy of six year old, with the great thing;
Or 't may be he has the fleas that run at tilt   25
Upon a table, or some dog to dance?
When saw you him?
   1 Neighbor.   Who, sir, Jeremy?
   2 Neighbor.   Jeremy butler?
We saw him not this month.
   Lovewit.   How!
   4 Neighbor.   Not these five weeks, sir.

---

11 TEACHING . . . NOSE *i.e. preaching, in the nasal tones thought characteristic of Puritans.*
12 BILLS *signs, billboards.*
14 DRUM *to draw a crowd to a show.*
15 DEVICE *sideshow.*
21 GING *crowd.*
22 MOTION *puppet show.*
24 THING *i.e. penis.*
25 RUN AT TILT *tilt with, charge one another.*

[6] *Neighbor.* These six weeks, at the least.

Lovewit.   Y'amaze me, neighbors!

30 *5 Neighbor.* Sure, if your worship know not where he is,
He's slipped away.

6 Neighbor. Pray God he be not made away!

Lovewit. Ha? It's no time to question, then.

He knocks.

6 Neighbor.   About
Some three weeks since, I heard a doleful cry,
As I sat up a-mending my wife's stockings.

35 *Lovewit.* This's strange that none will answer! Did'st thou hear
A cry, sayst thou?

6 Neighbor.   Yes, sir, like unto a man
That had been strangled an hour, and could not speak.

2 Neighbor. I heard it, too, just this day three weeks, at two o'clock
Next morning.

Lovewit. These be miracles, or you make 'em so!

40 A man an hour strangled, and could not speak,
And both you heard him cry?

3 Neighbor.   Yes, downward, sir.

Lovewit. Thou art a wise fellow. Give me thy hand, I pray thee.
What trade art thou on?

3 Neighbor. A smith, an't please your worship.

Lovewit. A smith? Then, lend me thy help to get this door open.

45 *3 Neighbor.* That I will presently, sir, but fetch my tools—

[*Exit.*]

1 Neighbor. Sir, best to knock again afore you break it.

38 JUST . . . WEEKS "*three weeks ago today.*"

Act V Scene 2

Lovewit. I will. [*Knocks again loudly.*]
    [*Face, dressed as Jeremy the butler, opens the door.*]
Face.   What mean you, sir?
1, 2, 4 Neighbor.   O, here's Jeremy!
Face. Good sir, come from the door.
Lovewit.   Why! What's the matter?
Face. Yet farder, you are too near yet.
Lovewit.   I' the name of wonder!
What means the fellow?
Face.   The house, sir, has been visited.
Lovewit. What! With the plague? Stand thou then farder.
Face.   No, sir,   5
I had it not. [*He closes the door and comes into the street.*]
  Lovewit. Who had it then? I left
None else but thee i' the house!
Face.   Yes, sir. My fellow,
The cat that kept the butt'ry, had it on her
A week before I spied it; but I got her
Conveyed away i' the night. And so I shut   10
The house up for a month—
  Lovewit.   How!
Face.   Purposing then, sir,
T'have burnt rose-vinegar, treacle, and tar,
And ha' made it sweet, that you should ne'er ha' known it;
Because I knew the news would but afflict you, sir.
  Lovewit. Breathe less, and farder off! Why this is stranger!   15

2 FROM *away from.*
12 *a form of fumigation.*

Act V Scene 2

The neighbors tell me all, here, that the doors
Have still been open—
    Face. How, sir!
    Lovewit. Gallants, men and women,
And of all sorts, tag-rag, been seen to flock here
In threaves, these ten weeks, as to a second Hogsden,
In days of Pimlico and Eye-bright!
20   *Face.* Sir,
Their wisdoms will not say so.
    Lovewit. Today, they speak
Of coaches and gallants; one in a French hood
Went in, they tell me; and another was seen
In a velvet gown at the windore! Divers more
Pass in and out.
25   *Face.* They did pass through the doors then,
Or walls, I assure their eye-sights, and their spectacles;
For here, sir, are the keys, and here have been,
In this my pocket, now, above twenty days!
And for before, I kept the fort alone, there.
30   But that 'tis yet not deep i' the afternoon,
I should believe my neighbors had seen double
Through the black pot, and made these apparitions!
For, on my faith to your worship, for these three weeks,
And upwards, the door has not been opened.
    Lovewit. Strange!
    1 Neighbor. Good faith, I think I saw a coach!

17 STILL *always, constantly.*
19 THREAVES *great numbers—twenty-four sheaves made a threave.* HOGSDEN
    *holiday place near London. Johnson is supposed to have killed a fellow actor in a
    duel there.*
20 PIMLICO . . . EYE-BRIGHT *two famous drinking places at Hogsden.*
24 WINDORE *old form of window.*
30 DEEP *far gone.*
32 BLACK POT *leather tankard for beer.*

174

2 Neighbor.   And I too,   35
I'd ha' been sworn!
    Lovewit.   Do you but think it now?
And but one coach?
    4 Neighbor.   We cannot tell, sir; Jeremy
Is a very honest fellow.
    Face.   Did you see me at all?
    1 Neighbor. No. That we are sure on.
    2 Neighbor.   I'll be sworn o' that.
    Lovewit. Fine rogues to have your testimonies built on!   40
            [*Enter Third Neighbor, the smith.*]
    3 Neighbor. Is Jeremy come?
    1 Neighbor.   O yes; you may leave your tools;
We were deceived, he says.
    2 Neighbor.   He's had the keys,
And the door has been shut these three weeks.
    3 Neighbor.   Like enough.
    Lovewit. Peace, and get hence, you changelings.
            [*Enter Surly and Mammon.*]
    Face. [*Aside.*]   Surly come!
And Mammon made acquainted? They'll tell all.   45
How shall I beat them off? What shall I do?
Nothing's more wretched than a guilty conscience.

Act V Scene 3

            [*In the street outside the door.*]
    Surly. No, sir, he was a great physician. This,
It was no bawdy-house, but a mere chancel.

    2 MERE CHANCEL *absolute church—the chancel is just outside the sanctuary of a
    church.*

You knew the lord, and his sister.

  Mammon.   Nay, good Surly—

  Surly. The happy word, "be rich"—

  Mammon.   Play not the tyrant—

5 *Surly.* Should be today pronounced to all your friends.

And where be your andirons now? And your brass pots,

That should ha' been golden flagons, and great wedges?

  Mammon. Let me but breathe. What! They ha' shut their doors,

Methinks!   *Mammon and Surly knock.*

  Surly. Ay, now 'tis holiday with them.

  Mammon. [Shouting.]   Rogues,

Cozeners, imposters, bawds!

10 *Face.*   What mean you, sir?

  Mammon. To enter if we can.

  Face.   Another man's house?

Here is the owner, sir. Turn you to him,

And speak your business.

  Mammon.   Are you, sir, the owner?

  Lovewit. Yes, sir.

  Mammon. And are those knaves, within, your cheaters?

  Lovewit. What knaves? What cheaters?

15 *Mammon.*   Subtle, and his Lungs.

  Face. The gentleman is distracted, sir! No lungs

Nor lights ha' been seen here these three weeks, sir,

Within these doors, upon my word!

  Surly.   Your word,

Groom arrogant?

  Face.   Yes, sir, I am the housekeeper,

20 And know the keys ha' not been out o' my hands.

  Surly. This's a new Face!

  Face.   You do mistake the house, sir!

16–17 LUNGS . . . LIGHTS "*lights*" *are animal lungs sold for food.*
21 FACE *role.*

What sign was't at?

   Surly.   You rascal! This is one
O' the confederacy. Come, let's get officers,
And force the door.

   Lovewit.   'Pray you stay, gentlemen.

   Surly. No, sir, we'll come with warrant.

   Mammon.   Ay, and then   25
We shall ha' your doors open.

                         [*Exeunt Mammon and Surly.*]

   Lovewit.   What means this?

   Face. I cannot tell, sir!

   1 Neighbor.   These are two o' the gallants
That we do think we saw.

   Face.   Two o' the fools?
You talk as idly as they. Good faith, sir,
I think the moon has crazed 'em all. [*Enter Kastril.*]

                 [*Aside.*] O me,   30
The angry boy come too? He'll make a noise,
And ne'er away till he have betrayed us all.

                Kastril knocks.

   Kastril. What, rogues, bawds, slaves, you'll open the door anon.
Punk, cockatrice, my suster! By this light,
I'll fetch the marshal to you. You are a whore,   35
To keep your castle—

   Face.   Who would you speak with, sir?

   Kastril. The bawdy Doctor, and the cozening Captain,
And Puss, my suster.

   Lovewit.   This is something, sure!

---

22 SIGN *distinguishing signs hung over the doors of inns and brothels.*
24 STAY *hold on.*
30 MOON *thought to drive men mad, lunatic.*
34 COCKATRICE *a fabled beast whose glance could kill; slang for "whore."*
38 PUSS *diminutive for young girl.* SOMETHING *a solid fact.*

Face. Upon my trust, the doors were never open, sir.

40　　*Kastril*. I have heard all their tricks told me twice over,

By the fat knight and the lean gentleman,

　　Lovewit. Here comes another.

[*Enter Ananias and Tribulation.*]

Face.　　　　　　　　[*Aside*.] Ananias too?

And his pastor?

　　Tribulation. The doors are shut against us.

They beat, too, at the door.

Ananias. Come forth, you seed of sulphur, sons of fire!

45　　Your stench, it is broke forth; abomination

Is in the house.

　　Kastril.　　　Ay, my suster's there.

　　Ananias.　　　　　　　　The place,

It is become a cage of unclean birds.

　　Kastril. Yes, I will fetch the scavenger, and the constable.

　　Tribulation. You shall do well.

　　Ananias.　　　　　　　　We'll join to weed them out.

50　　*Kastril*. You will not come then, punk device, my suster!

　　Ananias. Call her not sister. She is a harlot verily.

　　Kastril. I'll raise the street.

　　Lovewit.　　　　　Good gentlemen, a word.

　　Ananias. Sathan, avoid, and hinder not our zeal!

[*Exuent Ananias, Tribulation, and Kastril.*]

　　Lovewit. The world's turned Bedlam.

　　Face.　　　　　　　These are all broke loose,

---

41 KNIGHT . . . GENTLEMAN *i.e. Sir Epicure and Surly.*

44 SEED . . . FIRE *i.e. alchemists and devils—sulphur was one of the prime materials of alchemy, as well as hellfire.*

47 UNCLEAN BIRDS *see N. to IV.7.53.*

48 SCAVENGER *official responsible for street cleaning.*

50 PUNK DEVICE *absolute whore.*

52 RAISE *arouse.*

Out of St. Katherine's, where they use to keep   55
The better sort of mad-folks.

   1 Neighbor.   All these persons
We saw go in, and out, here.

   2 Neighbor.   Yes, indeed, sir.

   3 Neighbor. These were the parties.

   Face.   Peace, you drunkards. Sir,
I wonder at it! Please you to give me leave
To touch the door; I'll try an' the lock be changed.   60

   Lovewit. It mazes me!

   Face.   Good faith, sir, I believe
There's no such thing; 'tis all *deceptio visus.* [*Trying the door.*]
[*Aside.*] Would I could get him away.

                Dapper cries out within.

   Dapper.   Master Captain, Master Doctor.

   Lovewit. Who's that?

   Face. [*Aside.*] Our clerk within, that I forgot!—

                        I know not, sir.

   Dapper. [*Within.*] For God's sake, when will her Grace be at
    leisure?

   Face.   Ha!   65
Illusions, some spirit o' the air! [*Aside.*] His gag is melted,
And now he sets out the throat.

   Dapper. [*Within.*]   I am almost stifled—

   Face. [*Aside.*] Would you were altogether.

   Lovewit.   'Tis i' the house.
Ha! list. [*Another cry.*]

---

55 ST. KATHERINE'S *an old asylum—apparently somewhat more fashionable than*
   Bedlam. USE *are accustomed.*

61 MAZES *bewilders.*

62 DECEPTIO VISUS *an illusion.*

67 SETS . . . THROAT *shouts.*

Face. Believe it, sir, i' the air!

Lovewit.   Peace, you—

Dapper. [*Within.*] Mine aunt's grace does not use me well.

70   *Subtle.* [*Within.*]   You fool,
Peace, you'll mar all.

Face. [*Whispers through the door.*]
                Or you will else, you rogue.

Lovewit. [*Overhearing.*]
O, is it so? Then you converse with spirits!
Come, sir. No more o' your tricks, good Jeremy.
The truth, the shortest way.

Face.   Dismiss this rabble, sir.

[*Aside.*] What shall I do? I am catched.

75   *Lovewit.*   Good neighbors,
I thank you all. You may depart.   [*Exeunt Neighbors.*]
                Come, sir,
You know that I am an indulgent master;
And, therefore, conceal nothing. What's your med'cine,
To draw so many several sorts of wild fowl?

80   *Face.* Sir, you were wont to affect mirth and wit—
But here's no place to talk on't i' the street.
Give me but leave to make the best of my fortune,
And only pardon me th'abuse of your house:
It's all I beg. I'll help you to a widow,

85   In recompense, that you shall gi' me thanks for,
Will make you seven years younger, and a rich one.
'Tis but your putting on a Spanish cloak;

69 PEACE *be quiet!*
74 SHORTEST WAY *plainly.*
79 WILD FOWL *geese (fools).*
80 WONT TO AFFECT *"accustomed to delight in."*
82 *"Allow me the right to make the most of opportunity."*
87 'TIS BUT *"it only requires."*

I have her within. You need not fear the house,
It was not visited.
    Lovewit.   But by me, who came
Sooner than you expected.
    Face.   It is true, sir.   90
'Pray you forgive me.
    Lovewit.   Well, let's see your widow.
                [*They go inside the house.*]

89 VISITED *i.e. by the plague.*

Act V Scene 4

             [*Subtle leads in Dapper blindfolded.*]
    Subtle. How! ha' you eaten your gag?
    Dapper.   Yes, faith, it crumbled
Away i' my mouth.
    Subtle.   You ha' spoiled all then.
    Dapper.   No,
I hope my aunt of Faery will forgive me.
    Subtle. Your aunt's a gracious lady; but in troth
You were to blame.
    Dapper.   The fume did overcome me,   5
And I did do't to stay my stomach. 'Pray you
So satisfy her Grace.
             [*Enter Face dressed as Captain.*]
             Here comes the Captain.
    Face. How now! Is his mouth down?

6 STAY *quiet.*
8 DOWN *open.*

181

Subtle. Ay! He has spoken!

Face. [*Aside.*] A pox, I heard him, and you too.

[*Aloud.*] He's undone then.

[*Face and Subtle push Dapper aside and whisper.*]

10 I have been fain to say the house is haunted

With spirits to keep churl back.

Subtle. And hast thou done it?

Face. Sure, for this night.

Subtle. Why, then triumph and sing

Of Face so famous, the precious king

Of present wits.

Face. Did you not hear the coil

About the door?

15 *Subtle.* Yes, and I dwindled with it.

Face. Show him his aunt, and let him be dispatched;

I'll send her to you. [*Exit Face.*]

Subtle. [*Aloud.*] Well, sir, your aunt her Grace

Will give you audience presently, on my suit

And the Captain's word that you did not eat your gag

In any contempt of her Highness. [*Takes off the blindfold.*]

20 *Dapper.* Not I, in troth, sir.

[*Enter*] *Dol like the Queen of Faery.*

Subtle. Here she is come. Down o' your knees and wriggle:

She has a stately presence. [*Dapper kneels and inches forward.*]

Good! Yet nearer,

And bid, "God save you."

Dapper. Madam!

Subtle. And your aunt.

Dapper. And my most gracious aunt, God save your Grace.

---

11 CHURL *the hick—i.e. Lovewit, who has been living in the country.*

14 PRESENT *living.* COIL *hubub.*

18 SUIT *request.*

Dol Common. Nephew, we thought to have been angry with you,   25
But that sweet face of yours hath turned the tide,
And made it flow with joy, that ebbed of love.
Arise, and touch our velvet gown.

Subtle.   The skirts,
And kiss 'em. So! [*Dapper kisses her hems.*]

Dol Common.   Let me now stroke that head.
Much, nephew, shalt thou win; much shalt thou spend;   30
Much shalt thou give away; much shalt thou lend.

Subtle. [*Aside.*] Ay, much indeed!—Why do you not thank her
    Grace?

Dapper. I cannot speak, for joy.

Subtle.   See, the kind wretch!
Your Grace's kinsman right.

Dol Common.   Give me the bird.
Here is your fly in a purse, about your neck, cousin;   35
Wear it, and feed it, about this day sev'n-night,
On your right wrist—

Subtle.   Open a vein, with a pin,
And let it suck but once a week; till then,
You must not look on't.

Dol Common.   No, and, kinsman,
Bear yourself worthy of the blood you come on.   40

Subtle. Her Grace would ha' you eat no more Woolsack pies,
Nor Dagger furmety.

Dol Common.   Nor break his fast

25 THOUGHT *expected.*
33 KIND WRETCH *"natural fellow."*
34 RIGHT *true.*
34–35 BIRD . . . FLY *the familiar spirit he can command to do his bidding.*
36 THIS . . . NIGHT *i.e. in a week.*
40 ON *from.*
41 WOOLSACK *a London inn.*
42 DAGGER FURMETY *spiced pudding as made at the Dagger, a London inn.*

Act V Scene 4

In Heaven and Hell.
    Subtle.   She's with you everywhere!
Nor play with costermongers at mumchance, traytrip,
45 God-make-you-rich (when as your aunt has done it); but keep
The gallant'st company, and the best games—
    Dapper.   Yes, sir.
    Subtle. Gleek and primero; and what you get, be true to us.
    Dapper. By this hand, I will.
    Subtle.   You may bring's a thousand pound
Before tomorrow night, if but three thousand
Be stirring, an you will.
50   *Dapper.*   I swear, I will then.
    Subtle. Your fly will learn you all games.
    Face. [*Within.*]   Ha' you done there?
    Subtle. Your Grace will command him no more duties?
    Dol Common.   No;
But come and see me often. I may chance
To leave him three or four hundred chests of treasure,
55 And some twelve thousand acres of Faery land,
If he game well, and comely, with good gamesters.
                  [*She turns away from him.*]
    Subtle. There's a kind aunt! Kiss her departing part.
But you must sell your forty mark a year now.
    Dapper. Ay, sir, I mean.
    Subtle.   Or, gi't away; pox on't!
60   *Dapper.* I'll gi't mine aunt. I'll go and fetch the writings.
    Subtle. 'Tis well; away.   [*Exit Dapper.*]

43 HEAVEN AND HELL *two taverns in Westminster.*
44–47 N.
50 AN *if.*
56 COMELY *stylishly.*
58 SELL . . . MARK *i.e. sell his capital, which yields forty marks per year in income.*
60 WRITINGS *legal papers.*

184

[*Enter Face.*]

Face. Where's Subtle?

Subtle. Here. What news?

Face. Drugger is at the door; go take his suit,
And bid him fetch a parson, presently.
Say he shall marry the widow. Thou shalt spend
A hundred pound by the service!   [*Exit Subtle.*]

                                Now, Queen Dol,   65

Ha' you packed up all?

Dol Common.   Yes.

Face.   And how do you like
The Lady Pliant?

Dol Common. A good dull innocent.

                    [*Enter Subtle.*]

Subtle. Here's your Hieronimo's cloak and hat.

Face.   Give me 'em.

Subtle. And the ruff too?

Face.   Yes; I'll come to you presently.   [*Exit.*]

Subtle. Now he is gone about his project, Dol,   70
I told you of, for the widow.

Dol Common.   'Tis direct
Against our articles.

Subtle.   Well, we'll fit him, wench.
Has thou gulled her of her jewels, or her bracelets?

Dol Common. No, but I will do't.

Subtle.   Soon at night, my Dolly,
When we are shipped and all our goods aboard,   75
Eastward for Ratcliff, we will turn our course

---

62 SUIT *the Spanish costume he has gone to borrow.*

64–65 SPEND . . . SERVICE *"make a hundred pounds by doing it."*

71 DIRECT *squarely contrary.*

72 FIT *pay him in his own coin.*

To Brainford, westward, if thou sayst the word,
And take our leaves of this o'erweening rascal,
This peremptory Face.

   Dol Common.   Content; I'm weary of him.

80   *Subtle.* Thou'st cause, when the slave will run a-wiving, Dol,
Against the instrument that was drawn between us.

   Dol Common. I'll pluck his bird as bare as I can.

   Subtle.   Yes, tell her
She must by any means address some present
To th' cunning man, make him amends for wronging

85 His art with her suspicion; send a ring,
Or chain of pearl; she will be tortured else
Extremely in her sleep, say, and ha' strange things
Come to her. Wilt thou?

   Dol Common.   Yes.

   Subtle.   My fine flitter-mouse,
My bird o' the night! We'll tickle it at the Pigeons,

90 When we have all, and may unlock the trunks,
And say, this's mine, and thine, and thine, and mine—

                     They kiss.
                     [*Enter Face.*]

   Face. What now, a-billing?

   Subtle.   Yes, a little exalted
In the good passage of our stock-affairs.

---

77 BRAINFORD *Brentford, up the river from London—the opposite direction from Ratcliff.*

78 O'ERWEENING *proud, tyrannous.*

79 CONTENT *agreed.*

81 "*Contrary to the agreement (the 'venture tripartite') we three made.*"

87 STRANGE THINGS *spirits (?) dreams (?).*

88 FLITTER-MOUSE *bat; another "bird o' the night" like Dol.*

89 PIGEONS *the Three Pigeons Inn at Brainford. Later kept by John Lowin, the actor who first played Mammon.*

93 STOCK-AFFAIRS *the joint capital of the company.*

Face. Drugger has brought his parson; take him in, Subtle,
And send Nab back again, to wash his face.   95
    Subtle. I will. And shave himself?
    Face.   If you can get him.

                                      [Exit Subtle.]

    Dol Common. You are hot upon it, Face, whate'er it is!
    Face. A trick that Dol shall spend ten pound a month by.

                      [Enter Subtle.]

Is he gone?
    Subtle.   The chaplain waits you i' the hall, sir.
    Face. I'll go bestow him.   *[Exit.]*
    Dol Common.   He'll now marry her, instantly.   100
    Subtle. He cannot yet, he is not ready. Dear Dol,
Cozen her of all thou canst. To deceive him
Is no deceit, but justice, that would break
Such an inextricable tie as ours was.
    Dol Common. Let me alone to fit him.

                  [Enter Face.]

    Face.   Come, my venturers,   105
You ha' packed up all? Where be the trunks? Bring forth.
    Subtle. Here. *[Shows the chests.]*
    Face.   Let's see 'em. Where's the money?
    Subtle. *[Opens a chest.]*   Here,
In this.
    Face. Mammon's ten pound; eight score before.
The Brethren's money, this. Drugger's, and Dapper's.
What paper's that?
    Dol Common.   The jewel of the waiting maid's,   110
That stole it from her lady, to know certain—

---

100 BESTOW *conduct him to the proper place.*
105 VENTURERS *partners; merchants who risk or venture capital.*

    Face. If she should have precedence of her mistress?
    Dol Common.   Yes.
    Face. What box is that?
    Subtle.   The fishwives' rings, I think,
And th'alewives' single money. Is't not, Dol?
115   *Dol Common.* Yes, and the whistle that the sailor's wife
Brought you to know and her husband were with Ward.
    Face. We'll wet it tomorrow; and our silver beakers
And tavern cups. Where be the French petticoats,
And girdles, and hangers?
    Subtle.   Here, i' the trunk,
And the bolts of lawn.
120   *Face.*   Is Drugger's damask there?
And the tobacco?
    Subtle.   Yes.
    Face.   Give me the keys.
    Dol Common. Why you the keys?
    Subtle.   No matter, Dol, because
We shall not open 'em before he comes.
    Face. 'Tis true, you shall not open them, indeed;
Nor have 'em forth. Do you see? Not forth, Dol.
125   *Dol Common.*   No!
    Face. No, my smock-rampant. The right is, my master
Knows all, has pardoned me, and he will keep 'em.

---

112 PRECEDENCE *a higher place socially. By means of such details Jonson suggests how universal are greed and the desire for status.*

114 SINGLE MONEY *loose change.*

116 WARD *a famous pirate.*

119 HANGERS *carriers attached to belt for swords.*

120 LAWN *a light fine cloth.*

125 FORTH *out of the house.*

126 SMOCK-RAMPANT *i.e. furious whore. In heraldry an animal "rampant" stands on its hind legs, in an aggressive posture, attacking with its head and front legs.*

Doctor, 'tis true—you look—for all your figures.
I sent for him, indeed. Wherefore, good partners,
Both he and she, be satisfied; for here   130
Determines the indenture tripartite
'Twixt Subtle, Dol, and Face. All I can do
Is to help you over the wall, o' the back-side,
Or lend you a sheet to save your velvet gown, Dol.
Here will be officers presently; bethink you   135
Of some course suddenly to 'scape the dock;
For thither you'll come else.
                    Some knock. Hark you, thunder.
   Subtle. You are a precious fiend!
   Officers. [*Without.*]   Open the door!
   Face. Dol, I am sorry for thee, i' faith. But hear'st thou,
It shall go hard, but I will place thee somewhere: 140
Thou shalt ha' my letter to Mistress Amo.
   Dol Common.   Hang you—
   Face. Or Madam Caesarean.
   Dol Common.   Pox upon you, rogue,
Would I had but time to beat thee!
   Face.   Subtle,
Let's know where you set up next; I'll send you

---

128 FOR . . . FIGURES "*despite all your horoscopes (you couldn't foretell this would happen)."*
129 HIM *i.e. Lovewit—the play gives no other indication that Face did send for him.*
131 DETERMINES *ends.*
133 O' THE BACK-SIDE *at the back (of the house).*
134 SAVE *protect.*
135 OFFICERS *police.*
136 DOCK *trial—the accused stood "in the dock."*
138 PRECIOUS *rare, extraordinary.*
140 GO HARD *be difficult.* PLACE *get a position for.*
141 LETTER *i.e. of recommendation.*
141–42 AMO . . . CAESAREAN *type names for whorehouse madams.*

145 A customer, now and then, for old acquaintance.
What new course ha' you?
    Subtle.   Rogue, I'll hang myself,
That I may walk a greater devil than thou,
And haunt thee i' the flock-bed and the buttery.

                                         [*Exeunt.*]

146 COURSE *scheme, swindle.*

148 FLOCK-BED *mattress stuffed with cheap material, flock. The suggestion is that in his return to life as butler, Jeremy will again spend his time sleeping and eating in the buttery.*

Act V Scene 5

    [*Inside the house. Enter Lovewit, disguised as Spaniard, with a Parson. Mammon and Surly, with officers, batter at the door and shout from without. Kastril, Ananias, and Tribulation join them.*]
    Lovewit. What do you mean, my masters?
    Mammon.   Open your door,
Cheaters, bawds, conjurers.
    Officer.   Or we'll break it open.
    Lovewit. What warrant have you?
    Officer.   Warrant enough, sir, doubt not,
If you'll not open it.
    Lovewit.   Is there an officer there?
    Officer. Yes, two or three for failing.
5   *Lovewit.*   Have but patience,
And I will open it straight.
                [*Enter Face as Jeremy.*]
    Face.   Sir, ha' you done?

5 FOR FAILING *as insurance against failing.*

Is it a marriage? Perfect?

   Lovewit.   Yes, my brain.

   Face. Off with your ruff and cloak then; be yourself, sir.

              [Lovewit takes off his disguise.]

   Surly. *[Without.]* Down with the door.

   Kastril. *[Without.]*   'Slight, ding it open.

   Lovewit. *[Opening the door.]*   Hold!

Hold, gentlemen, what means this violence?   10

   [Mammon, Surly, Kastril, Ananias, Tribulation and Officers enter.]

   Mammon. Where is this collier?

   Surly.   And my Captain Face?

   Mammon. These day-owls.

   Surly.   That are birding in men's purses.

   Mammon. Madam Suppository.

   Kastril.   Doxy, my suster.

   Ananias.   Locusts

Of the foul pit.

   Tribulation.   Profane as Bel and the Dragon.

   Ananias. Worse than the grasshoppers, or the lice of Egypt.   15

   Lovewit. Good gentlemen, hear me. Are you officers,

And cannot stay this violence?

   Officer.   Keep the peace!

   Lovewit. Gentlemen, what is the matter? Whom do you seek?

   Mammon. The chemical cozener.

   Surly.   And the captain pander.

  9 DING *batter.*

11 COLLIER *coal hauler—i.e. alchemist, who coaled his fires.*

12 DAY-OWLS . . . BIRDING *the owl hunts "birds" by night, but these birds of prey hunt by day. "Owl" may suggest the grave wisdom pretended to by Subtle.*

13 SUPPOSITORY *i.e. whore—suppositories are plugs inserted in the vagina for medical purposes.* DOXY *floozy.*

14 BEL . . . DRAGON *N.*

15 GRASSHOPPERS . . . LICE *two of the plagues visited upon Egypt in Exodus.*

19 CHEMICAL *alchemical.*

 Kastril. The nun my suster.

 Mammon.   Madam Rabbi.

20 *Ananias.*   Scorpions,

And caterpillars.

 Lovewit. Fewer at once, I pray you.

 Officer. One after another, gentlemen, I charge you,

By virtue of my staff—

 Ananias.   They are the vessels

Of pride, lust, and the cart.

 Lovewit.   Good zeal, lie still

A little while.

25 *Tribulation.* Peace, Deacon Ananias.

 Lovewit. The house is mine here, and the doors are open;

If there be any such persons as you seek for,

Use your authority, search on o' God's name.

I am but newly come to town, and finding

30 This tumult 'bout my door, to tell you true,

It somewhat 'mazed me; till my man here, fearing

My more displeasure, told me [he] had done

Somewhat an insolent part, let out my house

(Belike presuming on my known aversion

35 From any air o' the town while there was sickness),

To a doctor and a captain; who, what they are,

Or where they be, he knows not.

 Mammon.   Are they gone?

 Lovewit. You may go in and search, sir.

     They enter [the interior of house.]

         Here, I find

---

20 NUN *ironical slang for "whore."* MADAM RABBI *i.e. Dol with her rabbinical learning.*

23 STAFF *a rod of office, showing the authority of the bearer.*

24 CART *the open wagon in which convicted criminals were displayed on the way to punishment.*

The empty walls, worse than I left 'em, smoked,
A few cracked pots, and glasses, and a furnace;   40
The ceiling filled with poesies of the candle,
And madam with a dildo writ o' the walls.
Only, one gentlewoman I met here,
That is within, that said she was a widow—

   Kastril. Ay, that's my suster, I'll go thump her. Where is she?   45

                        [Goes in.]

   Lovewit. And should ha' married a Spanish count, but he,
When he came to't, neglected her so grossly,
That I, a widower, am gone through with her.

   Surly. How! Have I lost her, then?

   Lovewit.   Were you the don, sir?
Good faith, now she does blame y' extremely, and says   50
You swore, and told her you had ta'en the pains
To dye your beard, and umber o'er your face,
Borrowèd a suit and ruff, all for her love;
And then did nothing. What an oversight
And want of putting forward, sir, was this!   55
Well fare an old harquebusier yet,
Could prime his powder, and give fire, and hit,
All in a twinkling!   *Mammon comes forth.*

   Mammon.   The whole nest are fled!

   Lovewit. What sort of birds were they?

   Mammon.   A kind of choughs,

---

41 POESIES . . . CANDLE *traces of smoke—perhaps also graffiti written with candle smoke. A "posy" was a short verse.*

42 MADAM . . . WRIT *either an obscene poem—a "dildo" is an artificial penis—or a crude drawing of a woman using a dildo.*

48 GONE THROUGH *i.e. married (as Surly originally promised).*

56 HARQUEBUSIER *soldier; an harquebus was a hand gun.*

59 CHOUGHS *"chuffs," crows. Crows and daws steal bright objects to put in their nest.*

60 Or thievish daws, sir, that have picked my purse
Of eight score and ten pounds within these five weeks,
Beside my first materials; and my goods,
That lie i' the cellar, which I am glad they ha' left,
I may have home yet.

    Lovewit.   Think you so, sir?

    Mammon.   Ay.

65   *Lovewit.* By order of law, sir, but not otherwise.

    Mammon. Not mine own stuff?

    Lovewit.   Sir, I can take no knowledge
That they are yours, but by public means.
If you can bring certificate that you were gulled of 'em,
Or any formal writ out of a court,

70 That you did cozen yourself, I will not hold them.

    Mammon. I'll rather lose 'em.

    Lovewit.   That you shall not, sir,
By me, in troth. Upon these terms they're yours.
What should they ha' been, sir; turned into gold all?

    Mammon.   No.
I cannot tell. It may be they should. What then?

75   *Lovewit.* What a great loss in hope have you sustained!

    Mammon. Not I; the commonwealth has.

    Face. [*Aside.*]   Ay, he would ha' built
The city new; and made a ditch about it
Of silver, should have run with cream from Hogsden;
That every Sunday in Moorfields the younkers

80 And tits and tom-boys should have fed on, gratis.

    Mammon. I will go mount a turnip-cart and preach

---

62 MATERIALS *the coals and chemicals needed to start the experiment.*

79 MOORFIELDS *open fields for recreation just outside London walls to the north.*

80 TITS *young girls.*

81 TURNIP-CART *rough farm cart—a suitable moveable platform for an itinerant preacher.*

The end o' the world, within these two months.—Surly,
What! in a dream?

 Surly.   Must I needs cheat myself
With that same foolish vice of honesty!
Come, let us go and hearken out the rogues.   85
That Face I'll mark for mine, if e'er I meet him.

 Face. If I can hear of him, sir, I'll bring you word
Unto your lodging; for in troth, they were strangers
To me; I thought 'em honest as myself, sir.

         [*Exeunt Surly and Mammon.*]
   They [*Ananias and Tribulation*] *come forth.*

 Tribulation. 'Tis well, the Saints shall not lose all yet. Go 90
And get some carts—

 Lovewit.   For what, my zealous friends?

 Ananias. To bear away the portion of the righteous,
Out of this den of thieves.

 Lovewit.   What is that portion?

 Ananias. The goods, sometimes the orphans', that the Brethren
Bought with their silver pence.

 Lovewit.   What, those i' the cellar, 95
The knight Sir Mammon claims?

 Ananias.   I do defy
The wicked Mammon, so do all the Brethren,
Thou profane man. I ask thee with what conscience
Thou canst advance that idol against us
That have the seal? Were not the shillings numbered 100
That made the pounds. Were not the pounds told out,

---

82 END O' THE WORLD *then, as now, there were many who predicted the early end
of a wicked world. Mammon is a man of extremes, shifting from a belief in endless
progress to a radical pessimism about the future.*

83 WHAT . . . DREAM *"pay attention, stop dreaming!"*

85 HEARKEN OUT *seek.*

100 SEAL *the mark of being God's Chosen.*

Act V Scene 5

Upon the second day of the fourth week,
In the eighth month, upon the table dormant,
The year of the last patience of the Saints
Six hundred and ten?

105   *Lovewit.*   Mine earnest vehement botcher,
And Deacon also, I cannot dispute with you,
But if you get you not away the sooner,
I shall confute you with a cudgel.
   Ananias.   Sir.
   Tribulation. Be patient, Ananias.
   Ananias.   I am strong,
110 And will stand up, well girt, against an host
That threaten Gad in exile.
   Lovewit.   I shall send you
To Amsterdam, to your cellar.
   Ananias.   I will pray there,
Against thy house: may dogs defile thy walls,
And wasps and hornets breed beneath thy roof,
115 This seat of falsehood, and this cave of coz'nage!

                       [Exeunt Ananias and Tribulation.]
                   Drugger enters.

   Lovewit. Another too?
   Drugger.   Not I, sir, I am no Brother.
   Lovewit. Away, you Harry Nicholas! do you talk?
                He beats him away.

102–03 *See N. to III.2.132.*
103 DORMANT *still; i.e. a fixed table.*
104 LAST . . . SAINTS *the last period of one thousand years which the Brethren
would have to endure before the coming of God's kingdom on earth.*
105 SIX HUNDRED AND TEN *the date of the play, 1610.*
111 GAD IN EXILE *i.e. the exiled Brethren—see Genesis 49:19.*
117 NICHOLAS *Hendrik Nicklaes, an Anabaptist and head of " The Family of Love"
sect.*

Face. No, this was Abel Drugger. *To the Parson.*

Good sir, go
And satisfy him; tell him all is done.
He stayed too long a-washing of his face.   120
The Doctor, he shall hear of him at Westchester;
And of the Captain, tell him, at Yarmouth, or
Some good port-town else, lying for a wind.

[Exit Parson.]

If you get off the angry child, now, sir—
[Enter Kastril and Dame Pliant.]

Kastril. Come on, you ewe, you have matched most sweetly, ha'
you not?   125
Did not I say, I would never ha' you tupped
But by a dubbed boy, to make you a lady-tom?
'Slight, you are a mammet! O, I could touse you now.
Death, 'mun you marry with a pox?

Lovewit.   You lie, boy;
As sound as you; and I am aforehand with you.
[Lovewit draws his sword.]

Kastril.   Anon?   130

Lovewit. Come, will you quarrel? I will feize you, sirrah.
Why do you not buckle to your tools?

Kastril.   God's light!
This is a fine old boy as e'er I saw!

119 ALL *i.e. the marriage with Dame Pliant, which Drugger expected.*
121 WESTCHESTER *the town of Chester, a good distance from London.*
122 YARMOUTH *a port in the northeast—rather farther than Drugger is likely to go.*
123 LYING *waiting.*
126 TUPPED *topped, referring to sheep.*
127 DUBBED BOY *knight.* LADY-TOM *wife of a knight.*
128 MAMMET *doll or puppet; without a will (?).* TOUSE *tousel, beat.*
129 'MUN *must; country dialect.* POX *diseased man.*
130 SOUND *healthy.*
131 FEIZE *deal with.*

Lovewit. What, do you change your copy now? Proceed;
135 Here stands my dove: stoop at her if you dare.
  Kastril. 'Slight, I must love him! I cannot choose, i' faith!
And I should be hanged for't! Suster, I protest,
I honor thee for this match.
  Lovewit.   O, do you so, sir?
  Kastril. Yes, and thou canst take tobacco, and drink, old boy,
140 I'll give her five hundred pound more to her marriage
Than her own state.
  Lovewit.   Fill a pipe-full, Jeremy.
  Face. Yes; but go in and take it, sir.
  Lovewit.   We will.
I will be ruled by thee in anything, Jeremy.
  Kastril. 'Slight, thou art not hide-bound, thou art a jovy boy!
145 Come, let's in, I pray thee, and take our whiffs.
  Lovewit. Whiff in with your sister, brother boy.
             [*Exeunt Kastril and Dame Pliant.*]
              That master

That had received such happiness by a servant,
In such a widow, and with so much wealth,
Were very ungrateful if he would not be
150 A little indulgent to that servant's wit,
And help his fortune, though with some small strain
Of his own candor.
     [*He steps forward and speaks to the audience.*]

134 CHANGE ... COPY "*change your tune.*"
135 DOVE *perhaps Dame Pliant; but more likely an ironic term for his sword.* STOOP
  attack; a hawking term; "Kastril" means a small hawk.
140 MORE *i.e. as a dowry.*
141 STATE *estate.*
144 JOVY *jovial.*
147 THAT "*that man who.*"
152 CANDOR *unspotted reputation.*

Therefore, gentlemen,
And kind spectators, if I have outstripped
An old man's gravity, or strict canon, think
What a young wife and a good brain may do: 155
Stretch age's truth sometimes, and crack it too.
Speak for thyself, knave.
   Face. [*Advancing.*]   So I will, sir.
                       Gentlemen,
My part a little fell in this last scene,
Yet 'twas decorum. And though I am clean
Got off from Subtle, Surly, Mammon, Dol,   160
Hot Ananias, Dapper, Drugger, all
With whom I traded; yet I put myself
On you, that are my country; and this pelf
Which I have got, if you do quit me, rests,
To feast you often, and invite new guests.   165

153 OUTSTRIPPED *gone beyond.*
154 STRICT CANON *the absolute demands of critical decorum which required, among other things, that a character run true to type, e.g. that old men be consistently grave and solemn.*
158–59 MY ... DECORUM *N.*
162–63 PUT ... COUNTRY *"submit to the judgment of you, my countrymen." An appeal for a jury of one's peers.*
163 PELF *loot.*
164 QUIT *acquit.* RESTS *remains. Here and throughout his epilogue, Face is subtly involving the audience in his swindles.*

Notes

DEDICATORY LETTER

SIDNEY'S *Lady Mary Wroth, sometimes spelled Worth, was the daughter of Robert Sidney, first Earl of Leicester, and the niece of Sir Philip Sidney. Jonson had close connections with this family, wrote a famous poem,* To Penshurst, *praising their country house, and dedicated several poems to Lady Mary* (Epigrams *103* and *105, and* Underwood *28). He believed her to be "unworthily married on a jealous husband"* (Conversations *355–56).*

TO THE READER

TAK'ST UP . . . COMMODITY *A reference to the "commodity-swindle," in which, to avoid the usury laws, a foolish or desperate borrower was forced to take part of his loan in money and part in some undesired "commodity," such as wax or paper, which was valued at a very high rate. For another reference to this practice see II.1. Jonson is here comparing the undiscriminating reader of plays to the fool who "takes up a commodity," with the plays as the "commodity" and many of them—excepting Jonson's—as worthless and exorbitantly valued.*

RUN AWAY FROM NATURE *Jonson thought of himself as the reformer of English drama, and in this preface he makes his usual charges against its debasement, fondness for the spectacular, love of romantic plots, multiplicity of events and words, and, in general, its shapelessness or lack of form. Jonson was one of the first of the English neoclassical critics and for him these faults are all summed up as a failure to follow Nature, by which he meant in part a failure to depict the social world as it actually appears to our senses—realism—but more importantly, a failure to select and order the work in accordance with those rules which he thought of as being natural to art, if not to life. He constantly offered his own plays as models of following the rules of Nature in art, and to some degree they do so, but any modern reader will find them, I believe, more Elizabethan than neo-classical in flavor, for all their adherence to the rules.*

Shakespeare is, of course, one of the playwrights Jonson attacks here, and our admiration for his work should not obscure the fact that most of the many plays written at this time by other dramatists were as foolish and as poor as Jonson thought them.

Jonson's emphasis on the importance of the artist following Nature, here and elsewhere in his writings, is of particular interest in connection with The Alchemist, *where those other artists—the alchemists and Mammon—aim at speeding nature up, to "firk nature up in her own center" (II.1.28).*

SCATTERED . . . COMPOSED *Literally "fragmented" as opposed to "structured." Jonson is referring here to that extraordinary multiplicity and range of places and persons—Africa and Europe, the passage of generations in the course of a single play, the mixture of kings and clowns on the same stage—which were characteristic of most drama of the period, including Shakespeare's. Against this kind of sprawl the neoclassical critic, like Jonson, proposed a much more controlled and carefully "composed" (brought together) work. In* The Alchemist, *for example, though the characters may seem "scattered" they are carefully managed within a single plot, the scene limited to one room in a house and the street outside, and the time from beginning to end only the space of a few hours. This is "composition."*

THE ARGUMENT

10 NEWS *In the absence of newspapers, and with a growing need and curiosity to know what was going on in the world, the desire for news became a mania of the times, more noticeable perhaps because men had not previously had this appetite. It was during this period that several commercial newsletters were started, and Jonson, always the skeptical conservative, satirized the search for news in a later play,* The Staple of News.

PROLOGUE

1 TWO SHORT HOURS *The usual time specified in contemporary documents for the performance of a play. See, for example,* Romeo and Juliet, *Prologue to I.1. Even in cut versions these plays take over three busy hours on the modern stage,*

and if a two-hour playing time was a reality, not a poetic convention, in the Renaissance English theater, then the delivery must have been very rapid, the entrances and exits swift, and the pace fast in all respects. There were, we believe, no scene changes or movement of sets, which occupy so much time in the modern theater. The total effect must have been one of theatrical virtuosity, pure theater, make-believe with the minimum of props: only words, costumes and action, the same theatrical tools Face and Subtle use to create their little world of pretense.

9 HUMORS *A man's "humor" was originally thought to be the result of his physical chemistry, and according as one fluid or another predominated he was said to fall into one of four types: choleric, sanguine, phlegmatic, or melancholy. Jonson had himself helped to make this conception of character popular on the English comic stage in several of his earlier plays, but he had redefined "humor" to mean a psychological obsession, "some one peculiar quality" that so possesses a man as to draw all his powers "to run one way"* (Every Man Out of His Humor, *Induction, 105–08). Though the use of the term "humors" in connection with comedy was peculiar to the Elizabethan theater, Jonson rightly points out in the following lines that the character obsessed with some one thing—money, sex, food, learning, horses—has always been the standard character type of comedy. Henri Bergson in* Laughter (De Rire) *has taken this idea to its logical conclusion and shown that we laugh always at the mechanical, the non-adaptive, the automatic single-mindedness ("humors") which pursues its one goal, to the exclusion of all else, like a woundup toy.*

19 APPLY *Then, as now, it was a favorite game of critics to see in comic and satiric stage characters parodies of particular, identifiable people. Jonson, who was sharply satiric and constantly engaged in personal controversies, had already been accused several times of attacking his contemporaries in his plays. The charges may have been just, but here and elsewhere Jonson makes the usual defense of the comic and satiric writer, that he attacks follies not men, and that if any spectator sees himself in one of the characters it is his own guilt, not the author's malice, that makes the identification.*

Act I, Scene 1

1 [FACE.] *In the folio edition (F) of his plays printed in 1616, which Jonson himself saw through the press, the first speech ascription in each scene is omitted. In the present text these ascriptions are supplied after this first scene without the brackets which indicate editorial emendation. F also lists all characters appearing in a*

scene in a group at the beginning of the scene, but does not usually mark individual entrances and exits. In this text the opening list is omitted and separate exits and entrances are given within brackets, to distinguish these additions from Jonson's own stage directions (SD).

5 SOVEREIGN, GENERAL Here and throughout the play, Dol uses such elevated political terms to describe the agreement these rogues have entered into to cheat the public. Such imagery cuts two ways: first, it suggests the grandeur to which these swindlers pretend; and second, it implies that actual governments may be more than a little like a con game. In this alchemical world of grandiose pretensions, even the relatively hard-headed con men think they can make themselves over into kings, queens, and generals.

17 FRIARS The area of Blackfriars, just north of the Thames at the present Blackfriars station, got its name from the Dominicans or Black Friars who had a monastery there until the Reformation. Jonson lived there about this time, and, more interestingly perhaps, the players who first performed The Alchemist, The King's Men, had a "private" or indoor theater in this area. They also continued to play on the other side of the river at their "public" theater, the Globe. It is not certain at which of these theaters The Alchemist was played.

52–53 As butler, Face has been cheating the poor to acquire capital. "Chippings," leftover scraps of bread and crusts, and "dole beer," beer given to the poor, were supposed to be distributed free to beggars at the "buttery-hatch" of such wealthy houses as Lovewit's. Face has kept these for himself and sold the beer to distillers, "aqua vitae men," who made hard spirits from beer and wine.

74 QUARRELING DIMENSIONS Rules for conducting an argument, leading perhaps to a duel, in the right or fashionable manner. The English were, at this time, imitating the French and Italians in the elegant conduct of these matters, and it is this art which Kastril, later in the play, comes up to London from the country to learn. Shakespeare's Touchstone parodies this foreign nicety in As You Like It, and Mercutio in Romeo and Juliet displays scorn for Tybalt, the "Prince of Cats," who is a practitioner of the code of the duello.

94–99 "Coz'ning with a hollow coal" involved hollowing out a coal, filling the opening with gold or silver, "dust, scrapings," then stopping the hole with wax. When the alchemist added this coal to his fire, the wax melted, the metal ran into his pot, and the gullible victim would think that "projection" had taken place before his eyes. Chaucer described this trick in The Canterbury Tales, "Canon's Yeoman's Tale." "Sieve and shears" was a trick for finding "things lost" by sticking the blades of opened scissors into a wooden sieve, holding the sieve in *the air, reading out biblical verses, and then pronouncing names of suspected thieves. When the right name was sounded, the sieve would spin around. "Erecting figures" involved constructing a horoscope, the "houses" being the signs of the zodiac. The "glass" is either a mirror or crystal ball in which the seer saw spirits or "shadows" and queried them about the future. Face threatens to expose all these tricks in a vividly printed poster, "told in red letters," with a drawing of Subtle's face hideously done on it. Gamaliel Ratsey was a highwayman, executed in 1605, who wore a very ugly mask during robberies.*

112 STATUTE *A law prohibiting the practice of sorcery, including alchemy, passed in 1541, the thirty-third year of the reign of Henry VIII. The same law had been confirmed again in 1604, a few years before* The Alchemist *was written, and was not repealed until 1689.*

170–74 DON PROVOST . . . WORSHIP *A provost was a judicial officer, but here seems to be the hangman, who as part of his fee received the clothes of those he hanged. Dol is saying, "let him go on wearing his old clothes and not get even so much as a new garter from us." "Crewel" is a type of worsted cloth, and she puns from that meaning to "worsted worship," meaning the worst kind of gentleman, the hangman.*

Act I, Scene 2

17 READ'S MATTER *Simon Read, who had earlier been in trouble for practicing without a license, was charged with dealing with spirits in 1608, but pardoned. He had invoked these spirits to find out who had stolen a sum of money from one Toby Matthew.*

26 TURK WAS HERE *In 1607 a Turk named Mustapha arrived in England and persuaded people that while his title was only "chaush" or messenger, he was indeed an ambassador from the Sultan at Istanbul. He was royally treated, but the whole thing was a swindle, and the verb "to chouse" came to mean "to cheat."*

47–48 *"Five-and-fifty and flush" is a perfect hand, scoring fifty-five all in the same suit, in the card game of primero. Face is saying that Dapper is not one of those who look good but in fact reveal everything at the first chance, spitting out secrets as a man would spit out boiling hot custard he had taken a mouthful of.*

56–57 XENOPHON . . . POCKET *The quarto (Q) reading "Testament" was changed in F to "Xenophon," and the change from a reference to the Bible (the Greek New Testament) to a merely literary text like* Anabasis *is usually explained* by editors as a part of Jonson's attempt to meet in the 1616 text the government's prohibition in 1606 against swearing and blasphemy on the stage. In F, for example, he softened the oaths of Q, though Q was itself printed in 1612. But a reference to the "Greek Testament" seems hardly blasphemy, even in so profane a context. It seems more likely that the substitution strengthens the picture of Dapper as an aspiring young humanistic scholar who knew, or pretended to know, Greek and carried one of the basic texts around in his pocket to show his learning. That he took his oath in court on this book, rather than the Bible, may show that he really couldn't tell one from the other, or merely that he used any book handy for this purpose.

58 OVID *The Roman poet Ovid was popular at this time, particularly for his works dealing with love, such as* The Art of Love. *Reading him would show not only an educated ability to read Latin—a far more common skill than Greek—but a fashionable interest in love poetry. A young man struggling to be* au courant *like Dapper might well address his young lady in phrases drawn from Ovid's instructions on the art of loving. If so, it apparently had no effect, since the lady "forsook" him. See III.5.45.*

109 DEAD HOLLAND, LIVING ISAAC *John and Isaac Holland were Dutch alchemists of the fifteenth century, both presumably dead by 1610, so the "living Isaac" may refer to some other magician. To see the relationship between alchemists like the Hollands and gambling it is necessary to remember that such men, of the type Subtle is also pretending to be, were Magi, Hermetic Philosophers, for whom alchemy was only a physical manifestation of a larger command over the secrets of the universe. Thus they could as well call spirits and gamble successfully as change lead to gold, because they understood and commanded the spirits and powers which controlled all life.*

Act I, Scene 3

24–27 SACK-LEES . . . CLOUTS *Tobacco, still a fashionable rarity in England, usually arrived dried out and crumbled. There were different ways of increasing its weight, moistening, softening, and adding to its bulk, and, therefore, its price. Sack-lees are crumbled material;* muscadel *is the Spanish wine, muscatel;* grains, *a type of spice.*

30–31 MAPLE . . . JUNIPER *All first-rate equipment for a tobacconist. Leaf was cut and shredded on the maple block, smoked in the best pipes which were made in Winchester, lighted with a hot, sweet-smelling coal of juniper wood, which was held with silver tongs.*

55–57 *According to* Herford and Simpson, *Subtle has made a mistake here; but, more likely, he is using astrological jargon to create his own code or thieves' cant. The House of Life is governed by the sign ascending the horizon at the time of birth, and the "lord" is the planet which rules that sign. Libra is, however, ruled by Venus, not Mercury. But, leaving astrology aside, Mercury and Libra are both appropriate here. Mercury is the god of thieves, as well as the chief metal in alchemical experiments; while Libra is the scale used by merchants like Drugger to weigh merchandise. What Subtle is actually saying in an encoded fashion is that nimble thieves like himself and Face will rule gullible tradesmen like Drugger. This is only one of several places in the play in which the rogues use jargon or technical terms to bewilder their victims and to describe the con game they are working. For another example see II.3.102ff. Face and Subtle, like many con men, take a perverse delight in walking on the very edge of disaster and describing for the dupe the very swindle they are working on him, if only he were bright enough to understand.*

65–68 *These are the names of various angels or spirits governing east and north, respectively, when Mercury is dominant, as it is said to be in Drugger's horoscope. These good spirits are therefore "Mercurial" and will protect Drugger's stock from getting flyblown. Subtle, and Jonson, according to* Herford and Simpson, *are here making use of a particular book dealing with magic and spirits, the* Elementa Magica *of Pietro d'Albano, published about 1567.*

100 SMOKY PERSECUTOR OF NATURE *Smoky because of the soot from the alchemical furnace. The alchemist persecutes nature in the sense that he "follows" or "investigates" it in trying to turn base metals into gold; but "persecute" seems always to have carried the sense of some malignancy or wrong-doing, and so here the suggestion is surely that Subtle's art or science perverts nature, tries to make nature do what it does not properly or "naturally" do. This would run counter to Subtle's argument against Surly (II.3.130ff.) that alchemy only speeds up the workings of nature itself in changing base metals to gold.*

Act I, Scene 4

19 DISPENSING *The Philosopher's Stone, which changed base metal to gold, was also believed to be capable of healing all diseases, including old age. When used medicinally the Stone was usually known as "the med'cine" or "the elixir." As explained in Appendix I, changing metals to gold was believed to be a perfection of their original imperfect or unbalanced natures, and since sickness*

was also thought to be an imperfection or chemical imbalance, the Stone could function equally well on man or metal.

26–27 NATURE . . . STEP-DAME *The question dealt with in these lines, and again in the following scene, is crucial not only to this play but also to larger philosophical questions central to the Renaissance. What is involved is the relationship of art and science, the skill of men, to the workings of nature prior to the interference of art. To the romantic or the conservative, nature is the truer way and man's arts only pervert the workings of nature by interfering with her processes; but for an optimistic humanist such as Subtle pretends to be, or Mammon, though art may be a " step-dame" she is capable of speeding up the workings of nature (make her "ashamed of her long sleep") and thus giving men many more things and sooner than would be the case if nature were left alone. In one of the modern forms which this perennial question takes, Mammon would be on the side of those who want to control the environment with dams, fertilizer, and factories against those who favor ecology. Jonson's own more complex view in this matter is dealt with in Appendix I.*

Act II, Scene 1

2 NOVO ORBE *This term, carrying as it does some of the Renaissance excitement about the new worlds discovered by explorers and astronomers, links that excitement over the breaking beyond frontiers to the anticipation of wealth, knowledge, and power felt by the new science or philosophy, represented here by alchemy, and the general expectation of endless progress and endless profits felt by such entrepreneurs as Mammon. It is through such imagery as this, linking exploration, science, art, and mercantile aspiration, that we become aware that Jonson's true subject matter in this play is not some mere swindle, but nothing less than the optimistic spirit of the Renaissance itself, that general feeling of confidence felt in so many areas of life that the world was vast and rich, and that its space and riches were available to man through his art and his daring.*

4–5 OPHIR . . . THREE YEARS *One of the allegories of alchemy, of the type discussed by Mammon in II.1.89–104, was that Solomon was an alchemist who had found the stone and used it to manufacture great wealth at Ophir in Arabia. A passage in I Kings 10:22 describing the return of Solomon's fleet every three years with great treasure was taken to mean that the alchemical work required three years for projection.*

11–14 LIVERY-PUNK . . . COMMODITY *No two editors agree on the exact meaning of these difficult lines which conflate two additional ways in which young men "on the make," like Surly, managed to make a precarious living. The first of these practices is pimping, providing professional whores (who wear the "livery" or uniform of their trade) for rich young roisterers (the "young heir") who may desire a woman at any time and quickly ("in his shirt"). Although the* Oxford English Dictionary (OED) *does not list this meaning, "seal," from the shape of a seal's handle, could mean to have sexual intercourse. But "seal" in these lines seems also to refer to the second practice, the commodity swindle explained above in a note to "To The Reader." In this context the "seal" would be the emblem affixed by the young heir with his signet ring on the contract to borrow a sum of money, part of which was paid in "commodities." The passage suggests that bullies like Surly might be employed to beat the heir if he balked at the contract, and the heir might in turn, out of rage at being forced to accept the swindle, beat the messenger who brought him such useless items as vinegar, lute strings, etc. The passage remains difficult.*

17–21 *Mammon's inflated language, mixing epic and biblical terms, expresses his own superheated imagination, his tendency to transform even the meanest of events to poetic gold, just as he intends to transmute base metals into literal gold. But the exact sense of what he is saying is hard to come by. He is describing a scene at some gaming house and brothel in which the tough adventurers who are trying to make their fortune in London by fighting and gambling ("The sons of sword and hazard") have assembled to drink and shoot dice ("fall before the Golden Calf"). When they are broke they have to take up the only other trade available to them and join the army for the wars in the Netherlands ("after drum and ensign").*

64 NATURE NATURIZED *F. H. Mares in his* Revels *edition of the play points out that this is the created or artificial nature, natura naturata, of the scholastic philosophers, and therefore opposed to the creating force of nature itself, natura naturans. While this scholastic terminology is doubtless the source of the phrase, it would seem that by "naturized" Mammon means not a lesser form of nature but a more intensive "super-nature," nature "firked up in its center" as he puts it elsewhere. His understanding of the stone expresses the standard alchemical view that in making the stone no violation of nature is involved but only a discovery of the way nature works and the use of that knowledge to speed up the process.*

81–83 MOSES . . . ADAM *Writers on alchemy claimed that the heroes of earlier myths and legends had possessed the philosopher's stone and that their stories were properly interpreted as allegories of alchemical experiments. Moses and his sister, Miriam, along with Adam, were supposed to have worked miracles with the stone and written about its mysteries.* The Song of Solomon *was argued by some to be a disguised explanation of alchemy. Sir Epicure's version, below, of the story of Jason and the Golden Fleece demonstrates the way this method of explanation worked in detail.*

89–103 JASON'S FLEECE . . . DEMOGORGON *In his usual breathless way, Mammon is here giving a dense summary of various myths which the alchemists and magi argued were allegorical versions of the process by which base metals were changed to gold. The golden fleece, from a ram which was originally the present of Hermes or Mercury and for which Jason and the Argonauts adventured, was said to be in truth a manuscript revealing the secrets of alchemy. The Greek mathematician and mystic, Pythagoras, was believed to have a golden thigh. "Pandora's tub" is the famous box containing all the evils of the world, which she released through her curiosity. Medea, a sorceress controlling powerful magic or "charms," helped Jason to get the golden fleece and then returned with him to Greece. The Hesperian garden contained golden apples which Hercules found and took in his eleventh labor. Cadmus founded the city of Thebes by sowing the teeth of a fierce dragon he had killed. From the teeth armed men sprang up. The majority of them killed one another, but five remained to help build the city.*

Jove came to visit Danaë, of whom he was enamoured, disguised as a shower of gold. King Midas turned all that he touched to gold. Argus with his hundred eyes guarded Io, who had been turned to a cow by a jealous Juno, but was charmed asleep by Hermes, or Mercury. As a metal, mercury was the crucial ingredient in alchemy, and the fabulous figure Hermes Trismegistus was thought to be one of the original founders of alchemy and the hermetic philosophy. In Boccaccio's De Genealogia Deorum *Demogorgon is said to be the primal god or origin of all things; in other words, the "nature" sought by the alchemist.*

Lines 93–100 are an extended analogy, of a standard kind, of the story of Medea and Jason and the work of the alchemist. Jason was promised the golden fleece by the King of Colchis if he could first harness two fire-breathing, brass-footed bulls, plow a field with them, sow the furrows with teeth from the dragon killed by Cadmus, survive the attack of the armed men who would spring from the teeth, and then overcome a dragon which guarded the fleece. Jason accomplished all these feats by means of charms given him by Medea, the king's daughter, in return for a promise to marry her and take her back to Greece. He did take her back but did not marry her, with tragic results. Indeed, most of these stories about obtaining gold have unhappy endings, of which Mammon seems unaware.

In Mammon's interpretation Medea's magic is the alchemist's skill; his furnace the fire-breathing bulls; the argent-vive *or mercury, the dragon killed by Cadmus; and the teeth "mercury sublimate" or mercury which has been distilled and refined many times until something near its pure essence remains, is "fixed." Many details can be worked out, but the basic pattern of the comparison involves an arduous and dangerous task requiring many steps to win the gold.*

Act II, Scene 2

43–44 TIBERIUS . . . ELEPHANTIS *In the* Tiberius *(43) of the Roman writer Suetonius, several rooms furnished with indecent pictures and statuary by the Emperor Tiberius in his palace at Capri are described. Some of the works came from Elephantis in Egypt. The detail of the "beds blown up" (air mattress?) in line 41 is taken from another classical author, Lampridius, Elagabalus, 25. Jonson often borrowed such details from the classics.*

44 DULL ARETINE *Pietro Aretino, Italian poet and satirist (1492–1556) was notorious in England for his so-called "Postures" (Sonnetti Lussurioso, 1523), sixteen poems illustrated by pornographic drawings by the artist Guilio Romano. Mammon calls Aretino "dull," i.e. flat or stupid, because his work does not rise to the heights of Mammon's own imagination in sexual matters.*

48 MISTS *A device for achieving this luxurious effect is described in Suetonius, Nero, 31. Perfume, which Mammon proposes to waft about, was even more expensive then than now.*

50 LOOSE *This word can mean either "loose" or "lose" in Jonson, and most editors choose the latter meaning and change the Folio spelling. This makes sense, but I have chosen to keep the original spelling because its effect of "letting the self loose" or freeing the imagination totally seems more in keeping with what is happening in these lines. It is equally true, of course, that Mammon is indeed losing himself in this imaginary luxury. This ambiguity carried by the word "loose" in Jonson's English has been lost in modern spelling.*

63 WRIT . . . FART *In 1607 Henry Ludlow M.P. replied to a message brought from the House of Lords in a "peculiar manner." A poem, " The Fart Censured in the Parliament House" was written shortly afterwards, and Jonson in Epigram 133 refers to the matter:*

> *And sure, it was th' intent*
> *Of the grave fart, late let in parliament,*
> *Had it been seconded, and not in fume*
> *Vanished away. (107–110)*

Notes, Act II Scene 3

77 APICIUS *Marcus Gabius Apicius, a Roman gourmet (circa A.D. 30), noted for his gluttony and interest in exotic foods.* Apicius: The Roman Cookery Book *(trans. B. Flower and E. Rosenbaum, 1958) contains many of the rare foods referred to by Mammon. Apicius ate his way through an immense fortune and then hanged himself.*

Act II, Scene 3

30–31 TRIPLE ... SPIRIT *In making the stone or the "med'cine" the aim was an essence purified of all the grossness and imperfections of earth, all the imbalances of natural things. It would therefore be pure or "triple soul," "glorified spirit," the very idea of gold, not ordinary gold, whose power could then "project" itself into base metals and turn them to natural or ordinary gold.*

32 ULEN SPIEGEL *Til Ulenspiegel was a trickster and practical joker like Reynard the Fox, Br'er Rabbit, or Coyote. He first appears in German stories in the fourteenth century, and some of the tales were Englished in 1528. Subtle is primarily using the name for its solemn foreign sound to impress Mammon; but at the same time the name establishes the relationship of these con men, Face and Subtle, to that ancient line of tricksters who live by their wits and survive by fooling those who think themselves wise and important.*

96–99 FOR ... KEMIA *Here is another of those many places in the play in which the jargon, while remaining technically correct, is really being used by the rogues to describe the swindle they are working. The two "inferior works" at "fixation" are Dapper and Drugger—inferior because they will yield less gold than Mammon, and fixed because as much as possible has been extracted from them for the moment and they have been sent away with their hopes. The third work is, of course, Mammon who is very much in "ascension" as his greed leads him on to give more and more money. The "oil of Luna" may be bubbling merrily in the retort, but so is Mammon's lunacy actively leading him on to being swindled.*

This kind of dual signification of alchemy, identifying the chemistry with the swindle, helps to establish alchemy as not just the means of an elaborate confidence game but the governing symbol of the play which contains, defines, and judges all the various actions and persons of the drama.

102–07 EXALT ... VIRTUE *These lines describe the characteristic slow, step-by-step refining process the alchemists used to make the stone. But they also describe the ancient and traditional method by which the confidence man and his associates bring their victim (the "mark") to the point where he yields, even insists on giving, the maximum amount of money. The process is always one of whetting the greed of the mark by a series of encouragements interrupted by doubts and discouragements (dissolvings and congealings) until the climactic moment is reached.*

135–37 LEAD ... FURTHER *In accordance with Aristotelian views, it was believed that gold was the perfect state toward which all metals were moving. In nature the process took place slowly, and the alchemist merely speeded it up. He was therefore working in accordance with nature, as Subtle argues, not against it.*

142–70 Herford and Simpson (X.46) *point out that this argument is derived, word for word in places, from the Latin of Martin Del Rio,* Disquisitiones Magicae *(Louvain, 2 vols., 1599–1600). What is involved is a basic alchemical explanation of the workings of nature to produce metals. "Remote matter," the most basic material, is said to be composed of a kind of oily water and heavy earth. Nature itself is in the process of working slowly toward the development and refinement of this crude material, and if in that process the "elementary matter" which is common to all materials loses some of its moisture, it becomes a stone. If it loses some of its earthiness it turns into a mineral such as sulphur or mercury. In sulphur, which is a male or active principle, a fatty, earthy quality predominates; while in mercury, which is the female or passive principle, the airy, oily qualities predominate. Out of these two metals in some combination all the seven identified metals are made. The alchemist in his laboratory intensifies this natural process and makes gold, which is the end toward which nature herself is working; but that gold, Subtle says, is more truly gold than any which nature makes.*

199–200 ART ... ART *In our own time, when it is believed that the purpose of art and science is to make the mysterious clear and widely understood, it is difficult to understand a tradition in which it was thought necessary to obscure meanings to prevent the mysteries they explained from being profaned. But many writers in the Renaissance and earlier, believing that they were in touch with the infinite, thought of their writings as revelations which should only be understood by a select few of the initiates. The alchemists were among this group, and they had in addition the more practical reason that if their secrets were generally known, everyone would be able to make gold.*

208 SISYPHUS *A figure in Greek mythology who was condemned for his crimes on earth to roll forever a great stone up a steep hill in the underworld. Whenever he reached the top, the stone escaped him, rolled to the bottom, and he had to begin*

all over again. By interpreting Sisyphus' stone as the alchemical stone, Mammon illustrates the theory stated a few lines earlier that the "fables of the poets" were "Wrapped in perplexèd allegories."

230–33 PARACELSIAN ... RECIPES Paracelsus, Theophrastus Bombastus von Hohenheim (1493–1541), was one of the revolutionary figures in alchemy and science. He was chiefly noted as a physician and developed a theory about the use of chemical medicines or "mineral physic" as most effective in curing diseases. There was a good deal of magic mixed with some real science in Paracelsus' writings, and he could therefore be said to "deal all with spirits," but "spirits" may also refer to chemicals, especially since Paracelsus first used the term "alcohol" (Arabic, al-kohl, black eye paint) to denote distilled spirits. Galen (A.D. 130–210) was a Roman doctor whose "tedious recipes" or prescriptions were mostly herbal and formed the basis of the practice of medicine during the Middle Ages and much of the Renaissance. Paracelsus publicly burned Galen's writings in a pan of chemicals to show his contempt for the older herbal medicines.

238–41 BROUGHTON'S ... GENEALOGIES Hugh Broughton (1549–1612) was a scholar of the Bible and of the Hebrew language. In his A Concept of Scripture (1590) he attempted to establish the chronology of the Bible, and dealt therefore with the "genealogies" or long catalogues of "begats" listing the generations and ages of Old Testament figures, particularly in Genesis. Jonson puts a parody of Broughton's style in Dol's mouth in IV.5., where it becomes clear that this type of elaborate argument and strange scholarly jargon is another example of the many specialized "languages" spoken by the characters of the play; and another of many attempts of learned ignorance to pretend to absolute knowledge of the mysteries of the world.

329–30 BENCH ... VERMIN The general sense of getting a high office for Face, or Lungs, is clear, but which office is not so certain. Most editors have taken the meaning from "chain," which would be the chain of office worn by a steward in a great household. The combination of "bench," "chain," and "vermin," with its play on "ermine"—"vermin" was a term for weasel—could also suggest that Face is to be made a judge. It should be noted that the words "weasel" and "vermin" in this speech remind us that Face is in fact the ferret of line 80 who is sent into the rabbit's hole to drive him out into Subtle's net. As usual, Jonson makes his fools speak more truth than they know.

Act II, Scene 4

20 ANABAPTIST Jonson has chosen his representatives of Puritanism from the extreme left of that movement. The Anabaptists were one of the more rigid and extreme

sects of Puritans and violent against the established church, Roman, English, or Lutheran. They first appeared in Germany in the early 1500s and by the middle of the century were in England. They took their name from their belief in adult baptism, by immersion, and believed in community of goods.

Act II, Scene 5

8 LULLIANIST . . . ARTIS *Subtle pretends that Ananias means "brother" to refer to an initiate of alchemy, and he now wants to know which one of the many schools of alchemy Ananias follows. Raymond Lull, or Lully, was a thirteenth-century Spanish scientist, while George Ripley was an English monk of the fifteenth century who wrote a number of works on alchemy. "Filius Artis"—son of the art—would apply to any professional practitioner of the art of alchemy.*

28 TRINE . . . SPHERES *The seven spheres are the seven planets, including sun and moon, and a "trine circle" is a circle divided into three parts of 120° each. The times at which three of the planets were positioned to create such a trine were thought to be particularly favorable to earthly endeavor. Face seems to be saying that this particular part of the alchemical experiment should take place only when the planets are located in trine. Alchemy and astrology were always closely related, as they are in this play where Subtle practices both, because it was believed that all nature was one and all its parts sympathetic. The power which changed base metals to gold was a power ultimately derived from God or nature, which beamed itself through the stars and planets, whence it was focused by the alchemist on his experiment.*

37–39 ELEMENTS . . . DRY *The master-knowledge, Face is saying, is knowing how to change the elemental composition of materials in order to change one metal to another. In Aristotelian physics all earthy materials are thought to be some combination of four basic qualities, hot, cold, dry, and wet. A perfect substance, like gold, is usually said to contain all these qualities in exact balance, while more imperfect substances have a predominance of one quality or another, as wetness predominates in water. The task of the alchemist would then be to make gold by achieving an exact balance of qualities, and it is this shifting of elements which Face describes.*

47 DEAL *Jonson was among the first to notice that there is a close association between Puritanism and capitalism. Here Ananias tries to cover the fact that his sect drives hard bargains, even trades in stolen goods, by the hypocritical pretense that they only help out poor widows and orphans by buying their possessions. The "Saints" they must account to are the members of their own religion, since*

Notes, Act II Scene 6

> Puritans thought the traditional saints of the Catholic church a Popish abomination.

82–83 BISHOPS . . . HIERARCHY *The majority of Puritan sects, and particularly the Anabaptists, were violently opposed to the hierarchical government of the Roman Catholic church—Pope, cardinals, bishops, etc.—and therefore to the retention of bishops in the Anglican church. Finding no justification for these positions of authority in the Bible, the Puritans favored more democratic methods of church government such as the consistory mentioned above.*

Act II, Scene 6

1 SPIRITS *Subtle, as noted in the Introduction, is not merely an alchemist but a Renaissance magus as well, a man attempting to master all the secrets of the universe and control the power of the cosmos by what Jonson calls "panarchic knowledge." As such it was necessary for him to deal with the spirits who, below God, operated through the stars to influence the world of nature in which man lives. If the spirits with whom Subtle is busy are angels, then he is practicing natural or white magic; if they are demons or devils, then it is black magic. But Subtle's frequent references to working with nature and to the necessity for the magus-alchemist being a holy man place him in the tradition of white magic.*

20 DEE *Dr. John Dee (1527–1608) was an English mathematician, philosopher, and magus. He was deeply read in all areas of philosophy and science, and was consulted by many members of the court, including the Queen. He is thought by some scholars to have been the model for Subtle and he was involved, though perhaps innocently, with a sinister figure, Edward Kelley, who became his medium or "scryer," to produce alchemical gold for the Emperor Rudolph II in Prague. Kelley, who may have been the model for Face, is referred to in IV.1.90.*

24 HIEROGLYPHIC *The ancient Egyptian writing had not at this time, of course, been interpreted, but its mysterious and intriguing signs were thought to be symbols of great magical power—not the representations of phonetic qualities we now know them to be. Some hieroglyphs were known from certain alchemical and magical religious tracts thought to be written by a fictitious Egyptian sage Hermes Trismegistus, but actually written in the centuries immediately after Christ. Egypt in general was thought, then as now, to be the home of ancient mysteries and supernatural knowledge.*

61 QUARREL . . . WITS *Just as his sister has come to London to learn the latest fashions in manners and dress, Kastril the country squire has come up to learn the*

proper style of duelling, presumably from an Italian or French master, and the correct way of managing a quarrel, insults, challenges, etc. For a Shakespearean parody of this elegant way of quarreling see Touchstone's speech in As You Like It, *V.4.94 ff. As for "living by his wits" what presumably is meant is that Kastril wishes to learn the witty and clever ways of speaking considered appropriate for courtiers and young men of fashion, for example the way Romeo and Mercutio or Hamlet and Ophelia play witty word games.*

Act III, Scene 1

6 CANAAN *The Puritans found in the* Old Testament *not only the truth about God, but a history of the trials that they felt they themselves must undergo. In their reading they became the chosen people and their wanderings and sufferings identical with those of the Jews leaving Egypt. The Canaanites were heathen worshipers of idols who originally inhabited part of Israel. In the mouths of Tribulation and Ananias this biblical terminology becomes another of the many jargons or cant languages used in* The Alchemist *to pretend to great wisdom to cover base motives.*

33 MENSTRUOUS . . . ROME *Violently opposed to any symbolism or display of wealth in church or divine services, the Puritans hated the vestments worn by the Roman Catholic priests and retained by the established English church. Insofar as it makes any sense at all, the "rags of Rome" are "menstruous" or bloody because the Roman Church was identified as "the Whore of Babylon" and because the church was stained with the blood of the persecuted Puritans.*

Act III, Scene 2

23 HOLLANDERS *The Dutch had a powerful navy at the time which was largely used to protect their colonies in the East Indies. Subtle is suggesting that the Puritans can use their gold to hire mercenaries and use the Dutch fleet to attack England and set up their own religion.*

78–97 SCRUPULOUS BONES *The Puritans, partly to show that they were God's elect, and partly to manifest their desire for simplicity and plainness in all things of this world, concerned themselves at great length with matters such as these. They were against hawking and hunting because these were the sports of the nobility. Their women were forbidden to dress their hair in elaborate styles; or to wear the then-fashionable doublet or tight jacket, because it was originally the dress of a man and the Bible forbade either sex to wear the clothing of the other; or to use starch in their collars because this was a form of worldly vanity, as well as an aping of high fashion.*

The Puritans regularly attacked in print and speech the bishops of the Church of England, whom they considered remnants of Papism; and for these attacks they were sometimes punished by having their ears clipped, "shortened," in the stocks. They were notorious for the length of their sermons and prayers, particularly the grace before meat, which, Subtle says, was drawn out as "fine" (lengthy) as a piece of metal being spun into wire. Puritans were particularly vehement in their attacks on the theaters and playing because they believed the theaters to be the ultimate places of sin and vanity, where men pretended to be persons they were not in plays which showed wrong and immoral actions. These attacks earned them the undying hatred of playwrights like Jonson, but made them the allies of the aldermen and merchants of the City of London, who had Puritan leanings themselves and further disliked the theaters because they were sources of trouble, spread the plague, and provided workers with a way to waste time. For some reason aldermen seem always to be associated with "custards," deep pastrys covered with cream.

The extraordinary biblical and allegorical names the Puritans chose for themselves were a source of much amusement, and Jonson's best efforts to mock this practice—Zeal-of-the-Land Busy and Win-the-fight Littlewit—scarcely exaggerate the reality of such names as the famous Praise-God Barebones.

103–06 ART . . . SPIRITS *This passage may be taken as a series of generalized praises of the wonders of alchemy, but it is also a specific reference to the elaborate Hermetic and Cabalistic philosophies which were prime sources of Renaissance magic. Alchemy was but the practical or paradigmatic form of a much more elaborate system of thought which proposed to tap and use by various magical methods the powers of the stars and even God Himself. The Cabala, a medieval Spanish development of Hebrew mystical thought, sought through the arrangement of symbols and letters to invoke and use the numerous angels who were identified as controlling the various spheres of the heavens and radiating certain beneficial powers. Thus Subtle, Jonson's parody figure of the Renaissance magus, can speak of the stone as being "the art of angels." The knowledge that can make gold from baser metals was thought to be the essential energy and secret of the universe itself, the true working of God, not merely a scientific theory experimentally arrived at. It was therefore "the divine secret that doth fly in clouds." It moves from "east to west" not only because this was the geographical direction in which knowledge and civilization were thought to move, but because the knowledge of alchemy was thought to begin with the writings of Hermes*

Trismegistus in Egypt (the east). The "tradition Is not from men but spirits" because the secrets are revealed to men by spirits, and Hermes passed on not experimental knowledge but revelations he received of the mysterious workings of the universe.

113–14 REVELATION . . . TRUTH *The Puritans, to a greater or lesser degree depending on the sect, believed that a man knew the truth, particularly religious truth, not from education, tradition, or social custom, but in his own heart, by revelation. Religion was thus a matter between the individual and God, and no church or other form of moral authority was competent to tell or dictate to a man what is right or wrong. Only the Bible, which was the direct word of God, could be of help in achieving that sudden, necessary sense of identification with God. It is easy to see how such beliefs would outrage a learned traditionalist, a humanistic scholar, and a very social man like Ben Jonson.*

132 NINTH MONTH *Puritans sometimes refused to use the usual names for the months because they were derived from pagan gods and festivals. Ananias is using March as the first month of the year because Puritans believed it to be the month in which God made the world. The date he thus arrives at, using his nonconformist calendar, is November 1, which could be the date of the composition of the play or its performance. In V.5.102–03, however, he calculates the date as October 23.*

Act III, Scene 3

33 *This is the opening line, after the Induction, of a famous tragedy, Thomas Kyd's* The Spanish Tragedy *(1587–88). By 1610* The Spanish Tragedy *was a favorite joke, a representative of the old-fashioned, heroic ranting dramatic style of an earlier age. The line must, however, have had special poignance for Jonson since he apparently played the leading part in the play as a young actor in the late 1590s, and as an author may later have made certain additions to the play to bring it up to date.*

Act III, Scene 4

30–35 *See N. to II.6.61. There were such books as Face is describing here which dealt with the exact and proper way to manage a quarrel. The most popular was* Vincentio Saviolo His Practise. In Two Books, The First Intreating of the Use of the Rapier and Dagger. The Second, of Honor and Honorable Quarrels *(1595). It is in this second matter that Kastril is interested, and Face, using the image of an astrolabe or some other navigational instrument, is saying that the Doctor's "instrument" can tell you how seriously a quarrel is to be taken; whether honor is sufficiently involved that a death, "mortality," will be required; and whether a particular slight or insult should be met head-on or can be treated in a roundabout or oblique manner.*

38–39 OBLIQUE . . . DIAMETER *A man of honor might not have to fight if it were suggested in an indirect, "oblique," or roundabout, "circle," way that he lied. But he could not "take the lie," that is he would have to challenge, if he were directly and openly, "in diameter," called a liar.*

81 BOY *How widespread homosexuality was during the Renaissance is questionable. References to it in plays are not uncommon, but it generally appears in a sensational context and is treated as an extravagant vice, not a commonplace.*

90–99 COMMODITY *Face and Subtle are masters at working swindles on three or four levels at once. For example, having bilked Mammon of all his household goods, they then proceed to sell them to the Anabaptists, and are looking about for a third party to sell them to again. In these lines Face is describing a second-level swindle working off the commodity swindle described in the note to "To The Reader." The young man who took part of his loan in such commodities as pepper, soap, woad (a blue dye), etc., having no use for these things, usually left them in the warehouse. Knowing who owns them, where they are, and who will buy them, Kastril, Face suggests, can pick the goods up and sell them for ready money, without any danger of being discovered.*

142–47 SHILLINGS *Because the amount of precious metal in coins of the same de-nomination varied from reign to reign, it was necessary to name the ruler, whose face appeared on the coin and during whose reign it was minted, in order to know the value. Dapper has obviously dug deep into his hoardings for every odd coin he could scrape up, and they are from the reign of every ruler since Henry VIII, except Queen Mary I, who ruled jointly, in name at least, with Philip of Spain. Face remedies this by forcing him to dig deeper and produce a few from this period as well. The only real point to this numismatic history of English kings is, I believe, Dapper's extraordinary stinginess: he hangs on to every coin he gets. A "Harry sovereign" was worth ten shillings; a groat was fourpence (the small coin from Elizabeth's reign may suggest her famous parsimony); a noble came to six shillings and eightpence.*

Act III, Scene 5

SD PRIEST OF FAERY *It is difficult to imagine how one of the attendants of the Faery Queen would be dressed, but some outlandish costume suggesting magic is called*

*for. Though the trick played on Dapper here seems unbelievable, apparently a
similar swindle was actually worked at this time on one Thomas Rogers.*

Act IV, Scene 1

69 PHOENIX *A mythical bird of Arabia which begot itself. At the end of its five
hundred years of life it consumed itself in fire, and from the ashes took renewed
life again.*

85–89 *Mammon repeats here the basic view of alchemy given several times in the
play. The alchemist understands divine powers, and he recreates in the temperate
heat of his furnace the same powers, "virtues and miracles," which in nature the
sun uses to turn slowly the base elements to gold. But nature is slow, "dull," and
does not understand its own workings. The alchemist speeds up the process and
develops the theory.*

89–91 EMP'ROR . . . KELLEY . . . HIM *See N. to II.6.20. Edward Kelley, born
Talbot (1555–95), was the medium for the English mathematician and magus
Doctor John Dee, and the two of them may have been the models for Face and
Subtle. (See Appendix II on sources and stage history.) Kelley was first a
lawyer, but had his ears cropped for coining and forgery, and then persuaded Dee
that he could bring him voices from the spirit world, particularly from the angel
Uriel. The two went abroad together, but eventually quarreled and broke up.
By now Kelley claimed to be an alchemist and said he had the stone, which he
had received at Glastonbury. The Emperor Rudolph II invited him to come to
Prague to make gold for him, presumably enticing him with gifts such as the
"medals and chains" mentioned here; but when Kelley failed to produce gold,
the chains became the iron ones of a dungeon. Kelley tried to escape, broke his leg,
and died from the wound.*

133–34 CONSTABLE'S . . . ESSEX *A "hundred" was a judicial division of a county,
with its own court. Presumably the constable's wife might serve as the doctor in
some such small remote district in a county like Essex, to the northeast of London.
Such an ordinary life, of a kind that most people did and do in fact live, is not for
Mammon, who dreams of the luxuries of ancient Rome and the power of
empires. This passage shows perfectly Jonson's characteristic technique of quietly
opposing the reality of actual life to the incredible, unrealistic dreams of his heroes
about what life might be if only man had unlimited wealth and power.*

154 IDLE FEAR *Since the making of unlimited quantities of gold would destroy the
economy of any state, and the power of its ruler, alchemists were in fact imprisoned from time to time to prevent any threat of flooding the country with gold.*

Act IV, Scene 2

7 CURTAIN *It is generally believed that drop or draw curtains, of the sort Face seems to have in mind here, were not used in the Elizabethan and Jacobean theater. There are references, however, to the use of a curtain in theatrical situations in Volpone V.2.84 and in the stage direction in the same play at V.3.9. It may be that Jonson, who was actively staging masques in the court, is thinking of the use of drop cloths of painted scenery.*

23–28 *Face had earlier used geometrical and navigational terms to construct an "angry tongue" or language of quarreling. Subtle now draws on formal scholastic logic to break up and analyze the various steps by which quarrels were to be understood and conducted. In this way the basic fact of fighting is formalized and made complex and elegant. Jonson is here laughing at—and revealing as a sham, for the language makes little sense—that characteristic tendency of the Renaissance to transmute the basic realities of the world and human life into something very rare and complicated by constructing elaborate theories and learned languages around it. This instruction in the art of quarreling is of course but one instance, in little, of the basic theme of the play: false alchemy, the vain attempt to use art for the wrong motives and in the wrong way to outdo nature.*

43–47 RIVO FRONTIS, ETC. *A mixture of phrenology and palmistry. The "rivo frontis" is the frontal vein of the head. The "linea fortunae" is the line of fortune in the palm still examined by fortune tellers. The "stella" is a starlike mark on the "monte veneris" or "Venus' mount," the fleshy area at the base of the thumb, supposedly showing a disposition to love. The "junctura annularis" is the joint of the ring finger, which would receive the wedding ring. All these details, as a competent actor would make clear with his actions, suggest a readiness for passion or "pliancy."*

Act IV, Scene 3

46 MONSTERS . . . LION *This line more or less means "you shall see all the sideshows (displaying monsters of various kinds) in the fair and the biggest tourist attractions in town." "Lion" refers to the lions who were kept in the Tower of London and much visited.*

Act IV, Scene 5

2–3 PERDICCAS . . . PTOLEMY *Alexander's four generals, Perdicas, Antigonus, Selucus, and Ptolemy, divided his empire after his death. They fought among themselves, and Ptolemy and Selucus eventually destroyed the other two and founded the empires known by their names.*

4–16 TWO LEGS . . . JAVAN *The details of Dol's raving are taken for the most part from Hugh Broughton's* Concent of Scripture *(1590) in which he attempts to establish the historical chronology of the Bible. The passage involved here is that in which Broughton deals with Daniel, the interpretation of Nebuchadnezzar's dream of a great image with a head of gold, body of silver, thighs of brass, and legs of iron mixed with clay. A stone appears, breaks the image into many pieces, and then grows into a great mountain. As Daniel interprets the dream, the different portions of the image are the successive pagan empires, each less distinguished than the last, which eventually crumble away and give place to the kingdom of God, the stone mountain, i.e. the kingdom of the God of the Jewish people. Broughton sees the Ptolemaic empire (Egypt, the south) and the Selucid empire (Syria and the north) as the fourth kingdoms of the image, the two legs of iron and clay, which crumble at last to "Gog-dust" and "Egypt-dust." "Gog" (a corruption of God?) is the name of a pagan ruler who threatened the Jews (Ezekiel 38: 2–3), and thus suggests any pagan ruler. Broughton divided history into four periods or "chains," and destruction comes at the end, "the last link," of the fourth period. "These" who "be stars in story" refers to Broughton's description of those who bore witness to the true God, the Jews, "rabbins," and Greeks, "the heathen Greeks" or philosophers, of "Salem" (Jerusalem) and Athens, who understood Hebrew and Greek, "the tongue of Eber and Javan."*

This flood of jargon need not, of course, be understood in any more detail than the jargon of alchemy used by Subtle and Mammon. It is merely one more of the cant or specialized languages which fill the play. But as such it is also another instance of Jonson's central satiric target in The Alchemist: *the foolish attempt of men to know more than is truly possible by claiming some special inspiration or some elaborate science which penetrates the mysteries of nature and history. In Jonson's scheme, here and elsewhere, such attempts always mask the basest of motives—greed, lust, aggressiveness—and the mask always takes the form of a specialized and obscure language, such as Broughton's. This verbal masking has its physical equivalent in the play in the disguises or costumes worn by many of the characters, particularly Face, Subtle, and Dol, who shift, like the great actors they are, from one costume and role to others with lightning speed.*

34 FIFTH MONARCHY *The fifth Kingdom, the mountain of stone, referred to in N. to IV.5.4–16. This happy apocalyptic state when the world will be made perfect is referred to frequently in the Bible, e.g. in Revelations where it becomes the*

> *Millenium, and was still confidently expected by certain Puritans in Jonson's
> time and later, when there was a sect known as "The Fifth Monarchy Men."
> Mammon's Fifth Monarchy is not, of course, a state founded on religion but a
> new utopia; to use his term, a* Novo Orbe, *to be built with wealth and science.*

62–63 AS . . . PROVE *The alchemists are using against Mammon the tradition of
alchemy referred to earlier (II.2.97–105) which requires that those involved in
the experiment be as morally perfect as the gold they hope to achieve is physically
perfect. For further explanation see Appendix I. Face and Subtle are, of course,
only using the requirement of moral perfection to keep Mammon on the hook
longer by delaying the day when he would expect to see actual gold, but the
tradition of moral perfection does serve by its introduction here to provide an
ironic comment on the hopes of all these rogues and fools. Transformation of
themselves and the world to a golden state will come about only when men are
morally perfect, which is to say, never.*

Act IV, Scene 6

37–39 *This trick seems to involve using a boot, treated beforehand with brimstone,
as a touchstone. When gold was rubbed against it, it did not leave the distinguishing mark that true gold would on a real touchstone. This swindle sounds rather
unpromising.*

42 CLOSE *The trick here is to put some of the client's gold in a retort and switch it
without being noticed for one filled with mercury sublimate, which then explodes
when heated. Since the gold is supposedly lost in the explosion, it cannot be
returned to the owner.*

46 FAUSTUS *Doctor Faustus, originally an itinerant German sixteenth-century quack,
was, largely because of Christopher Marlowe's play* Doctor Faustus (1592),
*the archetype of the Renaissance magus, the man who risked his soul in a
bargain with the Devil in order to achieve a power which "stretcheth as far as
doth the mind of man." Subtle is the comic version of this tragic figure, and of
that other great magus of Renaissance drama, Prospero in Shakespeare's*
Tempest. *Prospero, like Subtle, but not like Faustus, practices white magic,
in which power is derived from good angels, not demons, and work is carried on
in conjunction with Nature, not contrary to its laws.*

49–53 BAWDS . . . SICKNESS *Subtle has, or is accused of having, a network which
sends him women with various troubles, usually sexual, for magical treatment.
He provides abortions, probably with some kind of medicine; makes charms for*

barren women to make them fertile; and cures young women of anaemia,
"green sickness." This latter disease is frequently associated with virgins, so sex
may be involved here too. At any rate, Subtle is functioning in these practices
as a male witch, or warlock.

Act IV, Scene 7

21–22 SPIRIT . . . IT *The magus drew down his powers from the heavens by invoking*
the various spirits or angels who governed the spheres of the cosmos. These were
God's angels doing his bidding, but there was always a danger that evil spirits,
demons and devils, would break into the communications. Face is saying that
one of these demons is controlling Surly, though he can only "trouble" the work
of Doctor Subtle, not really "harm" it, since in the Christian scheme of the
world evil powers cannot ever destroy the good.

53 UNCLEAN . . . SEVEN *This passage has never been satisfactorily explained.*
Seventy-seven may be a mistake for 1588, the year of the Spanish Armada, or
1567, the year the Duke of Alva invaded the Netherlands to quell the Protestant
uprising. It has been suggested that the line may refer to some strange birds with
ruffs found in Lincolnshire and described in a pamphlet of 1586.
"Unclean birds" with ruffs seems obviously, however, to suggest some
scavenger, like a buzzard or vulture, eating the dead after some catastrophe.
It may also be a reference to Revelations 18: 2, which speaks of the "unclean . . .
bird" who inhabits Babylon after the fall of the city.

Act V, Scene 4

44–47 *Dapper is commanded not to play in little games with street peddlers (coster-*
mongers) but in the big games in the best places and with the best people.
"Mumchance" was a simple dice or card game played in silence, "mum";
"traytrip" was a dice game in which three was the winning number; "God-
make-you-rich" was a form of backgammon. "Gleek" and "primero" were
more fashionable card games.

Act V, Scene 5

14 BEL . . . DRAGON *The title of one of the books of Apocrypha, the uncanonical*
books of the Old Testament. It tells how the prophet Daniel overcame two idols
worshiped by Babylon: a brazen image (baal) and a dragon. This reference is
characteristic of Jonson's dramatic technique: on the first level it is simply noise,

the biblical cant of a pious hypocrite; but, without the speaker being aware of it, it comments on the main action of the play, which also deals with the worship of idols, the false gods of money (the brass image) and the dragon of alchemy and false science. The image may apply even further, for just as Daniel defeated the idols, so is Lovewit at this point exposing and driving out the false images of the various "heathen" of this play. Jonson's learning is elaborate and "curious" (to use his own term), but it is used precisely and this is, I believe, a good example of the kind of careful work that characterized true "art" for Jonson. It required extensive labor in composition, but in the end this kind of knowledge and work distinguished his own well-made comedies from the slovenly work of most of his contemporaries. As Jonson put it in his introductory verses to the Shakespeare Folio of 1623, "Who looks to cast a living line must sweat."

158–59 MY . . . DECORUM As a neoclassical critic and writer, Ben Jonson was most concerned to maintain the neo-Aristotelian rules for writing well, such as the unities of time, place, and action. Prominent among these "rules" was the principle of decorum, the requirement that a work or its individual parts be internally consistent. That is, that a low character speak in a low, not a high, style; or that kings and clowns should not appear in the same play (though they in fact did in most Renaissance English plays, to Jonson's great disgust). The aspect of decorum referred to here applies to the consistency of characters, who were supposed to maintain their leading type characteristic throughout a play, and not to change suddenly and radically as they do in many romances and Shakespearean plays. Face, and Jonson behind him, is concerned that his shift from the absolute rogue Face to the merely scheming Jeremy in the last act may be thought a "fall" in the part. But we are reassured that decorum has not been broken, which means, I take it, that Jeremy is as much a rogue as Face, and that he does good here at the end only with an eye to saving his own skin.

Appendix I: Jonson's Use of Alchemy and a Glossary of Alchemical Terms

While the practice of alchemy is very ancient, going back at least to the workshops of old China and of first-century A.D. Greek Alexandria, whose theories were transmitted by the Arabs to the Christian West in the eleventh or twelfth centuries, it is well to remember that alchemy was never, as we would define it, a true science. Therefore, though a multitude of books and treatises were written on alchemy between the first and the eighteenth centuries, there was not and never could be any agreement on the exact meaning of certain basic terms, nor on the processes and techniques of alchemy. As a result, as Surly notes in the play, we cannot ever be sure precisely what terms mean, nor can we expect that the explanations of how alchemy works will be completely logical or in agreement with one another. In what follows, I merely offer the most common knowledge about the subject of alchemy, knowledge which Jonson took for granted, and supply those explanations which fit most closely the system of alchemy referred to in the play.

With his usual thoroughness, Jonson prepared himself to write *The Alchemist* by reading a number of books on the subject. He was, for example, familiar with Chaucer's "Canon's Yeoman's Tale," and with the dialogue "De Alcumista" from the *Colloquies* of Erasmus, as well as the *Disquisitiones Magicae* of Martin Del Rio. Those interested in further information about Jonson's alchemical sources should consult Volume X, pages 46–47, of *Ben Jonson*, edited by C. H. Herford and Percy and Evelyn Simpson (Oxford, 1950), and an article by E. H. Duncan, "Jonson's *Alchemist* and the Literature of Alchemy," *PMLA* 6 (1946). While Face and Subtle may use the language of alchemy only as a spiel to take in the gullible, Jonson saw to it that the terms and the theories they used were authentic.

Whether Jonson actually believed in alchemy or not is now, I believe, impossible to say with certainty. In his own age, there were many skeptics on the subject, such as Sir Francis Bacon, while there were other distinguished thinkers up to and including Newton who believed that it was indeed possible to turn lead into gold by alchemical methods. When, for example, Sir Walter Raleigh was imprisoned in the Tower of London, he engaged in alchemical experiments, and Queen Elizabeth hired at least one alchemist to produce gold for the state. The views on the subject, then, were mixed; but our concern should probably not be with the unanswerable question of whether Ben Jonson the man believed in alchemy, but with how Jonson the dramatic poet used alchemy in his play. And on this point, the evidence is, I believe, clear. As Face and Subtle use alchemy it is a pure swindle, a lot of meaningless big words and a fake laboratory. And as Sir Epicure Mammon and the Brethren understand alchemy, it is an impossible scheme for getting rich and powerful as quickly as possible, an image of the confidence of the new men of the Renaissance in their ability to change their world absolutely by means of trade, science, and art to a condition of endless riches and pleasure.

But Jonson is the supreme ironist always, and in all of his plays the flood of big words and bright images which his characters spout have meanings deeper and more extensive than the speakers know. In *The Alchemist*, the language of alchemy is at the first level only the patter of the con man, designed to impress and hypnotize the victim so that he may be more easily swindled. But gradually, the audience becomes aware that the terms of alchemy are constructing behind the play a great scheme of an evolutionary Nature working in her own right, ever so slowly, toward the perfection of the world and man. Jonson, himself the great artist who always emphasized the power of art, obviously believed, as his literary criticism clearly shows, that art—and the art of the poet, particularly the comic poet, is not so different from the art of the alchemist—could work in conjunction with nature to improve the world. For Jonson, however, as for Shakespeare, true art was not invented but derived from nature, and it worked in the same way nature did to achieve the same ends. It is this concept of art and alchemy, this scheme of the true workings of Nature, which takes shape gradually below and behind the surface of the play, to provide ultimately a savage judgment on the greed of the characters and their wild notions about being able to transform themselves, life, and the world into the purest gold, instantly and magically. To understand this basic conception of nature lying behind the play it will be necessary to look briefly at the basic alchemical ideas which Jonson used.

Alchemy was based to a large degree on Aristotelian chemistry. In the Aristotelian system all materials ultimately derived from some crude, basic, primary stuff, which in *The Alchemist* is called "remote matter." This remote matter developed first into the four basic elements which compose the universe: water, earth, air, and fire, listed here, as was usual, in ascending order of purity. There was sometimes said to be a "quintessence," or fifth element, more pure or spiritual than the others, and the source of form in the others. These elements were defined as mixtures of four qualities, wet, cold, dry, and hot. Water is, of course, a mixture of cold and wet, while fire is dry and hot, etc. All other matter, including all metals, was made of some combination of these basic qualities and elements. The alchemists also assumed that the basic elements first took the form of two fundamental materials, mercury and sulphur. In a later chemical system, that of Paracelsus, a third basic material was added, that of salt. The metals were ranked according to purity and value, with lead being the lowest and gold the highest. Perfection was said to result from a perfect balance of the basic qualities and elements. In other words, the lower on the scale the metal, the more one quality or another will predominate; but in gold, the perfect metal, the elements were said to be in absolute balance.

The world of matter was not thought of as fixed and unchangeable but as in constant movement, with one metal changing to another. Underlying this flux in nature, however, there was believed to be a fundamental movement toward perfection, which in practice meant that nature was on its way, slowly, toward changing all other materials into gold. Existing gold was simply that material which had already arrived at the end of the natural process. It was considered the business of the alchemist simply to speed up this natural process, or as Mammon puts it, "to firk up nature in her own center."

The actual technology of alchemy, while incredibly elaborate in its details, was really quite simple in its basic operation. (Since it never worked, the details tended, of course, to become more and more elaborate.) The alchemist's basic materials were mercury or quicksilver, which was believed to have the volatility or changeability necessary to the experiment; sulphur, which was believed to have the combustibility and right color for making gold; and, at least in the Paracelsian system, salt of some variety, believed to be necessary to fix the golden color on the mercury base. Working with these basic materials, the essential process of alchemy, no matter how elaborate the various steps, involved the refinement of the initial material by repeated application of heat of varying intensity. I think it would not be wrong to say that the essential process was one of distillation, but a distillation repeated again and again and again, with the product of each stage subjected to further refinement. Most of the variety of names given to the alchemical processes are simply variant terms for some refining process. The desired ultimate result was the destruction of all impurities and the achievement of the perfect balance of the basic elements and qualities to produce the "philosophers' stone" by which other materials could be changed into gold. The sequence of colors through which the materials passed during the experiment was considered of crucial importance. While authorities did not, of course, agree on what the exact sequence should be, the general pattern begins with black and moves through a number of other colors to intense red, the last considered the color announcing the climax of the experiment. It should be understood that the philosophers' stone was not merely ordinary gold but, somehow, the quintessential gold, the very essence or form of gold. Because it was this spirit or essence of gold, a mere touch of it on baser metals was sufficient for "projection," that is, the transformation of lower matter into gold. In another form, usually called "the elixir," the end product of alchemy was thought of as being the supreme medicine, capable of making a man healthy by balancing his various "humors" or bodily fluids, just as the stone brought the qualities of metals into perfect balance.

If this were the end of the matter, alchemy would be simple. But so far we have spoken of only the chemical side of the art, and to complete our discussion we must say at least something about the esoteric or magical side of alchemy. Modern science has achieved remarkable results by being as objective as possible and isolating its objects of investigation from all unnecessary connections with other things to achieve the condition of "laboratory purity." But the human mind does not ordinarily work in this logical fashion to isolate things; it seeks instead to build up systems of relationships between things, as intricate and as extensive as possible, as in poetry. The psychiatrist C. G. Jung understood alchemy as just such an attempt to unite subjective and objective. And he was right, for alchemy was in actuality the most incredible union of magic, astrology, religion, and a host of other arcane arts. Its theory was drawn from the esoteric writings of the Egyptians, the Babylonians, the Greeks, the Jews, and the Arabs. The actual chemistry of the alchemical experiments was, to put it one way, no more than a symbol or visible material form for a much larger and extensive process in which all things are ultimately linked to all other things, and all powers interact with all other powers. Thus Subtle is not only the alchemist but the learned Doctor, the man who has mastered palmistry and phrenology, who can concoct love potions, command spirits to aid the gambler, and manipulate astrological symbols and signs to magical ends. In alchemy, each thing was a part of all things and corresponded with specific events or things on other levels of being. Thus, for example, mercury is female, influenced by the movements of the planet Mercury, related to all other white things, and linked closely to the human emotions of excitability and changeability. It was the business of the alchemist, or the "magus" as he would have been called in his larger role, to line up all of the correspondent parts of the universe in a favorable fashion in order to make the experiment work. The result of such proper alignment would be that the powers which were diffused from God through the angels and essences above would flow down through the appropriate stars to the experimenter (who must be in the proper moral or equivalent emotional state), and then ultimately into the metals or raw materials being worked on in the experiment. Gold was the most perfect of metals, and therefore the man who made it must be in the most perfect moral state, as pure as the fiery sun which is the astrological equivalent of gold. Only if all of the proper elements were in conjunction or correct alignment could base metal be changed into gold. It is this mystical belief, which has little to do with chemistry but a great deal to do with magic, which is frequently referred to during the course of the play. Surly and Mammon refer to this tradition in II.2; and Face and Subtle use it to cheat Mammon in IV.5, where the entire experiment is conveniently destroyed because Mammon has had lustful thoughts about Dol, and thus was not as morally pure as the gold he was trying to make.

As the play notes, the making of gold was a dangerous business, and alchemists were looked on with great suspicion by rulers whose currency might be destroyed by an excessive amount of gold appearing in the state. But the alchemists took advantage of this political fact to argue that most of the alchemical documents of the past had necessarily been written in some sort of code or under the cover of allegory, of the kind Mammon describes to Surly in II.1, in order to preserve the secrets and the safety of the alchemist. The art was believed to be very old, going back as far as the time of Adam and Eve and known to the Patriarchs of the Bible as well as such mythical figures as the strange Hermes Trismegistus. It was generally believed by Renaissance scholars that the knowledge of the ancients, who knew more because they lived at the beginning of things and therefore closer to God, had been lost in the Fall and in the process of sinful time, but that a sufficient amount of reading and industry would enable the philosophers of the present to unlock the old secrets and the old stories with keys discovered through long study. Alchemy, at least during the period that Jonson wrote about it, was then a part of that larger Renaissance dream of the ability of man through the power of his art and knowledge to rediscover and use the secrets of God Himself to change the universe to conform to his own desire.

Those who wish to know more about the details of alchemy will find it convenient to begin their study in two books: Wayne Shumaker, *The Occult Sciences in the Renaissance, a Study in Intellectual Patterns* (Berkeley, 1972); and E. J. Holmyard, *Alchemy* (Baltimore, Penguin Books, 1957). Those wishing a Renaissance discussion of alchemy may find it helpful to consult Elias Ashmole, *Theatrum Chemicum Britannicum* (London, 1652).

GLOSSARY OF ALCHEMICAL TERMS

ABLUTION washing away impurities.

ADROP lead.

ALEMBIC vessel for distilling, consisting of a globular flask for heating and a long tube or HELM for carrying away the vapor.

ALUDELS pear-shaped pots, open at both ends, which were fitted together, joints sealed, to make a condenser.

AMALGAMA joining other metals with mercury.

AQUA REGIS "noble water," i.e. acid.

ASCENSION refinement.

ATHANOR furnace designed to maintain a constant slow heat.

AZOCH mercury—from Arabic *az-zaug*.

BALNEO bath. A substance heated *in balneo* was placed in sand for a slow even heat. *Saint Mary's bath* was water, while *balneo vaporoso* involved suspension in steam or vapors.

BEECH considered the best source of charcoal used for heating furnaces.

BLOOD the deep red color indicating the near-culmination of the alchemical process.

BLUSH turn red.

BOLT'S-HEAD round flask with a long neck.

BUFO literally "the toad" (Latin). The black color appearing early in the experiment.

CALCINE reduction to a fine powder by process of heating and drying out a substance. The product is CALX.

CERATION mixing a fluid and a powder until a substance of waxlike quality is reached. From Latin *cera*, wax.

CHIBRIT sulphur.

CHRYSOPOEIA gold-making (Greek).

CHRYSOSPERM seed of gold.

CIBATION one of the major techniques of alchemy, involving the infusion of liquids into a substance which has been dried.

CINERIS firing, heating.

CITRON yellow, one of the colors reached at an advanced stage of the experiment.

COHOBATION repeated distillation process in which the distillate is again distilled, etc.

COMPLEXION the color of the experiment at any given time.

CONGEAL solidify, as when a liquid is heated until it becomes solid.

COR'SIVE WATER acid.

CRIMSON one of the hues of red, the climactic color of the experiment.

CROSSLET iron melting pot.

CROW dark blue or deep black, one of the promising colors in the sequence.

Appendix I

CROW'S HEAD refers to same color.

CUCURBITE retort.

DRAGON mercury, quicksilver.

DULCIFY sweeten, i.e. refine the salts from a substance.

ELIXIR the end product of alchemy, the "med'cine" or essence used to change base metals to gold. When called the elixir it often refers to a fluid which confers eternal life and health on anyone who takes it.

EQUI CLIBANUM gentle heat supplied by decaying horse manure.

EXALT raise up, process of continuing refinement of materials.

FECES dregs or sediment left over after refinement. Considered the basest of materials, which must necessarily be removed in order to reach the essence or soul of metals.

FERMENT a refined or purer form of a substance.

FIMUS EQUINUS the lowest and slowest form of heat, provided by decaying horse dung.

FIRMAMENT a blue stone or a blue color appearing at a stage of experiment (?).

FIXATION fixing a volatile substance into a stable compound.

FLOWER the essence of a substance, produced by repeated refinement. Thus, "flower of the sun" is the very essence of gold, the stone.

FLY OUT evaporate, explode and escape in fumes.

FUMO vapor.

FURNUS ACEDIAE "furnace of sloth" (Latin). The same as "Piger Henricus," a multiple furnace to which heat is supplied from a single fire.

GLORIFIED SPIRIT essence raised to its most intense form.

GREEN LION lime compound. One of the colors, and its animal analogy, like the black crow, or the blood of the lamb, reached during the process of the experiment.

GRIPE'S EGG an egg-shaped vessel used for boiling. A "gripe" is a vulture.

GROUND residue left over after distillation.

HEAUTARIT mercury (Arabic).

HELM the tube or trough leading out of the top of a flask used for distillation. Coming "over the helm" was the beginning of the process of evaporation, or refinement of spirit. "Jason's helm" is Jason's helmet, from which he sowed the dragon's teeth, but this is taken by Mammon as a cryptic reference to the alchemical helm.

HERMES' SEAL closing off a tube by heating and twisting closed.

HETEROGENE of more than one kind, i.e. a compound.

HOMOGENE of only one kind, i.e. an element.

IGNIS ARDENS the hottest fire, to which the material is subjected in the latter part of the experiment.

IMBIBITION saturation and supersaturation.

INCERATION see "ceration."

INCOMBUSTIBLE a sulphur, or some material incapable of reduction.

KEMIA (al)chemy; the alchemical process.

LAC VIRGINIS dissolved mercury.

LAPIS MINERALIS "the mineral stone": "perhaps . . . thought of as the *matrix* or mother of minerals" (F. H. Mares, *Revels edition*).

LAPIS PHILOSOPHICUS the philosopher's stone, the medicine or essence of gold used to transmute base metals into gold.

LATO brass-like compound.

LIMBEC see alembic.

LIQUOR liquid. "Liquor of Mars" is molten iron.

LUNA the astrological sign for silver.

LUNARY an herb, but here "silver."

LUTE clay used to pack joints in the chemical apparatus, making them airtight.

LUTUM SAPIENTIS a paste used for closing the mouths of vessels quickly.

MACERATE to soften by placing in liquid.

MAGISTERIUM "the mastery," the philosopher's stone or summit of the alchemist's work.

MAGNESIA a thick salty water.

MALLEATION hammering. The distinctive mark of metals is that they can be expanded by hammering.

MARCHESITE iron pyrites.

MARRY to combine. A good instance of the way in which metaphor was treated as scientific fact in alchemy.

MARS the astrological sign for iron.

Appendix I

MARTYRIZATION the various processes of reduction to which the materials were subjected.

MED'CINE the philosopher's stone or the great elixir; the essence of gold.

MENSTRUE solvent.

MENSTRUUM SIMPLEX the most basic form of solvent.

MOON astrological sign for silver, *luna*.

MORTIFICATION process of change or breakdown of materials into components.

NIP to seal a tube or vessel.

OIL any thick, as opposed to watery thin, liquid compound. "Oil of Luna" would be a thick silver mixture, while "oil of height" would be some variety of essential fluid.

OLEOSITY oiliness.

PANTHER "the spotted panther" was, along with "crow" and "toad," one of the animated colors appearing during the course of the experiment.

PEACOCK'S TAIL another of the colors appearing at a certain point in the experiment.

PELICAN glass or clay vessel with spout at top which curved to enter again at the bottom, thus permitting continuous refinement and recirculation.

PHILOSOPHER'S VINEGAR either mercury or a corrosive vinegar made from mead.

PHILOSOPHER'S WHEEL the various stages in the production of the stone were often represented in the form of a wheel or circle.

PHILOSOPHER'S WORK the stone or great med'cine.

PHLEGMA watery distillate.

PIGER HENRICUS a "lazy Henry," a multiple furnace requiring only one central fire.

PLUMED SWAN the color white, and its animal equivalent, achieved at an advanced stage of the successful experiment.

POWDER the philosopher's stone ground into powder form for projection.

PROJECTION interpenetration of the matter to be transformed by the powers of the stone—the act of transforming base metal to gold.

PUTREFACTION the breaking down of compounds and reduction of materials, one of the stages in production of the stone.

QUALIFY dilute.

QUINTESSENCE the "fifth essence," or the pure and spiritual component to be found in all matter along with the other four Aristotelian elements, earth, water, air, and fire. In a sense the "philosopher's stone" was the quintessence of metals or gold.

RECEIVERS vessels used to trap and contain distillates. Also slang for "fences," or "receivers of stolen goods."

RECEPIENT a "receiver" or vessel for containing distillates.

RECTIFY purify, refine, distill.

RED the climactic color toward which the experiment moved. Deep red was considered the color of gold, and its appearance in the proper color sequence of the alchemical process signalled success.

RED MAN sulphur, "red" because of its golden color, and "man" because in the union with mercury it represented the masculine or penetrating principle.

REGISTER damper controlling the flue and thus the heat of the furnace.

RETORT glass vessel with long curved neck used for distillation.

REVERBERATING heating with indirect or reflected heat.

ROBE "Bright Sol is in his robe": Sol or the sun is the essence of gold, and so to be "in his robe" means that he is ready to loose his power, i.e. that the "stone" is made.

RUBY an intense red, the climactic color in the sequence.

SAINT MARY'S BATH a soft form of heat achieved by placing materials in warm water.

SAL salt, considered, along with mercury and sulphur, by Paracelsus and his followers to be one of the three basic metals. In alchemy the function of salt was to fix the golden color of sulphur in the material transformed.

SALT OF MERCURY mercuric oxide.

SAND HEAT a "bath" of heated sand, or heating in a bed of sand.

SANGUIS AGNI "the blood of the lamb," one of the reds indicating the success of the experiment in producing the stone. "Blood of the Lamb" is also a name for Christ, Whose sacrifice to obtain eternal life for man was often treated as an analogue to the mortification of metals in alchemy to obtain the perfect and eternal metal, gold.

Appendix I

SAPOR taste. The "sapor pontic" is a sour taste, while "sapor styptic" is slightly sweeter.

SERICON a tincture of red.

SILVER POTATE silver in liquid form.

SOL the sun, the astrological sign for gold.

SOUL the essence or spiritual quality in a material. Alchemists sought the "soul" of gold, which was the stone or elixir.

SPAGYRICA a compound word meaning to separate and to combine. Used in connection with the alchemy of Paracelsus.

SPIRIT in alchemy the word refers to the spiritual, non-material essence informing matter.

STATE OF GRACE in the magical or esoteric type of alchemy used in this play by Subtle it was believed necessary to bring the raw materials and the spiritual condition of the experimenter into coordination. Thus, in order to achieve the purest and most spiritual of metals, the essence of gold or the stone, it was requisite that the alchemist be in an equally advanced moral condition, i.e. a state of grace.

STONE the philosopher's stone, great medicine, magisterium, or elixir, the essential gold which was the end sought in alchemy. A touch of it could turn base metal to gold.

SUBLIMATION vaporization and distillation to purify a substance.

SULPHUR one of the two basic materials on which the alchemist worked, and considered one of the fundamental metals, along with mercury, in the composition of all other metals. Its yellow-red color suggested a close association with gold. "Sulphur o' nature" is a very pure form of the element.

SUN the astrological sign, and astronomical equivalent, of gold.

SUSCITABILITY volatility.

TALC material in powdered form.

TERRA DAMNATA the sediment or residue left after distillation.

THIRD REGION the highest and purest plane of the universe.

TINCT, TINCTURE color, or, sometimes, quality.

TOAD bufo, the animal name given to the black colored sediment.

TREE OF LIFE the essence of gold (?). The knowledge of how to make the stone (?).

TRIPLE SOUL thrice refined or powerful essence. Three is an important number in alchemy, referring to the Trinity and the arch-alchemist, Hermes Trismegistus or "thrice great Hermes."

TURRIS CIRCULATORIUS "circulating tower." An elaborate apparatus for constantly refining and recirculating material for further refinement.

TUTIE impure zinc oxide.

VENUS the astrological sign for copper, often mixed with gold.

VEXATION the constant working and subjecting to fire of the materials used in the experiment.

VINEGAR used as mild acid in experiments.

VIVIFICATION refinement to extract pure metal from compound.

WHITE the swan, a pure white color produced during the process of experiment. The WHITE WOMAN is Mercury, the female principle. To say an experiment has a WHITE SHIRT on is to say that it has reached the color white. A white oil or talc would be substances turned white, or some compound of mercury.

ZERNICH trisulphide of arsenic (Arabic).

Appendix II: Text, Sources, and Stage History

The Alchemist was probably written and certainly produced in the year 1610. A quarto version (Q), the usual cheap form of printing of Elizabethan and Jacobean plays, appeared in the year 1612. In 1616 the first folio (F_1) a collected edition of Jonson's works written up through the year 1613–14, appeared, which included *The Alchemist*. A second folio (F_2) was printed in 1640. All three texts derive from one another: F_1 was printed from a corrected copy of Q, and F_2 was printed from F_1.

Renaissance English playwrights did not as a rule pay much attention to the care with which their plays were printed. Ben Jonson, however, considered himself "a dramatic poet," not a mere working writer of stage entertainments, and thought of his plays as being works of art. When it came to the printing of the 1616 folio edition of his works, he took the unusual step of preparing the texts himself, reading proofs, and even to some extent designing the book. As a result, we have in the 1616 folio text of *The Alchemist* the play, with the exception of a few errors, as the playwright himself wished to fix it and transmit it to us. The principles on which changes have been made in this original text in order to make it more useful to a modern reader are explained in the "Preface of the General Editors."

Despite Jonson's concern that the printers of the folio get his text right, the actual changes made in the original quarto text (Q) which he corrected are not as extensive as might be expected. There are a few excisions, some additions, and a number of substitutions of different words and phrasings,

241

none of which seriously affect meaning. (Where the changes are substantial and important they are recorded in the notes of the present text.) Perhaps the most noticeable change Jonson made was in the stage directions. Q contains only one stage direction, but F_1 has a large number of quite explicit directions for movement and action, which add a great deal to the play and give us some feel for the way Jonson conceived of movement on the stage. There had been at an earlier date a prohibition against the use of oaths and swearing on stage, and the F text removes and tones down a number of oaths appearing in Q, which might by this time have been considered offensive. (There is still, however, a good deal of swearing of a moderate sort left in the text.) In addition, Jonson also took a great deal of care with the punctuation of the F text. There are those scholars who believe that Jonson developed in F_1 a perfectly consistent though complicated system of punctuation which should be exactly reproduced in modern editions. It is my own belief that while Jonson did punctuate with great care, concerned less for logic and grammar than for an attempt to indicate the way in which the line should be pronounced, that he never really achieved anything so formal as a system. Furthermore, the fact is inescapable that the text must now be read—even before it can be acted—and that much of Jonson's original punctuation makes understanding difficult, at times nearly impossible. The present text frankly represents a compromise between Jonson's dramatic punctuation and modern expectations of logic; but any reader wishing to see the way in which Jonson actually pointed can refer to the almost exact reprint of the play in *Herford and Simpson*. A reader consulting this volume will also be able to see the elaborate typography which Jonson employed, presumably in an attempt to make his meaning even more explicit. He was a tenacious and a thorough man, determined that posterity would read *his* texts and understand *his* meaning.

SOURCES

Jonson also differed from other contemporary playwrights in the matter of sources. Most playwrights of the day, Shakespeare included, drew on old collections of stories and historical materials for their basic plots. In this practice, they were, of course, doing what most authors have always done. The Greek playwrights of the classical period, for example, did not invent their own plots but drew them from the store of mythical tales common to the culture. Inventiveness lay in the variation of common plot structure, not their creation. Jonson's practice, however, was not to borrow a story but rather to use a theatrical "type" plot as a central structure, fleshing it out with a great variety of details drawn from a wide range of sources, both classical and contemporary. In *The Alchemist* the fundamental plot is a farce-type of a familiar kind. The type has no name, at least so far as I know, but is well known in some form to every theater-goer. The plot always involves a pair of confederates, often a husband and wife, whose task it is throughout the play to make sure that several people, all of whom are coming and going rapidly, do not meet together on stage. When they do meet, as always happens from time to time to increase the tension, the confederates must find some plausible way of explaining the visitors to one another and then hustle them off-stage again as rapidly as possible. The conclusion of the plot always comes with the collapse of the scheme and the appearance on stage simultaneously of all the characters of the play demanding an explanation. This is not only the plot of *The Alchemist* but Jonson's most successful basic plot in other plays, and it is admirably suited to allow him to parade across the stage that cross-section of folly which is his most characteristic subject matter.

This farce plot is only the framework of the play, and on it Jonson hangs a remarkable number of references, details, characters, events, and verbal echoes from the world around him and from the classical literature he read with so much care and skill. In this play the mixture is unusually rich. A single scene, like II.2, in which Mammon describes the brave new world he plans to create once he has the stone, contains a wide range of references drawn from obscure classical authors mixed easily with an equally wide range of specific details from the contemporary London underworld and the geography of the city. In order to prepare himself for writing the play Jonson also read widely in alchemical literature (see Appendix I), and he may have taken some details and events from the play of the Roman comic writer Plautus, *Mostellaria*; from an Italian farce, *Candelaio*, printed in Paris in 1582; and from Erasmus' *De Alcumista*. Furthermore, he certainly knew and referred to the strange adventures of Dr. John Dee, the mathematician and magus, and his strange companion Edward Kelley (see note to II.6.20). Some critics have argued that Face and Subtle are based on Kelley and Dee, and that Jonson's entire play is a comic version of the adventures of these two strange men. This is probably going much too far, but the reader who may wish to pursue the matter will find remarkable parallels between the life of Dee and the events of *The Alchemist*, and may wish to refer to two recent books: Richard Deacon, *John Dee* (Frederick Muller, 1968); and Peter J. French, *John Dee, The World of an Elizabethan Magus* (Routledge & Kegan Paul, 1972). In the end, Jonson's play, despite all his extensive borrowing, is really a special world of his own creation and a uniquely comic version of London society and its hopes at the time of the Renaissance.

STAGE HISTORY

The Alchemist was one of the most popular of Jonson's plays during his lifetime and remained a favorite throughout the seventeenth century. Its popularity carried over into the eighteenth century, but early during the century it began to be cut for the stage and presented in revised and abbreviated versions, mostly because the original language and references had become too difficult for the audience to follow easily. It was also during the eighteenth century that the great actor Garrick became interested in the play and put it on annually for a number of years. Curiously enough, Garrick chose to play the part of Drugger, rather than Face or Subtle, and for many years the merchant was thought to be the most interesting character in the piece. Quite understandably, *The Alchemist* dropped out of the standard repertory during the nineteenth century, and it was only in the twentieth century that revivals of the play began. It is still played rather infrequently for despite its obvious greatness it is a most difficult play to perform on the modern stage, and actors and directors are always forced to make some adjustment in the play's language and to its obscure allusions if its vitality and ultimate power are to be successfully conveyed.

Selected Reading List

EDITIONS

Ben Jonson, ed. C. H. Herford and Percy and Evelyn Simpson. 11 vols. Oxford, 1925–52. Volumes I and II contain a life of Jonson and introductions to the individual plays. The text of *The Alchemist* appears in Volume V and the explanatory notes in Volume X. This is the standard text of this and other Jonson plays, being practically a reprint of the original printings, and providing mines of information on all topics dealing with Jonson.

The Alchemist, ed. F. H. Mares. The Revels Plays. London and Cambridge, Mass., 1967. A very scholarly and thorough text with excellent notes and editorial material.

CRITICISM

Arnold, Judd. "Lovewit's Triumph and Jonsonian Morality: A Reading of *The Alchemist*." *Criticism* 11 (1969): 151–66.

Barish, Jonas A. *Ben Jonson: A Collection of Critical Essays*. Englewood Cliffs, N.J., 1963. Contains a number of excellent articles on Jonson generally, as well as further bibliography.

———. *Ben Jonson and the Language of Prose Comedy*. Cambridge, Mass., 1960.

Chute, Marchette. *Ben Jonson of Westminster*. New York, 1953. A popular well-written biography.

Dessen, Alan C. "*The Alchemist*, Jonson's 'Estates' Play." *Renaissance Drama* 7 (1964): 350–54.

Selected Reading List

Duncan, Edgar Hill. "Jonson's *Alchemist* and the Literature of Alchemy."
    PMLA 61 (1946): 699–710.
Enck, John J. *Jonson and the Comic Truth.* Madison, Wisconsin, 1957.
Knoll, Robert E. "How to Read *The Alchemist.*" *College English* 21 (1960):
    456–60.
Partridge, Edward B. *The Broken Compass: A Study of the Major Comedies
    of Ben Jonson.* London and New York, 1958.
Thayer, C. G. *Ben Jonson: Studies in the Plays.* Norman, Oklahoma, 1963.